Carrie Gracie grew up in north-east Scotland and set up a restaurant before completing a degree in Philosophy, Politics and Economics at Oxford. In a BBC career spanning more than three decades, she has served as China correspondent and Beijing bureau chief, presenter on the BBC News Channel and host of the weekly BBC World Service programme *The Interview*. She has made many documentaries for TV and radio, winning prizes including a Peabody and an Emmy, and commentating at the 2008 Beijing Olympics. In January 2018, Gracie left her post as the BBC's China Editor in protest at unequal pay, publishing an open letter to BBC audiences and giving evidence before a parliamentary committee. Six months later, she won an apology from the BBC. She donated all her back pay to the gender equality charity, the Fawcett Society, to help low-paid women facing pay discrimination. She continues to serve as a BBC News presenter, and as a member of the BBC Women group, she campaigns for a more equal, fair and transparent pay structure at the national broadcaster.

'Part instruction manual, part howl of rage, *Equal* tells a personal story that changed the public debate . . . The book is full of advice for others – there is a separate section at the end for employers, men and women . . . [Carrie Gracie's] decision to use her personal story for the public good has put the issue of equal pay firmly on the agenda' *Guardian*

'The BBC's former China editor recounts her hard-fought battle with the broadcaster for equal pay, artfully weaving in the history of gender inequality and tips for women – and men – who wish to continue her campaign for equitable treatment' *Financial Times* Best Books of 2019

'Carrie Gracie's . . . . . . her aim
of inspiring . . . . f being
underpaid and . . . . ng lives,
if not throughout it' *Mail on Sunday*

'Carrie Gracie pulls no punches in this account of how she clashed with the BBC over gender-pay inequality ... In the book, which is written with great clarity and backed up by a good deal of research, Gracie not only details her own experience but also weaves in studies showing how unconscious bias and gender stereotyping leave women undervalued at work' *Sunday Times*

'[Carrie Gracie's] important account of her struggle to win equal pay is full of sound advice for women ... Gracie understands all the various ways in which pay inequality can play havoc with a person's self-belief and peace of mind, and in her book she staples them to the page ... For me, the most resonant parts of her book have to do with her self worth' Rachel Cooke, *Observer*

'What I admire about Carrie Gracie is not just her bravery, though that is amazing, but more that she tells the story of her struggle and eventual triumph as a way of encouraging us, of changing our society, of giving us all courage. She shows what can happen when women work together to call out blatant injustice and to insist that all women are fairly and equally paid. It's hard to believe we're still having these conversations in 2019 but we are and that is why we need heroes like Carrie. *Equal* is a very important book' Sandi Toksvig

'A gripping personal story told with warmth and wit, combined with a "how to" guide for anyone who wants to ensure women are paid as true equals' Julia Gillard, former Australian Prime Minister

'*Equal* is an inspiring memoir exploring why women often find it difficult to assert their value in the workplace, as well as a practical guide to what women and men – employees and employers – can do to achieve pay equality for women now and in the future' *Stylist*

EQUAL

How We Fix the Gender Pay Gap

CARRIE GRACIE

virago

VIRAGO

First published in Great Britain in 2019 by Virago Press
This paperback edition published in 2020 by Virago Press

1 3 5 7 9 10 8 6 4 2

A CIP catalogue record for this book is available from the British Library.

ISBN 978-0-349-01225-4

Typeset in Garamond by M Rules
Printed and bound in Great Britain by Clays Ltd, Elcograf S.p.A.

Papers used by Virago are from well-managed forests
and other responsible sources.

Virago Press
An imprint of
Little, Brown Book Group
Carmelite House
50 Victoria Embankment
London EC4Y 0DZ

An Hachette UK Company
www.hachette.co.uk

www.virago.co.uk

To BBC Women, who have shown true grit in this struggle. And within our sisterhood, to the late Dianne Oxberry. Dianne once wrote, 'You can't do this alone. We are stronger together.' That solidarity drove our bosses to address many equal pay cases, including Dianne's. Sadly she died aged fifty-one feeling her fight was not yet won. But Dianne never gave up hope and her fellow BBC Women carry the fight forward.

CONTENTS

=

PREFACE

=

In some ways this is a very personal book about a workplace dispute, but in the writing I have tried to avoid score settling and instead to be guided by the editorial values the BBC has taught me over a career spanning more than three decades. Our values start with trust: 'Trust is the foundation of the BBC; we are independent, impartial and honest.' BBC journalists are also expected to strive for truth and accuracy. We are instructed to ask searching questions of those who hold public office and others who are accountable, and to infringe privacy only when that is in the public interest.

These values make a good compass to steer by. In telling my own story I have recounted some private conversations, but only where I have permission to do so or believe it is in the public interest to do so. Where I leave out names and other details it is because I feel revealing them would serve no legitimate purpose.

In recollecting events, I have relied on my own notes of conversations and my detailed diaries, as well as email exchanges, information that is already in the public domain and the recollections of the many colleagues and friends who were with me on the journey.

Interwoven with my own story, I have tried to present an honest account of what I have learned about unequal pay within the wider context of the gender pay gap. Having fought my own battle and witnessed the struggle of many other women inside the BBC and beyond, I have not sought to hide my conclusions on the subject. I do not expect all readers to agree with me on all points, but I am grateful to those who approach this topic with an open mind.

Gender pay triggers heated reactions. At various times I have been called a BBC-hater, a man-hater and a virtue-signaller. I am none of these things. I love the BBC, this story owes a lot to many great men, and I'm as susceptible to greed and fear as the next person.

As well as telling my own story and placing it in a wider context, I offer advice to readers. I have placed that advice where it falls most naturally in the story but I have also gathered it at the end of the book in case a summary can be helpful to individual women, men and employers. Some points are specific to the UK legal context but I hope others will feel relevant to readers wherever they are in the world.

The BBC expects its journalists to acknowledge their mistakes and learn from them. I have tried to avoid mistakes of fact or analysis. My research included extensive reading, and conversations with scores of lawyers, regulators, employers, unionists, HR professionals, politicians, historians, economists, statisticians, claimants, campaigners and colleagues. If I have made mistakes, they are mine alone and I will try to acknowledge them and learn from them.

On the subject of following BBC values, I can't help reflecting that my own story would have been different, and this book would not have been written, if my employer had applied to its own dealings with staff the same high standards it expects of them in dealings with others. The BBC is led by people who are trying to do their best, but on gender pay I think they made bad decisions and then tried to defend those decisions in a way that damaged trust.

However, all employers face difficult pressures; we live in a time of shifting expectations for women, and pay structures are complex things. I have sympathy for employers who would like to do better and men who would like to support female colleagues but don't know where to start.

Start here. I wrote this book for you. I also wrote it for the millions of women in the UK and around the world who are at grave risk of being undervalued and underpaid at some stage of their working life, if not throughout it. From having a conversation in the privacy of these pages, I hope we will go on to make a difference in our workplaces. Look how the women and men of the past changed the world for us, first by imagining a better future and then by working to bring it about.

On equal pay, I hope this generation will make change for the next.

PROLOGUE

UP OVER THE TOP

=

At 3.30 a.m. on 8 January 2018 a cab pulled up outside my home in south-west London. I was on my way to present one of the BBC's flagship radio shows, the *Today* Programme. The early editions of the morning newspapers were stacked on the back seat to help me prepare for the show. As I glanced at the front pages I flinched at seeing my own face staring back at me. 'BBC accused of breaking law as star quits over pay', 'Beeb's pay for women "illegal"' read the headlines.

On the inside pages of *The Times* was my whistle-blower letter in full. It felt strange to see it out in the world. It had lived inside my head for so long, crowding my days with self-doubt and my nights with bad dreams.

Dear BBC Audience,

My name is Carrie Gracie and I have been a BBC journalist for three decades. With great regret, I have left my post as China Editor to speak out publicly on a crisis of trust at the BBC.

The BBC belongs to you, the licence fee payer. I believe you have a right to know that it is breaking equality law and resisting pressure for a fair and transparent pay structure . . .

For BBC women this is not just a matter of one year's salary or two. Taking into account disadvantageous contracts and pension entitlements, it is a gulf that will last a lifetime. Many of the women affected are not highly paid 'stars' but hard-working producers on modest salaries. Often women from ethnic minorities suffer wider pay gaps than the rest.

The front-page story in *The Times* reported that more than 130 other women at the BBC endorsed my letter. Our movement had begun six months earlier, as an attempt by senior women to engage management on equal pay, but soon we were joined by colleagues at all levels, dismayed by what they saw as the BBC's unwillingness to abide by the law. We called our group BBC Women. I was the one who'd now resigned a high-profile post and condemned BBC pay culture as secretive and illegal, but many stood shoulder to shoulder in open mutiny.

As I sped into central London, I wondered what my bosses would do. Perhaps they would pull me from presenting the *Today* Programme? Sack me for breach of contract? Like many employment contracts, mine says I am not allowed to talk publicly about my workplace without permission. I got out of the taxi at BBC Broadcasting House and glanced up at the statue of George Orwell beside the entrance. Even shrouded in darkness I could make out his words engraved in the wall: 'If liberty means anything at all it means the right to tell people what they do not want to hear.'

Through the waiting TV cameras I marched into a long campaign of telling powerful people in that building what they didn't want to hear: my work and that of many other women was equal to the work of our male peers and must be paid equally. The shock for me was that even as a senior, high-profile woman working for an organisation publicly committed to equality, among female colleagues who showed great solidarity, and in a country with robust legislation, it proved almost impossible to get equal.

Pay discrimination is the gender pay gap's dirty secret. It doesn't get talked about enough, it doesn't get measured enough, and it rarely gets managed at all. A gender pay gap is usually measured as the difference between men's and women's average hourly earnings across an organisation, an industry or a national economy. The gap may be caused by many different factors, but when caused by paying men more than women for the same jobs or jobs of equal value it's called pay discrimination or unequal pay, and it's illegal.

Pay discrimination is hard to measure. There are no statistics on it because no employer wants to boast about breaking the law. Public awareness is hampered by the unavailability of hard facts. But gender pay gaps show a suspiciously large element that is 'unexplained'. This is where discrimination is hiding and only painstaking work by economists can begin to tease it out. One Australian study found that discrimination accounted for a full 38 per cent of the national gender pay gap. Likewise, an American investigation separated out occupation, work experience and education to put the role of outright gender discrimination at 38 per cent.

But such attempts to measure discrimination are very rare. Which allows some employers to insist that it is a problem of the past or one that doesn't apply to their organisation. If employers are not making choices that disadvantage women, women themselves must be making the choices which result in them earning less: their choice of occupation or industry, their choice to work unpaid at home caring for children or elderly relatives, their choice to work part-time or flexibly.

This is too binary. The gender pay gap is complex. It is not an either/or problem. It is a both/and problem, driven both by pay discrimination and women's choices – and by the many factors that constrain women's choices. In fact, the very employers who say there is no such thing as discrimination in their workplace often perpetuate the problem because they are unconscious of the way their own gender bias – and often ethnic bias – operates in recruitment, promotion and pay. They have choices too, as do male colleagues.

Women are far from equal at work. Across the world, 2.7 billion are still legally barred from having the same choice of jobs as men and only six countries have legislation that gives women equal economic opportunity. Many countries have laws that prohibit pay discrimination but then leave it up to women to enforce those laws against overwhelming odds.

Pay discrimination is almost impossible for individual women to correct. It is unjust and economically inefficient. It is also pervasive.

Gender pay gaps, in which discrimination plays a significant role, afflict many millions of women across the world. They also afflict our partners and children, and they afflict the women who come into the workforce after us. For each individual, the personal financial cost is stark. In the United States, for example, an average woman will make nearly $600,000 less than a man over the course of her working life. The resulting inequality then follows her into retirement. In the UK, women receive nearly 40 per cent less from pensions than men.

But this is not a women's problem. Gender pay gaps are a blight on employers too. Those who narrow them report a measurable return in engagement and loyalty from employees and there is growing evidence that companies with strong female leadership perform better. At the global level, deploying women to their full potential would be transformative. In 2015 one major study estimated that if all countries matched the progress towards gender parity of the fastest-improving country in their region, it would boost global GDP by $12 trillion. 'In a "full potential" scenario in which women play an identical role in labour markets to that of men, as much as $28 trillion, or 26 per cent, could be added ... roughly equivalent to the size of the combined Chinese and US economies today.'

Unlocking that potential seems a distant dream. In 2018 the World Economic Forum said global gender economic parity was 202 years off. 'The overall picture is that gender equality has stalled,' said Saadia Zahidi, the WEF's head of social and economic agendas: 'The future of our labour market may not be as equal as the trajectory we thought we were on.'

Women know this only too well from personal experience. On 8 January 2018, many wrote and told me so. Within hours of my own protest letter detonating in the media, hundreds of email messages poured in from around the UK and across the world. Letters arrived in the BBC post room and women stopped me on buses and at the supermarket to tell me their stories of workplaces large and small, public and private. From Germany to Australia, Tanzania to South Korea, China to the United States, my experience resonated. One woman in the UK financial sector wrote that when she asked if she was receiving equal pay, her female manager replied, 'Run a bath, get in the bath, and then when you let the water out, let all thoughts of this run away with the water.'

Another wrote that she'd recently found out she was paid less than colleagues doing exactly the same work: 'Even though we all (including my male colleagues) urged my boss (a woman) to pay us equally, she refused.'

A manager in a professional association wrote that when she asked for equal pay with men who shared the same job title, her employer deleted all relevant emails and then made her redundant 'under a so-called strategic refocus'.

All were energised by my protest letter: 'Some wars are worth waging. You KNOW that every woman on the planet is behind you – and pushing HARD.'

In some messages, frustration with men was palpable:

What is so great about the XY chromosome? Do they report the news better? They don't. Become better lawyers? Nope. Perform surgery more meticulously than their female counterparts? Definitely not. Clean the streets faster? HELL NO!

Why do men think this is acceptable? Oh yes, it's because they get the better end of the deal.

But it turned out many men do not think it's acceptable. Three-fifths of the messages of support I received were from women but two-fifths were from men. This one made me laugh:

Good luck . . . you are quite right. As a Stone Age bloke, I find shortlists stashed for gender equality abhorrent. However, having got the job on merit, one should be paid for it.
   Rgds
   Dodgy old bugger
   Bill

Thank you, dodgy old bugger Bill. I did get the job of BBC China Editor on merit. Over my career, I have been privileged to work with some immensely talented journalists and, hand on heart, I can say the women have been every bit as good as the men. In other spheres, women have proved themselves as surgeons and soldiers, cooks and cleaners, police officers and pilots.

But when it comes to deep-rooted patterns of power and money, history shows time and again that justice for women does not come through patient persuasion. Instead women must find their power and use it. In January 2018, I went over my employer's head to write directly to the public because I wanted an end to pay discrimination in my workplace and my bosses weren't listening. The answering echo from women everywhere made me feel the BBC was a mirror of the society it served. My experience was commonplace. The sooner women, men and employers acknowledge this and put our heads together to fix it, the better for all of us. Hence this book.

I know not all readers will be in paid employment. Some work in unpaid roles at home, some are self-employed, others may be trying to find a job. But I hope my experience will still be useful, as it's a rare woman who will not face the risk of pay discrimination at some point in her life, and for many it will be compounded by discrimination on race, ethnicity and class as well.

Unequal pay is a complex problem and resolving it will take honest listening and patience on all sides. Gender inequality is entrenched in many pay structures and in the biases and habits of those who operate them. Even small differences in the treatment of women can become self-amplifying, with effects which are cumulative. Too often efforts by women to enforce the law on equal pay become a battle against impossible odds. One side commands the information and resources and also controls the other side's income and career prospects. Regulation is weak and external scrutiny rare.

Do you think this is good enough? I don't. In the pages to follow, I will look at what governments, employers and male colleagues can do to help. I will also offer advice that individual women can put into practice immediately, because I believe that until workplace culture changes, women remain at very real risk of being underpaid, especially in the second half of their working lives. Because of the way pay history often follows individuals into new roles, even one episode of pay discrimination can have lifetime consequences. In circumstances where there is no effective cure, prevention is the only course. If you're a woman and currently doing little to protect yourself, I urge you to start.

If you're a man, there's much you can do to help. Men are often the powerful people in the pay conversation. They can advance gender justice in the workplace or they can obstruct it. Some men are waking up to the fact that their own work–life balance is at stake. In this book, you will meet male heroes as well as men of the other kind.

I also hope to talk to open-minded employers. They know they need to attract and hold talent, regardless of gender. Women care about workplace culture. Pay is personal, but it's also a power relationship. Abuse of power is hard to forgive or forget. Often the damage to trust is compounded if powerful people then refuse to acknowledge the problem or correct it. Just as I published my open letter on unequal pay, the #MeToo movement was breaking workplace silence around sexual harassment. The 'problem people' in both stories were those who refused to listen to female employees or to enforce just processes and offer redress.

As with #MeToo, so with unequal pay. More women will have to tell their stories for things to change. Silence-breaking is a big ask. For many people, talking about pay at all is taboo, let alone talking about it publicly. Victims of pay discrimination may feel low self-esteem about being valued less, they feel anxious about washing dirty linen in public, uncomfortable about playing the washerwoman at all, and afraid of punishment by a vindictive employer. But if true stories are not told, it leaves all of us ignorant of the facts of life and vulnerable to becoming victims or abusers in turn.

This is my story. It's no more important than any other. My employer is also no worse than any other. Quite the contrary. The BBC employs more women in senior roles than most workplaces and has a smaller gender pay gap. My workplace became the equal pay story only because our pay was slightly more transparent than most and women were less afraid of being victimised for asking questions. Elsewhere, pay is often too opaque and the odds too overwhelming. But in the essentials, BBC Women were just like women anywhere. We had the motivation to fix inequality but lacked the means, while our employer had the means but seemed to lack the motivation.

In one sense this is a familiar story of trying to hold the powerful to account. I am a BBC reporter. Holding the powerful to account is my job, along with telling stories that are true and important. The BBC is one of the UK's most trusted institutions. Its mission is to bring the country together and help it understand itself. I hope that in this book, by reporting my personal experience of a problem that is so commonplace, I am doing my professional duty by other means. When I resigned my post as China Editor I did not resign from the BBC because I felt a duty to help it be the best it can be. That requires treating women and men equally and telling the truth when things go wrong.

This is how things went wrong for me. It all began with a painful reckoning.

I

GET REAL

=

Reality punched me from behind on 19 July 2017.

Many of us never find out what the person next to us is paid, and some of us only find out by chance. Like most employers, mine had long resisted greater openness about salaries. But the BBC was spending public money and transparency was supposed to be one of its core values – alongside trust. The average income of the audiences who paid for its programmes through a compulsory licence fee was less than £30,000 a year. They had just endured a decade of economic austerity while over the same period the BBC resisted parliamentary pressure for more transparency around the salaries of its stars. It warned of a 'poacher's charter', saying if rival broadcasters knew what BBC stars were earning they would offer a little more and the net effect would be inflationary.

Eventually the government lost patience. Under the terms of the BBC's new Royal Charter, in 2017 the broadcaster was obliged to publish all salaries higher than the Prime Minister's £150,000.* At which point the news story became not just how

---

* All BBC pay from public money was published in £50,000 bands: Chris Evans between £2.2 and £2.25 million, Gary Lineker between £1.75 and £1.8 million, Graham Norton between £850,000 and £900,000 and so on. The highest-paid woman was Claudia Winkleman at between £450,000 and £500,000.

much money the BBC was paying its top people, but who those people were. It turned out that the highest-paid stars were all white men. There were very few women or ethnic minorities on the list at all, and they were mostly clumped towards the bottom.

It's worth spelling out that this reporting requirement was different from the gender pay gap. A gender pay gap shows only the average for men and women. It does not give individuals enough information about colleagues doing the same work to see whether they themselves are being underpaid. But these revelations at the BBC about the pay of named individuals meant that, for the first time, some women could see that some men doing the same work were earning much more than them.

When this pay story broke, it was the last thing I wanted to think about. I was three days into a much-needed summer holiday. I'd just finished a massive reporting project on China's strategic plans for Asia. I'd produced TV news films, radio features, an immersive long read for the website, a TV documentary. I'd been travelling thousands of miles and working round the clock. I was exhausted and I hadn't seen my children in months. Now we were finally together in a cottage in southeast Scotland.

The day before the pay bombshell was my son Daniel's nineteenth birthday, and in the aftermath of his party I just wanted to lie on the grass, gaze out across the glittering North Sea and listen to the happy chatter of young people. One of my oldest friends, Jackie Kemp, was sitting beside me, squinting into her mobile phone and scrolling through the BBC's own news story about its high-pay disclosures: 'The North America Editor is on this list. And the Middle East Editor. Economics Editor, Home Affairs . . . I've never even heard of *this* guy! What does he do?'

I closed my eyes and grunted. But Jackie was also a reporter. 'All the top salaries are for men. The numbers are outrageous.

Why aren't you even on this list? I thought you'd insisted on equal pay when you took the China job! How do you feel about this?'

How did I feel? Resistant. Avoidant. Numb.

Four years earlier, when I had accepted what I knew would be a tough job as China Editor, I had demanded equal pay and been promised the same salary as the North America Editor. I now discovered that the North America Editor was earning at least 50 per cent more – and perhaps closer to double.

I had ignored the buzz of advance speculation about the pay story. I certainly agreed with the public and the politicians that top salaries at the BBC were too high, but in my mind this was filed under the heading 'Bad things I can't do anything about'. And after a long career at the BBC, I was good at not thinking about that list. It was a long-standing joke among staff that there was no crisis our bosses couldn't make worse.

But Jackie was right on the facts. Three and a half years earlier James Harding, the then Director of News, had begged me to become the BBC's first China Editor, saying we urgently needed to tell the story of a rising superpower and I was the only person who could do the story justice. The BBC had said the role was 'on a par with' the other international editors. I'd explicitly made equal pay with my male peers a condition of taking the job. Four years on, my salary was £134,000 but this pay list said the North America Editor was earning between £200,000 and £250,000.

Scenes flooded my memory unbidden. A brief meeting with James when I was back from Beijing in 2015. 'Carrie, it's always a joy to see you,' he said. 'You deliver so much and ask so little.'

Deliver so much and ask so little? That should have rung an alarm bell. But we only had fifteen minutes in his diary and I wouldn't get another chance to bend his ear until my next trip back from China. So I got on with talking about what I'd come to talk about – the China stories that mattered to our audiences and the production team I needed to tell those stories. I didn't stop to examine the ground under my feet.

Under the pressure of Jackie's questions I now reflected that this was poor. Asking questions is my job, after all.

I wasn't the only woman at the BBC getting a painful reality check that day. Imagine having to challenge your boss on national radio as it emerges that he's paying men more for doing the same job as you. Mishal Husain had to interview the BBC's Director-General Tony Hall on the *Today* Programme. He said: 'It's complicated. One person could be sitting next to someone doing the same job who earns more.'

Mishal's situation exactly. The Director-General swiftly explained that this second person could be doing 'other things'.

'Or they may not be,' countered Mishal.

The *Today* Programme ended at 9 a.m. and *Woman's Hour* started at 10 a.m. Its presenter Jane Garvey tweeted, 'I'm looking forward to presenting @BBCWomansHour today. We'll be discussing #GenderPayGap. As we've done since 1946. Going well, isn't it?'

In an interview on a rival station, the Prime Minister pulled no punches: 'We've seen the way the BBC is paying women less for doing the same job . . . I want women to be paid equally.'

The veteran Labour MP Harriet Harman said, 'It is very important that the lid has been lifted on this pay discrimination in the BBC . . . the old boys' network where they are feathering their own nests and each others' and there is discrimination and unfairness against women.'

Others blamed the women. Sir Philip Hampton, the co-chair of a government-commissioned review into getting more women into senior business roles, said women hadn't pressed hard enough for pay rises: 'How has this situation arisen at the BBC that these intelligent, high-powered, sometimes formidable women have sat in this situation? They are all looking at each other now saying: "How did we let this happen?" I suspect they let it happen because they weren't doing much about it.'

The truth is more complex. Any game that claims to be fair must have rules that are well understood and applied to all players equally. This is even more important in games with big winners and big losers. Like the pay structure of most large employers in the early twenty-first century.

We all know that the gender pay gap runs like an underground fault around the globe; it divides men and women across almost every workplace and every occupation. The gap tends to be wider for ethnic minorities and wider for all women as they get older or more senior. Over a career, it can cost life-changing amounts of money. Is pay a game with fair rules?

We can debate whether or not it is fair to have occupations and industries segregated by gender, more men in senior roles, and childcare responsibilities shared unequally. But these aspects of the gender pay gap are at least lawful. What is not lawful, and what most people now agree is not fair, is paying women less for equal work.

It may be unlawful and unfair, but in practice pay discrimination is commonplace. Women can't correct what they can't see. If pay secrecy means you don't know there's a pay gap between you and a man doing equal work, you can be a victim for years without having any idea.

I've always believed the old adage that sunlight is the best disinfectant. In the course of a 2009 TV interview about the Westminster expenses scandal, the Labour peer George Foulkes challenged me to reveal my salary on air. I didn't hesitate to tell him I earned £92,000 as a news presenter. Afterwards a BBC manager suggested that declaring our salaries was 'not really what we do'. In my diary for that day, I recorded my reply: 'If my salary is defensible, defend it. If it's too high, cut it. But we both know the real problem is not my salary but the BBC's can of worms on pay.'

Over the years, staff surveys and unions had repeatedly flagged up unease over pay. It was felt the BBC had too many fiefdoms in which managerial discretion seemed to go unchecked. Even before the disclosures in the summer of 2017, I don't think many staff felt our pay structure was equal or fair.

In my department, BBC News, pay often felt like an unspoken caste system. The only rough rules of thumb I could divine were as follows: presenters generally earned more than reporters; those who worked on national programmes earned more than those on international or local programmes; TV earned more than radio; people at the top earned ever-increasing multiples of the salaries of those further down the chain; people who worked in English earned more than those who worked in other languages; men earned more than women; and because they were not protected by UK employment law, staff on local hire contracts around the world often earned less than anyone.

I don't believe the BBC was unusual in having anomalies and unexamined discrimination embedded in its pay structure. It was perhaps only unusual in suddenly being forced to explain itself. On 19 July 2017 the lid was wrenched off the can of worms and what happened next is a cautionary tale for employers everywhere.

First, BBC bosses were taken by surprise. They'd expected headlines about fat-cat salaries, but when the figures revealed that these cats were all white men, bosses didn't foresee the rage of women and men of colour. Secondly, having undervalued women for many years, they underestimated them, failing to predict that shared outrage would drive action. Or that was how it looked to me.

Crisis? What crisis?

Linguists complain that it's not strictly accurate to say the Chinese word for crisis – 危机 – combines the pictograms for danger and opportunity. But it's so neat an idea that it sticks. The BBC was now facing a crisis but, blind to the danger, it missed the opportunity. It might have prepared for enforced transparency by getting its house in order. Instead it waited till the pay was published and then the Director-General claimed that our house was already in better order than those of our neighbours: 'On gender and diversity, the BBC is more diverse than the broadcasting industry and the civil service ... We've made progress, but we recognise there is more to do and we are pushing further and faster than any other broadcaster.'

The UK media regulator, Ofcom, took a less sanguine view. A few weeks after the BBC's pay disclosures, in its 2017 report on the UK broadcast industry, it said the BBC was behind all major UK broadcasters bar Sky on the proportion of women in its workforce, behind ITV and Viacom (owner of Channel 5) on women in senior roles, behind Channel 4 and Viacom on BAME staff, and behind Channel 4 on the proportion of disabled staff.

'As the UK's largest broadcaster, the BBC's position on diversity is likely to have a disproportionate effect on the wider industry. The BBC should be leading the way, but today's report shows its performance on most characteristics is behind that of Channel 4.'

The public seemed equally unimpressed. In one survey, 83 per cent of respondents said the gap between salaries of men and women at the BBC was unfair and 82 per cent said the BBC had not explained how it was addressing that gap.

Least impressed of all were the women in question. For years some had been demanding equal pay, only for bosses to tell them they were already 'roughly equal'; they should stop complaining and work harder. Now women realised that working harder would not lead to getting equal. We concluded we were second-class citizens – and not because our work was second class, but because we were women. Pay discrimination was real and, as Jane Garvey warned her followers on Twitter, 'If it's happened to us, it's happening to you.'

On 23 July 2017, four days after the high-pay disclosures, the Director-General received a letter signed by forty-four of the BBC's most senior on-air women and published in a national newspaper.

Dear Tony,

The pay details released in the annual report showed what many of us have suspected for many years ... that women at the BBC are being paid less than men for the same work.

Compared to many women and men, we are very well compensated and fortunate. However, this is an age of equality and the BBC is an organisation that prides itself on its values.

You have said that you will 'sort' the gender pay gap by 2020, but the BBC has known about the pay disparity for years. We all want to go on the record to call upon you to act now.

Beyond the list, there are so many other areas including production, engineering and support services and global, regional and local media where a pay gap has languished for too long.

This is an opportunity for those of us with strong and loud voices to use them on behalf of all, and for an organisation that had to be pushed into transparency to do the right thing.

We would be willing to meet you to discuss ways in which you can correct this disparity so that future generations of women do not face this kind of discrimination.

The letter was signed by well-known names in BBC News, Sport and Entertainment: Katya Adler, Samira Ahmed, Anita Anand, Wendy Austin, Zeinab Badawi, Clare Balding, Sue Barker, Emma Barnett, Fiona Bruce, Rachel Burden, Annabel Croft, Martine Croxall, Victoria Derbyshire, Lyse Doucet, Jane Garvey, Fi Glover, Karin Giannone, Joanna Gosling, Orla Guerin, Geeta Guru-murthy, Lucy Hockings, Mishal Husain, Alex Jones, Katty Kay, Martha Kearney, Kirsty Lang, Gabby Logan, Kasia Madera, Emily Maitlis, Annita McVeigh, Louise Minchin, Aasmah Mir, Sarah Montague, Jenni Murray, Sally Nugent, Elaine Paige, Carolyn Quinn, Angela Rippon, Ritula Shah, Kate Silverton, Charlotte Smith, Sarah Smith, Kirsty Wark. And me.

I can't divulge exactly who organised and drafted the letter because I believe jobs and careers might be at stake. Both then and now, safety in numbers is important in protecting against any danger of victimisation. But what I can say is that this was the beginning of the group called BBC Women and its first show of solidarity.

The message would have been even more powerful if it had included men. I think our bosses would have listened to men in a way they didn't listen to women. After all, they clearly valued them more as we could see from the pay disparities. And men renouncing privilege would have been immune to the charge laid against women, that their fight was motivated by narrow self-interest.

One male presenter, the TV historian Dan Snow, did try to organise an open letter from senior BBC men in support of the letter from women. He understood that however high-profile the women, their argument would hit harder and they would be safer in making it if they had powerful men alongside. But most of the men he invited to sign refused to do so. One warned it was a 'minefield', another said 'it's complicated' and a third 'better not to rock the boat'. The men's letter in support of women did not get off the ground. Instead, one BBC manager told me that after the pay gaps were revealed, 'The first people through my door were not the women but a queue of men complaining that they were earning less than other men.'

Men are not just half the population; they are the powerful half. And in any hierarchical workplace, they are likely to dominate the top positions. Which means they have more power than women to make change or to block it. In your workplace, if men acknowledge the structural problems that frustrate the drive for equality, it will be easier for you to dismantle them.

So men and employers, ask yourselves whether you have advocated any advance for women. A century ago would you have supported a woman's right to vote, to attend university or to sit on a jury? What would that kind of support look like today?

You probably say you believe in equal pay. But are you ready to inconvenience yourself for it? 'Deeds not words,' as the suffragettes once said. Principle is only a word unless you're prepared to pay something for it.

When BBC Women complained of unequal pay in the summer of 2017, we asked ourselves where the money might come from to make us equal. If women's pay was levelled up, it would be expensive. Job cuts and programme cuts were already never-ending. If men and managers levelled down, it would be less expensive. As we were about to learn, it's very hard for women to get equal without men and employers on side.

But Tony Hall replied to our open letter by changing the subject: 'Across the BBC, our provisional figures show that the pay gap is 10 per cent against a national average of over 18 per cent. I have committed the BBC to closing the gap by 2020 and if we can get there earlier then we will.'

Our protest letter wasn't about closing the gender pay gap,

urgent though that was. Instead we had accused our employer of paying women less for equal work, which is illegal. This charge the Director-General ignored.

The BBC Sport presenter Clare Balding tweeted: '1970: Equal Pay Act. 2010: Equality Act. 2020: BBC target. We're standing together to politely suggest they can do better.'

Clare Balding and Jane Garvey bore the brunt of the media pressure that day. The news journalists in the group felt they had to be more cautious because of the risk of being seen to breach the BBC's strict impartiality rules.

As for me, I was still trying to focus on my holiday. By this stage, we'd moved on from the cottage with Jackie and her children to spend a weekend in Edinburgh with my father and stepmother. It was at their kitchen table that I read and signed the BBC Women open letter. But I too refused interview requests and instead marched resolutely in the opposite direction from the media storm – onto a ferry bound for the Outer Hebrides and the second week of our summer holiday.

It was only on the Isle of Barra, as the Atlantic breakers surged over long empty beaches, that I finally allowed myself to confront what I found so personal and so painful about the pay shock.

Pay is about how others value us, and if we suddenly discover they value us much less than we thought, it feels like a betrayal. If you've ever experienced a partner's infidelity or a close friend's breach of confidence you'll know that betrayals force a re-examination of the past. Were you ever valued? At what point did your partner or friend start to betray your trust, and why? Did you ignore the tell-tale signs? And it's not just the past that needs re-evaluating. Betrayal forces us to examine our deepest values and make choices about the future. Can you forgive? Can you rebuild trust? Do you have any alternative?

In English law, every contract of employment has an 'implied term' that the employer 'shall not conduct itself in a manner, "calculated or likely to destroy" the "mutual trust and confidence" between employer and employee without reasonable cause'. Moreover, the BBC claims 'trust is the foundation of the BBC'.

Now I felt I had been lied to, and in this I was not alone. The radio presenter Sarah Montague later told a newspaper she was 'incandescent with rage' when she discovered her pay gap and 'felt a sap' for 'subsidising other people's lifestyles'. Another presenter, Samira Ahmed, said discovering the facts felt 'as though bosses had naked pictures of you in their office and laughed every time they saw you'. Anita Rani said the pay disparities were disappointing but the problem went beyond gender: 'It's difficult for everybody, but for me, as much as it's about gender I think it's about race and it's about class.'

Discrimination is painful, whatever its precise fingerprint and whatever the workplace and role. In direct response to the equal pay row at the BBC, Margaret Heffernan wrote an article for the *Financial Times* recounting how in the late 1990s she was the CEO of a tech start-up called iCast and the only female leader of the forty businesses under the conglomerate CMGI. An HR executive tipped her off that she was being paid half as much as her male peers. 'Being underpaid in relation to your peers in an organisation takes your abilities, experience, goodwill and dedication and casually degrades them. The contempt implied is beyond unnerving; you cannot but feel worth less. This anger should not be mistaken for self-pity or vanity because it is exactly the opposite: it is fury at oneself for having been fooled.'

Yes, that. My mind went back to 2013, when I was appointed BBC China Editor.

'On bended knee'

China coverage was always a problem for the BBC. A rising world power upending every dimension of the status quo, but doing it in imperceptible increments that often didn't quite make a daily news story. As a result, China was almost invisible on flagship news bulletins. In 2013, the BBC advertised for a China Editor to help the story punch through. The job ad made it sound attractive:

> The role of China Editor is at the most senior level of correspondent in BBC News, on a par with the World Affairs, Middle East, Europe and North America Editors overseas and the Political, Business, Home and Economics Editors in the UK.

No one applied. Unlike Washington DC, Beijing was a hard posting to recruit for. If St Augustine prayed 'O God, make me pure – but not yet', BBC programme editors vowed 'O God, make me cover China – but not today.' They acknowledged that China was important but something else usually seemed more urgent. I'd been covering China for the BBC on and off for a quarter of a century. I'd seen how China reporters often became invisible and demoralised, their personal brand tainted by a perceived failure to get the story across. To make it worse, heavy censorship and other obstructions meant that every piece of broadcast journalism in China required an investment of time, skill and stamina that programme editors in London could not easily imagine. Air pollution, police surveillance, an eight-hour time difference and a fiendishly difficult language didn't help.

But in 2013, the BBC appointed a Director of News obsessed by China. James Harding had once been a Shanghai reporter for the *Financial Times* and believed China was not just important but urgent. He wanted a China Editor and he wanted one fast.

Another big priority at the time was getting more women on air, especially older women. In 2011 the BBC lost a legal case against a fifty-three-year-old female journalist called Miriam O'Reilly. Miriam had presented the TV programme *Countryfile* until managers suddenly replaced her with a younger reporter. She sued the BBC for sex discrimination, age discrimination and victimisation. She won on the second and third counts. The case drew attention to how very few older women there were on screen at a public service broadcaster that claimed to reflect its diverse audiences. At the end of 2013, the top tier of news reporters was even more male than the top tier of presenters. There were no female on-air editors. No wonder James Harding came 'on bended knee', as he put it, to ask me to be China Editor. Fifty-one-year-old Carrie Gracie would kill two birds with one stone.

At first I said no. I certainly cared about the BBC's China coverage. I also cared about seeing women reporting the big stories. 2013 was the year of Sheryl Sandberg's *Lean In*. The book by the billionaire chief operating officer of Facebook triggered many questions about white or corporate feminism, but it also convinced me that I shouldn't sit complaining about a gender problem if I'd been invited to help fix it.

But the timing was bad. The plan for a China Editor had already been discussed in 2012. I'd warned the Foreign Editor that if the BBC wanted me to do the job I'd have to be appointed, and accredited in China, in time to move Rachel and Daniel before important exams. That moment passed and I concluded that the BBC still didn't take China seriously enough. When the post was finally advertised, I didn't apply, and when James came knocking at the end of 2013 I told him it was too late for me. I joked that he should do the job himself. After all, he always seemed more at home swapping news stories than working the levers of BBC management. He even looked like

Tintin, the young reporter of Hergé's comics. The conversation ended with me making a couple of serious suggestions for China Editor and wishing him luck.

But James was reluctant to take no for an answer, and he was good at persuasion. Rachel and Daniel also urged me to take the job. So did my ex-husband, Jin. They all knew how much I cared about the China story.

My obsession had begun straight after university, when I spent a year as a college teacher in provincial China. By 1991, I was back as a BBC reporter. The political mood had darkened after the Tiananmen Square democracy movement ended in a massacre. But economically, China was about to embark on the years of miracle growth that would catapult it from agrarian backwater to twenty-first-century superpower. It was a gripping story and I stayed for most of the nineties. But by 1999, I had a husband and two small children. When Rachel was diagnosed with childhood leukaemia I knew it was time to leave.

Fast-forward to the China Editor dilemma of 2013 and Rachel was a flourishing seventeen-year-old. Daniel was fifteen and already taller than his dad. Jin offered to move from China to the UK for a couple of years and lean into parenting, so that I could move to China and lean into reporting. Until then, I'd run the home and been primary parent. All of us knew switching roles would be a big upheaval.

In the end I said yes to the job, on three conditions. The first was to split the role two-thirds in China, one-third in London. The BBC's Middle East Editor and Africa Editor are both based in London. So is *The Economist*'s China Editor. The job didn't need me to be on the other side of the world all the time, and doing some of the work in London would enable me to spend time with Rachel and Daniel. The second condition I set was having a producer to help me craft compelling TV and radio pieces and persuade programme editors to run them. The third condition was equal pay.

Equal pay might sound like an unusual deal-breaker, but it made perfect sense to me. Like many women at the BBC, I had long suspected I was earning less than the men I worked alongside. But in an environment where pay was opaque and talking about it taboo, it seemed preferable to talk about the journalism. I'd never asked my peers directly what they were earning and never issued an ultimatum on pay.

I liked my male colleagues. It seemed invidious to challenge managers in a way that might impact the pay of people I liked. When I went through treatment for breast cancer, my bosses were kind to me. I reasoned that, in many ways, the BBC was a good employer.

In return, I had always tried to be a good employee. Every year I persuaded Jin to come back from Beijing and stand in at home for a few weeks so that I could do one big reporting trip to China, and I never demanded higher pay for all the prep and post-production. The BBC showed me goodwill and I showed it goodwill back. One of my documentary projects followed the transformation of China through the experiences of three families in a village that was being razed to make way for a city. This *White Horse Village* series won the BBC a Peabody Award and an Emmy. At the moment the Emmy was announced in New York, I was, quite literally, washing up at my kitchen sink. Rachel and Daniel were twelve and ten at the time and as I dried my hands and sat down to help with homework, I joked that I was a real-life Cinderella. But not being invited to the ball was a commonplace at the BBC. We had lots of people who did brilliant work for little recognition.

At fifty-one I felt I needed to be more careful. After all, I was being asked to move to the other side of the world to do a difficult job, one that my employer said only I could do. A key motivation for taking the post was to show that women can do the big jobs just as well as men. Hence insisting on equal pay.

The BBC had no other candidate for the post, let alone one who combined the necessary skills and experience in the way I did. I did not exploit any of that to ask for more money than my peers. I simply explained why I expected to be paid equally.

The then Head of Newsgathering, Fran Unsworth, responded by citing the salaries of the North America and Europe Editors, both of whom were men. She offered me £130,000. I was proud that I'd stood up for myself and won what I thought was a commitment to pay parity.

But equal pay is not in and of one moment in time. It's about relativities. A promise made to one employee can be broken by a later pay offer made to another. At least I had a job ad that said the roles were on a par, and I had notes of the contractual conversation. I'm a reporter, after all, and I make notes on almost everything. James Harding once joked there were two Carries, 'one who's fun to be around, the other writing everything down in a big black book'.

If I have any advice from this part of my story, it is this: when it comes to negotiating any new role, say that the principle of equal pay for equal work matters to you. Mean it. Benchmark your role where possible, as I benchmarked China against North America. Obviously it does not always follow that you will be paid the same as the person in the other role – your boss may cite factors such as experience and skill in paying them more – but having the conversation should nudge your employer towards accountability.

Many employers base pay on market-based 'pay ranges' provided by compensation consultancies. If these are not transparent within the organisation, you can ask for them. You can also get a good insight from recruitment agencies or executive search organisations. And there are websites you can look at, like Salaries.com and Glassdoor.

Take notes at the time, or immediately after the conversation. Don't trust your own memory and definitely don't trust your boss's. Share your notes the same day, even if only in an informal email that starts 'Thanks so much for the conversation. Here's a brief summary of what I think we agreed.' Forward the message to your private email account.

In an ideal world, you should get into a habit of keeping meticulous notes of all interactions with your bosses and with HR. However formal or informal, type up these notes and email them to those involved. Paper trails matter. Give any new boss an up-to-date copy of your CV so they know what skills you offer and what you might take to a rival.

As for me, the contract was signed. I was Beijing-bound and James Harding sent an all-staff email:

> The appointment of the BBC's first China Editor signals our determination to bring home to people the sweeping changes in the world's most populous nation, as well as the transformative impact that China is having upon the world and all of our lives. In Carrie, the BBC is fortunate to have someone who has profound knowledge of China, insightful judgement as a journalist and exceptional talent as a broadcaster.

I then did the BBC proud in China for the next four years.

So how did I come to be worth so much less than a man again?

At one level, the answer is very simple. Several months after my appointment, the BBC put a new editor into the North America post, paid him much more than the previous incumbent and never thought that was relevant to me, because it forgot the promise it had made and didn't consider the lawfulness of its pay decisions under equality law.

This is an employer's responsibility.

But I felt responsible too. There had been opportunities for me to check on pay: renewal of my China contract after two years, a performance evaluation, a couple of occasions when I discussed leaving my post and managers asked me to stay. Not once did I raise the topic of pay. I felt well paid, after all. I'd only ever wanted to be equal.

Now, in the aftermath of the BBC's pay disclosures, I judged the case and found myself guilty of wishful thinking and wilful blindness. I had wanted the BBC to have the equal and fair pay structure it laid claim to. I had failed to test promises against reality.

Ego was definitely there too. Unequal pay is a form of disrespect, and both my professional and my personal pride were hurt. The wiser voice in my head pointed out that if I'd said I wanted equal pay yet accepted substitutes like flattery, I shouldn't be surprised to end up with more of the flattery and less of the money.

So here I was now, in 2017, a woman of fifty-five reviewing her mistakes on a beach. I had grown up in a family of strong sisters. I was white, middle class and educated. I had studied politics and economics at university, on a course entirely taught by men, which at no point touched upon the political or economic struggle of women. Before having children, I mistook my privileged bubble for equality.

I'd suffered challenges in life. My mother had died of ovarian cancer when she was forty-two and I was seventeen. I had inherited the BRCA1 genetic mutation and gone through two episodes of breast cancer in my forties, the second requiring mastectomies and chemotherapy. I'd nursed my daughter through childhood leukaemia and my marriage had cracked under the strain. I thought of myself as resilient, and a career in journalism had taught me compassion for life's underdogs. But I had no experience of seeing myself as an underdog.

So I now found it hard to understand that I actually couldn't be equal in the pay game because I was a woman. As China Editor, I'd made my children take second place; I'd lived on the other side of the world for long periods, and behaved like a workaholic even when at home or on leave. The Director of News, Head of Newsgathering and Foreign Editor endlessly said I was brilliant and had 'an expertise and an affinity with the story and the place which we can't replicate'. I had delivered equal but been valued second best.

I gazed sightlessly out to sea. My dad once said I was a placid baby, the slowest of his five children to anger, 'But on the rare occasions that you did get angry, it was something to behold.'

I was angry now.

Daniel and Rachel jolted me back onto the beach as they emerged from the waves to peel off their wetsuits, build a fire and tease me for being distracted and wordless. Our holiday continued – cycling around Barra with a dog who had hurt his paw. We had to take turns carrying him in a rucksack on the back of our bikes. Rachel had a reaction to shellfish and did spectacular projectile vomiting in the bathroom of our bed and breakfast. The ups and downs of a family holiday. All very grounding.

When we got back to London, I was ready to bottle the rage and begin the research. After all, I reflected, what had happened to me and other women at the BBC was just another news story. If we applied the same professional skills we brought to any other reporting duty, we'd make sense of it in time.

Get sleuthing

I started by talking to some of the women behind the open letter to the Director-General. They were even angrier than me. Some said they had been told for years that their pay was 'about equal', only to find out in July how far from the truth this was. Exchanging experiences allowed us to see the patterns in which discrimination had thrived. Hearing detailed accounts from the union representatives in the group convinced me that we were not just a small elite but the tip of the iceberg. I wrote a personal letter to Tony Hall, warning that women were not an abstract set of statistics to be ironed out in the fullness of time. I used my own story to make the point:

> I am a cancer survivor in my mid-fifties who lost my own mother to cancer when I was a teenager and who nursed my own daughter through childhood leukaemia. I did not apply for the China Editor post, and was reluctant to take it, precisely because of the strains I knew it would impose on my family and my health. I agreed to do the job because I cared about our coverage of China and because I thought the BBC needed older women journalists to 'lean in'. I am bitterly disappointed to discover that my contribution as an editor is valued at so much less than my male peers.

I warned the Director-General that unless I was made equal I would resign.

I then worked backwards through the past twenty years of my career, asking male peers direct questions about pay. I chose not to tackle this face to face or on the phone, but to put questions in writing instead, as I felt this would allow me to be polite and clear and would allow them time to consider. My email explained that I realised they were under no obligation to disclose their salaries and might prefer not to, but that the recent revelations compelled me to ask in an attempt to make sense of my own pay story.

The responses were mixed. Some men, like the Middle East Editor Jeremy Bowen and the World Affairs Editor John Simpson, were generous with information. Others were less so. Asking became easier the more often I did it, and in the end I wished I had started years ago as it came to feel natural and collegiate, just something that all grown-ups should do. I felt grateful to those who shared. Theirs was a real-world demonstration of empathy, one of the simplest but most powerful things a man can do to help a woman achieve equal pay.

It is still rare. In many societies, talking about money is taboo. In the UK, people are much more willing to discuss their sex life, including their sexual partners, extramarital affairs and sexually transmitted diseases, than they are to discuss their salaries.

What makes it worse is that many employment contracts include pay secrecy clauses, which appear to bar employees from discussing their pay. They make women afraid to ask and men afraid to disclose. In fact, for any conversation in a given workplace relating to equal pay, these clauses are unenforceable in law. But recent research suggests that three in five employees remain uncomfortable asking colleagues what they earn, one in two believe their managers would respond negatively to more openness and one in three don't know that talking to colleagues about pay is not illegal.

'Pay discrimination is able to thrive and is more common than people realise because of a culture of pay secrecy,' said Sam Smethers, the CEO of gender equality charity the Fawcett Society which commissioned the research.

Women need to ask, men need to disclose, and employers need to consider that while pay secrecy may seem expedient in the short term, it has a long-term cost in economic justice and efficiency.

Men can be underpaid too. After researching my pay history, I was in turn able to help one or two male colleagues. In general, I became more conscious of how chaotic the BBC's pay culture was. And I learned that for the best part of two decades I had been paid much less than most of the men I worked alongside.

What about you? Do you know what men or women who do the same work as you earn? Do you often talk to colleagues about pay, bonuses, and benefits like health insurance, childcare vouchers, tuition fees and gym memberships? Do you know the reasons why you get paid more or less than a peer? If you ever ask for a pay rise, are you specific about the reasons and the amount? Do you ever consider other job options?

If the answer to some of these questions is yes, you're already in much better shape than I was. If the answer to all of these questions is no, you may want to reflect on that. Fifty-five was quite late for me to get real, but I'm glad I didn't go to my grave ignorant.

Consider the cumulative cost of being paid less. Add up the years of pay, and perhaps pension too. It may be worth the short-term discomfort to face facts now. Understanding your reality doesn't commit you to any course of action.

In gathering facts, you could start by looking at pay websites to try to understand what's normal for your role. You might want to read your latest performance evaluation if you have one. List things you do that go unmentioned but add value. Keep listing them often, especially if the ways you add value are not obvious to your boss because of the nature of your role. If you work for a large UK employer, read your employer's gender pay gap report. Find opportunities to bring up the gender pay gap in a non-threatening way, perhaps by referencing a story in the news. Ask peers about pay. It may be easiest to start with someone who is leaving or has just left. Ask friends and family – women and men – about their experiences.

If there are male colleagues who don't initially want to discuss pay, try not to hold it against them. Play the long game. After all, not all women find it easy to be open about their salary either. Proceed with tact, and if you start sharing information among a small group, other colleagues may end up asking to join.

When you feel ready, ask for a pay meeting with your boss. If your employer has grades and bands, you could ask exactly where you sit and why. If you work for a small employer or in a context where everyone's pay is individual, discuss some of the less obvious ways you add value and check whether they are reflected in your pay. Whatever the size of your employer, you can talk about how you'd like to advance. If you have a specific pay rise in mind, say so. Support your case with as much data as you can muster. Don't expect an answer on the spot. Allow your boss time to think and respond. If you feel awkward about scheduling a special meeting to talk about pay, use your annual review or appraisal to raise the issue. Regular appraisals are not a legal requirement for employers, but many accept that they are good practice.

I know how difficult it can be to ask colleagues about their pay or to ask your boss about your own. But I discover it's rather like talking about other delicate subjects, such as sex or death. It gets easier the more you try. Don't beat yourself up if you don't manage the conversations exactly as you'd like or if you don't immediately get the outcome you want. Even just by starting down this road you're doing something for yourself and for women everywhere. Be proud. As the tennis champion Serena Williams pointed out in a personal essay in the summer of 2017, 'The cycles of poverty, discrimination and sexism are much, much harder to break than the record for Grand Slam titles . . .

Black women: be fearless. Speak out for equal pay. Every time you do, you're making it a little easier for a woman behind you.'

On the topic of difficult conversations, here's another: do you understand the law?

I'm ashamed to say that I didn't. Before I went to China, I'd simply demanded equal pay without knowing how it works. Legal systems may be different from country to country, but many of the underlying principles of equal pay legislation are essentially the same. It didn't take much reading for me to grasp the basics.

Under the UK Equality Act 2010, employers must give men and women equal treatment in the terms and conditions of their employment contract if they are employed to do 'equal work'. This can be one of three things: 'like work', which means work that is the same or broadly similar; work rated as equivalent under a job evaluation study; or work found to be of equal value in terms of variables like effort, skill or decision-making. That third category, equal value, enables an employment tribunal to compare very different jobs and still find them to be 'equal work'.

'Pay' means all and any sums payable in connection with employment that are within the scope of the Equality Act 2010, including basic pay, shift pay, allowances, pension, bonus, sick pay, redundancy and unfair dismissal compensation awards, whether payable under an express term of their contracts or otherwise.

To claim equal pay, an employee must name a 'comparator' – that is, an employee of the opposite sex working for the same employer whom they believe to be doing equal work. A woman should claim equal pay with a man and vice versa.

If an employer wants to resist an equal pay claim, they must show that the claimant is not doing equal work. Or, in cases where they accept that the employee is doing equal work, they must show that the difference in pay is due to a material factor and not based on the sex of the employee. These factors may include personal differences such as experience and qualifications; they may include geographical differences; or factors like unsocial hours, rotating shift work and night working. The employer must identify the factors and prove that they are the real reason for the pay disparity, and that they are not in themselves discriminatory. Discrimination does not have to be intentional to occur.

It seemed unlikely the BBC could deny I was doing equal work. It would be hard to argue that reporting from North America required more effort, skill or decision-making than reporting from China. Perhaps my managers would plead 'material factors', something to do with the market?

To get to the bottom of this I pored over judgments from employment tribunals and discovered that it's not an adequate defence for an employer simply to assert that they paid a man more because that was necessary to attract and retain him in the post. To defend a pay difference by reference to market rates an employer should have evidence of the market rate at the time of recruitment. They should also show that they applied a consistent rate to employees with the same skills.

Moreover, when employers pay men what they were earning in a previous job, they are potentially indirectly discriminating against female candidates by perpetuating the gender pay gap. Sometimes judges conclude that the real reason for a man's higher pay is simply that he asked for it and the employer gave it to him. These judges are not stupid, I thought to myself.

Employment tribunals also take a dim view of employers with no transparency around pay criteria. Again and again, judges urge the introduction of coherent, transparent, criterion-based pay systems. The BBC employs about twenty thousand people and I thought there might be parts of it which met this test, but

I knew that there were certainly no coherent, transparent criteria for the pay of presenters and senior reporters in BBC News. I half expected my bosses to come back after their August holidays saying that, on reflection, they wanted to admit mistakes and apologise. BBC staff are very loyal and our anger hadn't hardened. Many of us would have been glad to forgive the past in exchange for a route map to a better future.

Before going back to China in early September, I had separate meetings with the Director of News and the Director-General. There was no admission or apology from either.

It felt strange to be in conflict with James Harding. Usually when we met, he and I would share wry jokes about our China challenges. I once painted myself as the Frodo Baggins of the BBC, forced to leave the bucolic life of the Shire and set out to do journalism in Mordor under the jealous eye of Sauron.

China's already cool climate for freedom of speech had chilled further in the era of Xi Jinping. A handful of foreign reporters had effectively been expelled by having their credentials revoked. Occasionally foreign NGO staff or businesspeople went missing, only to turn up in detention or on a flight out.

Since 2015, I'd faced down repeated warnings from the Chinese authorities about my work. In early 2017 I made a podcast series called *Murder in the Lucky Holiday Hotel*. It was a narrative about the workings of elite Communist Party politics, told through a true-life murder story involving sex, corruption and espionage. Official outrage in Beijing was fierce. The risk of a brief detention seemed real enough to think about contingencies. I gave instructions to two close friends who'd both served as BBC Beijing producers on what to do in the event of my sudden disappearance.

As Director of News, James had got used to making the uncomfortably short walk from Broadcasting House to the Chinese embassy on the other side of Portland Place, where he would patiently endure a dressing-down from an irate ambassador about my work and that of other BBC reporters in China.

I was grateful to have a boss who understood the importance of the story while calmly sandbagging against the Chinese censorship pressures that lapped at our door and those of many other newsrooms, boardrooms and university campuses. James remained as fascinated by the China story as I was. Once when I popped in to see him just before Chinese New Year he asked what animal I was in the Chinese zodiac.

'Tiger,' I said.

'That figures,' he grinned. 'I'm a rooster.'

The astrologers say tigers are brave, impetuous and irritable. Roosters are confident, smart and like to succeed. Tigers and roosters are not always compatible.

There were no jokes when James and I met to discuss equal pay on 10 August 2017. He pleaded that he had wanted to pay me the same as the North America Editor from the start. But he also said he had 'bent over backwards' to make it possible for women like me to do high-profile reporting jobs. In the past I would have been disarmed because it was true. He had promoted women. But he had been just as flexible with senior men while paying them much more. Besides, by not moving my children to Beijing, I had saved the BBC a lot of money in housing, healthcare and education, and I had borne the costs of a second home in the UK. When in China I worked seven days a week to make up for not being there all the time. The team in the Beijing bureau described me as a workhorse and together we'd done a lot of very fine work. If I'd delivered less value than male peers, someone would have to explain how.

When I met the Director-General later that month, I warned him not to make BBC Women the enemy. I urged that salaries for top men in News should come down so that women could be equal without squeezing pay for everyone else. Tony Hall listened politely, but when I look back on that meeting I feel we inhabited competing realities.

If you experience this kind of parallel universe when you broach gender pay, don't be daunted. I imagine all important social change triggers these moments of incomprehension.

That same day I visited a different kind of leader, Jeremy Heywood, Cabinet Secretary and head of the Civil Service. Jeremy and I had been friends since we were at university. Now I found him in hospital on an intravenous drip. He'd begun outpatient chemotherapy treatment while continuing to attend weekly Cabinet meetings and working almost as hard as ever.

Jeremy always had one eye fixed on the future. On the table by his hospital bed sat a huge tome about how to achieve equality in the workplace, Iris Bohnet's *What Works: Gender Equality by Design*. We talked at length about his plans for a more diverse Civil Service and about the pay crisis at the BBC. And then he reduced me to helpless laughter with a comic account of the events of 9 June. He had received his cancer diagnosis the day after the 2017 general election, and the same day the UK woke to a hung parliament. The story of colliding personal and public crises shouldn't have been funny, but Jeremy told it brilliantly and without self-pity. As I left him to his chemo drip and equality textbook, I reflected on what a very special public servant he was.

The BBC is also a vital public service. The duty of its reporters is to tell the truth that matters without fear or favour. By this stage, a month had passed since the initial pay disclosures, stories of gross inequality were coming in from women across the organisation and bosses showed no urgency in tackling them. I decided it was time to escalate.

It wasn't hard. In the UK, an equal pay complaint is as simple as an email to HR in which an employee states that they believe they may not have received equality of pay or terms in accordance with the Equality Act 2010, naming a comparator of the opposite sex. I named the North America Editor Jon Sopel and, having pressed send on my complaint, I went back to China, worked harder than ever and waited for my employer's next move.

Little did I know that with one short email I was embarking on the toughest assignment of my BBC career.

2

STOP, THINK

=

Equal pay for equal work sounds straightforward. Children can certainly manage it, as an experiment in Norway demonstrated when it paired young boys and girls to test their response to unequal rewards.

First each girl and boy completed a task together, collecting plastic balls and sorting them by colour into tall vases. With the task complete, the adult in charge gave each child a jar of sweets. For the girls, initial joy turned to disbelief when they saw their male partner had a full jar, while they got only half. The adult explained that this was because they were girls.

At which point, it was the boys who took action. Each started by looking puzzled and uncomfortable. But then each gave up his privilege.

'She was just as good as me, so we should get the same reward,' explained one boy as he redistributed sweets from his jar into his partner's. When the jars looked about level, both children were smiling again. And so it went on with each pair.

This informal experiment was conducted by the Finansforbundet trade union and the video shown to their members and posted on Facebook under the caption 'What do these kids understand that your boss doesn't?'

Good question. In my workplace, the pay revelations of 2017 and the debate that followed meant we could now see that the sweet jars were unequal. Same task, different rewards. But the boys did not share their sweets and the adults were silent. There is no set time limit for an employer to respond to an equal pay complaint. I'd submitted mine on 22 August and the BBC had promised to resolve my case by the end of September, but its first response didn't come until 10 October. That gave me time to do what journalists are supposed to do: ask questions.

The big one: why do women still face unequal pay? I live in a country where women make up nearly half the labour force and equal pay has been the law for half a century. Pay discrimination shouldn't be happening. I embarked upon a lot of reading and thinking and this is the answer I came up with: unequal pay happens because pay is very complex and it's in the interests of some people to keep it that way.

Let me go back to the Norwegian experiment to explain. There, the comparison of the children's tasks and rewards was immediate and easy, but in the adult workplace, comparison is very hard. Often men and women are told they're putting balls of different colours into vases of different shapes, which makes it hard to form judgements about whether work is equal. The women are given an additional set of unpaid duties at home, which means they come and go at different times. When the sweets are handed out, they are in opaque jars not clear ones, and the adult warns that talking about sweets is forbidden. Will the boys share their rewards now? As the American writer Upton Sinclair observed in the early 1930s, 'It is difficult to get a man to understand something when his salary depends upon his not understanding it.'

Some things about pay are inevitably complex, but non-essential complexity and opacity are also ways for employers to retain control. They choose the balls, the vases, the rooms, the jars. They record the tasks completed and count out the sweets. The employer is often male and explains that pay gaps are largely because men dominate senior roles. But why is that? Pay is a game in which the winners set the rules and the next generation of winners tends to look rather like the previous generation.

In ancient Egypt, the priesthood established political control through orchestrating public ignorance of flood patterns; in medieval Europe, the Catholic clergy monopolised literacy. In the first decade of the twenty-first century, some people got rich from credit default swaps and collateralised debt obligations before others got poor from bubbles bursting. Making things complex is one of the ways elites entrench privilege and baffle the rest of humanity. But I'm not a conspiracy theorist. I'm not arguing that most employers consciously and deliberately pay women less just because they are women.

It is time to meet Mark and Elizabeth. In an illuminating study, hundreds of British veterinary employers were asked whether they thought women in their profession still faced discrimination. At the same time, they were invited to review the performance evaluation of a vet. For half of the participants, that vet was called Mark. For the other half, the vet was named Elizabeth. Apart from the name, the evaluation was identical.

Forty-four per cent of the respondents said they thought gender discrimination was a thing of the past. But when asked what salary was appropriate to Mark/Elizabeth, the very same people offered Mark significantly higher pay than Elizabeth. The more strongly employers believed gender discrimination was a thing of the past, the more they discriminated against Elizabeth on pay.

The same 44 per cent also rated Mark as significantly more competent than Elizabeth. They would be more likely to let Mark take on more managerial responsibilities and more strongly encourage him to pursue promotions. Mark's performance evaluation was exactly the same as Elizabeth's. These employers displayed what is called unconscious bias.

The more research I read on the effects of bias in the workplace the more I suspected that the same point holds not just for British vets but across many industries and occupations, and across the globe. Employers who think gender discrimination is not happening are in denial. Often they themselves are discriminators and through their own blindness are perpetuating the problem.

This makes them dangerous, but it does not make them wicked. Wherever humans are headed, we're a species with a patriarchal history, and most of our brain activity lies beyond conscious awareness. We make all kinds of assumptions unconsciously, and even more so in groups. As long as our experience confirms, or at least doesn't contradict, these assumptions, we tend to save on cognitive effort by holding onto them. After all, stereotyping is useful when it helps us to navigate the world without being overwhelmed by information. But stereotyping is a problem when it hardwires prejudices on gender – or for that matter on race, class, disability, sexual orientation or age. Precisely because so much bias is unconscious it's very difficult to see, let alone measure or fix.

Gender bias forms early, with TV programmes and toy catalogues reinforcing the message that men go out to work and women look after the home and children. Ask children anywhere to draw a firefighter, pilot or surgeon and they'll generally tell you the person in their picture is a man. Ask them to draw a nurse or hairdresser and they'll tell you that's a woman. Employers are just those children grown up.

In case you thought British veterinary employers were in a bias class of their own, similar findings come up in other sectors, and research in relation to race produces even more shocking results. One labour-market study found job-hunters from ethnic minority backgrounds had to send 80 per cent more applications than a white person of British origin to get a positive response from employers. These forms of discrimination then compound each other. In the UK, black women of African descent have seen virtually no progress in closing the gender pay gap with white men since the 1990s.

All victims of workplace discrimination are not just materially poorer from being knocked back in decisions on recruitment, promotion and pay. They are conditioned to internalise an inferiority complex and reflect back to the world the belief that they only ever deserved half a jar of sweets.

My research brought me to the book Jeremy Heywood had been reading on the day I visited him in hospital. In *What Works: Gender Equality by Design*, the behavioural economist Iris Bohnet offers an examination of academic research on unconscious bias in the workplace.

Take recruitment. Bohnet considers experiments showing that when a male candidate had more experience but less education than a female candidate, recruiters said they valued experience more; when the male candidate had more education, they inflated the relative value of education. Recruiters demonstrated similar ex-post justifications for race as well. 'They justified their decisions, made on biased social categories, by using information on experience and education selectively.'

Performance evaluation? Bohnet examines research suggesting that men evaluate themselves more positively than women do. And when it comes to evaluating others, there's an added twist. In one study, management students were asked to evaluate two entrepreneurs, Heidi and Howard, whose attributes were identical other than gender. They judged Heidi as competent and effective but they did not like her and did not want to work with her. Howard, by contrast, was both competent and likeable.

Bohnet writes: 'What is celebrated as entrepreneurship,

self-confidence, and vision in a man is perceived as arrogance and self-promotion in a woman.'

Pay? Of course. According to Bohnet, negative reactions to demanding job candidates are much larger when the pronoun 'she' is used in place of 'he'. 'Not only did employers counter women's already lower demands with more stingy counter-offers, they responded less positively when women tried to self-promote.'

This puts women in a bind, because the evidence suggests people who don't press for better pay are not just worse off than those who do, but considerably worse off.

The actress Jennifer Lawrence learned this the hard way after a hacker group released a huge cache of confidential data from the film studio Sony Pictures. In a piece entitled 'Why do I make less than my male co-stars?' she wrote,

> When the Sony hack happened and I found out how much less I was being paid than the lucky people with dicks, I didn't get mad at Sony. I got mad at myself. I failed as a negotiator because I gave up early ... I didn't want to seem 'difficult' or 'spoiled.' At the time, that seemed like a fine idea, until I saw the payroll on the Internet and realised every man I was working with definitely didn't worry about being 'difficult' or 'spoiled' ... I'm over trying to find the 'adorable' way to state my opinion and still be likable! Fuck that.

A sentiment that many women share, but the problem is that, Hollywood stars aside, even women who ask mostly still don't get.

At this point in my reading I felt puzzled. The evidence seemed overwhelming that gender bias in the workplace is real and – not always, but often – has a significant impact on pay. Human brains are simply trained to expect more for men: more attention, airtime, power ... and money. Much of the evidence is two or even three decades old. Large organisations stuffed with HR professionals should long ago have designed strategies to counter bias, whether in recruitment, progression or pay.

The answer is not suppression. According to Bohnet, suppression of bias doesn't work: 'In extreme cases, instructions to resist stereotypes had the opposite effect, making stereotypes more salient and leading to an increase in biased judgments.' What works, she writes, is a sustained awareness of the risk of bias, hard thinking about the ways it might operate in any given context, and consistent monitoring and feedback.*

Bohnet argues that transparency about what is negotiable helps. In a study of American MBA graduates going into their first job, female applicants who understood what was negotiable eliminated the gender pay gap. But where that was left ambiguous, men made about ten thousand dollars more than women from the very outset of their careers.

The catch is that those who are never the victim of the bias find it harder to believe it exists. In the study of veterinary employers, two-thirds of those who believed gender discrimination was no longer a problem – while actively discriminating against Elizabeth – were male. Because men are much less likely to experience a negative reaction when they attempt to negotiate, some argue that if women earn less it is because of their perverse unwillingness to bargain like men. According to the former newspaper editor Piers Morgan, 'Historically, in my experience, I would say women are far less pushy about valuing themselves in the way that men were leaping to do every five

---

* If you haven't done so already, it's worth starting down this road by taking the online bias tests created by Harvard University. They are available not just for gender, but also race, age and sexuality. https://implicit.harvard.edu/implicit/takeatest.html.

minutes. Men were far more aggressive at getting the better deals and women didn't like to have the confrontation ... I think women need to be more forceful about getting their value assessed properly.'

Should pay and promotion be decided by who is most forceful? That will tend to be elite white men for as long as class, race and gender privilege give them more confidence. Forcefulness and confidence do not equal competence. According to a study of US bankers, those more willing to negotiate advanced more quickly, but assertiveness did not predict performance. The more assertive employee, but not necessary the best performer, was being promoted.

The organisational psychologist Tomas Chamorro-Premuzic writes that 'because we (people in general) commonly mis-interpret displays of confidence as a sign of competence, we are fooled into believing that men are better leaders than women ... Yet arrogance and overconfidence are inversely related to leader-ship talent – the ability to build and maintain high-performing teams, and to inspire followers to set aside their selfish agendas in order to work for the common interest of the group.'

In her book *Invisible Women: Exposing Data Bias in a World Designed for Men*, Caroline Criado Perez points out all the ways our world is designed around what suits 'Reference Man', from workplace temperature to car seatbelts and heart attack protocols.

Negotiating for pay is on that list. As Iris Bohnet explained, forcefulness works for women only where the employer invites it. Signals from the employer set the rules of the game. If you are an employer, are you making a determined effort to send clear signals to women on what is negotiable? Or are you falling for the 'because I'm worth it' hype of the force-ful employee? Can you exorcise 'Reference Man' from your workplace to carefully measure who delivers what, and pay on that basis? Can you de-bias your recruitment and progression habits too?

Women will in fact do a lot of this work for you if you give them the information, but if you won't, they can't. I'd always instinctively been in favour of much more pay transparency but now I realised why it matters so much. Going back to our vets, Elizabeth and Mark, if they are recruited by the same employer, doing the same work and can see each other's pay, Elizabeth will soon spot a problem. She will ask Mark about his qualifications and experience, make her own assessment of whether these justify the pay gap between them, and if she feels they don't, she can query that with her boss.

The trouble is that in most workplaces Elizabeth does not know Mark's pay. She may have been hired with exactly the same CV but years, decades, an entire career, can go by without her finding out that she was paid less from day one and the gap has since widened because of the promotions and managerial responsibilities unequally offered to Mark. Employers often argue that pay secrecy has nothing to do with discrimination but simply allows them to exercise their discretion without every decision being questioned by every employee. This caution is understandable. Calculations around the value of each employee's skill, experience and market value are nuanced, and as we'd seen at the BBC, sudden transparency can have turbulent consequences. But handled well, transparency can build employee loyalty. The more people know about why they earn what they do and how that relates to their peers, the more satisfied they are and the less likely they are to chase higher pay elsewhere. And in conditions of pay secrecy, the onus is entirely on employers to carefully monitor, interrogate and challenge their own pay decisions for compliance with equality law.

Rigorous gender-neutral job evaluations and rigorous independent equal pay audits would be two ways of achieving this, but currently they are the exception rather than the rule. A job evaluation scores training and skills, conditions of work, effort required and decision-making. Points are then given under each heading and the score translated into a value. This allows very different jobs to fall within the same grade. A non-discriminatory job evaluation must not be influenced by gender stereotypes or attach less importance to certain qualities or roles. I've made it sound daunting but actually a job evaluation scheme is just a glorified marking scheme such as any examination board has to operate. What is daunting for employers is that introducing such a scheme can cause massive disruption to pay arrangements by highlighting underlying problems. To place their heads firmly in the sand may sometimes seem an attractive alternative, as this account by Robin Allen, QC, makes clear:

> I recall being instructed in the early 2000s by a small council that had undergone a job evaluation study but not yet published the results. The study showed a consistent pattern of overpayment of men relative to women through bonuses and special premia. The council wanted to know if it was permissible to ignore the result and continue as before. When I explained that the answer was no, the leading – as I recall, male – officers and councillors were appalled and argued that it would lead to the deepest unrest in their workforce. They could not afford to bring the women up to the men's rates. They accepted my advice as right but refused to consider implementing its consequences and did not instruct me further.

As for job evaluations, so for equal pay audits. The Equality and Human Rights Commission warns employers: 'It's not possible to know whether your organisation's pay system is compliant with equal pay legislation without undertaking an equal pay audit.'

But fearing that an equal pay audit might dislodge too many bricks in the Jenga tower of their pay structure, few employers heed the warning.

In the UK, I couldn't even find a national estimate of unequal pay. The only relevant publicly available measure was the 'unexplained' element of the gender pay gap. In 2017, the UK's gender pay gap was 18 per cent. Just over a third of that was explained by observed differences including age, industry and occupation. Sixty-four per cent was unexplained. The gender pay gap has narrowed since the Equal Pay Act of 1970, but in this century, progress has slowed. At the current rate, it will not close for another half-century. Many countries are even worse. I consoled myself that at least I wasn't in South Korea. Women there had the largest gender pay gap of the developed world, at 36 per cent, and that's despite achieving better qualifications than men.

In New Zealand, too, women outstrip men on education. There the Ministry for Women says around 80 per cent of the country's gender pay gap is now due to 'unexplained' factors. It adds bluntly: 'We, at the Ministry for Women, view these factors primarily as behaviour, attitudes, and assumptions about women in work, including unconscious bias.'

The size and persistence of the unexplained gender pay gap are now very striking in most developed economies. In 2017 the UK's Office for National Statistics warned that 'the unexplained element should not be interpreted as a measure of discriminatory behaviour, though it is possible that this plays a part'.

How could it not play a part, I wondered.

Measured against the span of human history, women's legal right to equal pay is a brand-new idea. Half a century later, we've barely begun to enforce it. And what a tremendous war of attrition that has been.

Unfinished business

For women of previous generations, the challenge was often to get into the paid labour force at all. The nineteenth century did see growing numbers working for wages in domestic service or textile factories, but mostly their roles were intermittent, part-time or casual, and the presumption remained that most women should work unpaid in the home. Limited legal status and property rights made it difficult for married women to operate businesses.

According to the historian Professor Mary Davis, the demand for equal pay first surfaced in the 1830s with one union journal, the *Pioneer*, arguing, 'The low wages of women are not so much the voluntary price she sets upon her labour, as the price which is fixed by the tyrannical influence of male supremacy.'

But the union movement was mostly male and mostly hostile. Unequal pay was the norm, with women only tolerated in the workforce when they didn't threaten men. Until the First World War, when women across Europe flooded into factories, farming and transport to fill the places of men who'd enlisted to fight. In 1919, women's contribution was recognised when the principle of 'equal remuneration for work of equal value' was written into the Treaty of Versailles that ended the war. But the backlash soon began, with opponents of equal pay arguing that women should earn less than men because they had no dependants and pay should be based on need. A century on, the stereotype of the male breadwinner still hovers over women when they ask for a pay rise, only for a boss to say, 'What do you need more money for?'

A second set of opponents insisted that women deserved lower pay because the jobs they did required less skill and experience. It took another world war and another spike in the demand for female labour to reinforce the point that women really could do the same jobs. From 1941 British women were conscripted and by 1943 almost 90 per cent of single women and 80 per cent of married women were employed in war work, many of them in roles that had once been the preserve of men.

The trend was global. Australian newsreels showed women in munitions factories and the US deployed the iconic image of 'Rosie the Riveter' to encourage women to believe they could do 'men's' work. India, Canada, Italy and Poland were among the many countries that enlisted women in their armed forces and the Soviet Union integrated them into main army units as anti-aircraft gunners, combat flyers and snipers.

But equal work still did not mean equal pay. Professor Davis writes that during the Second World War, British women earned on average 53 per cent of the pay of the men they replaced: 'Unequal pay was not new, but the overt injustice of it was all the more marked now that women had temporary access to the traditionally better paid all-male craft jobs.'

After the war, 'men's' work became men's again and women were driven back into gender-segregated roles where pay was generally lower. In the UK, no political party championed equal pay for women until the 1960s and trade unions often continued to defend male privilege, warning female members that higher pay for women would lead to job losses for men.

'You only come to work for pin money,' scoffed the men at the Dagenham car plant in 1968 when women there began a historic fight for recognition of their skills. There were 187 women to nearly fifty-five thousand men at what was then Ford's biggest factory in Europe.

'Can you work a sewing machine?' the women retorted. Their job was to make seat covers, and they'd gone on strike after their jobs were downgraded. Teenage boys sweeping the floors were earning more than skilled female machinists. When the women went out on strike, the stock of seat covers ran out and all car production stopped. Eileen Pullen later remembered the hostility of female neighbours: 'A lot of women jeered us. They didn't go to work and their husbands were at Fords and we'd put them out of work.'

For Gwen Davis, it was an awakening on more than equal pay: 'It made me realise that women can fight for their rights just like men.'

The strike lasted three weeks before Ford gave in and raised their pay. The Dagenham machinists had made history. Thanks in part to their struggle, the UK passed the Equal Pay Act in 1970. Other major drivers of equal pay legislation were the determination of the Labour politician Barbara Castle and the UK's impending entry to the European Economic Community (EEC). The forerunner of the European Union, its founding treaty declared that men and women should receive equal pay for equal work.

The big fights in history are often longer, harder and more complex than later generations care to remember. The Dagenham machinists may have won a pay rise in 1968, but they didn't actually get classed as skilled workers and win pay parity until a second strike sixteen years later. The Equal Pay Act was passed in 1970 but not implemented until 1976, to give employers time to adjust. According to Professor Davis, 'This meant that they had nearly six years to re-grade jobs in discriminatory ways thus rendering them immune from the very limited scope of the act.'

It's impossible to read this history without concluding that many politicians, unionists and business leaders have devoted great energy and ingenuity to letting women down. Certainly the complexities around defining and enforcing equal pay have offered plenty of places for employers to hide. What's called occupational sorting means that women are over-represented in low-paying sectors and occupations including social care, childcare and retail. Even when women are in similar occupations to men, employers have often created minor differences between roles and argued that as the work is not equal, there is no need for equal pay.

In 1975, the EEC passed a directive to enable women in all member states to claim that two roles are of equal value even if the work content is very different. Key to equal value claims is a careful gender-neutral job evaluation to score the roles for factors like training and skills, conditions of work, effort required and decision-making.

The UK dragged its feet until 1982, when the European Court of Justice instructed it to pass domestic legislation to make such claims possible. A series of test cases followed, ranging from speech therapists to canteen workers, fish packers and prison staff. In April 1985, fifteen fish packers were the first women in the UK to win an equal pay claim for work of equal value. The hero of their story was actually a man. Interviewed later for a TV documentary, Peter Allen of the Transport and General Workers' Union explained that what got him started was a nagging sense of injustice:

> I'm thinking to myself 70 per cent of my members are women, but I concentrate on looking after the men. Keep them happy and my job is easy. I decided there and then that I would be an officer to all my members ... No woman goes out ... filleting fish and trimming fish for the stimulating company. They go out for money ... So I started looking at the rates and that's when I realised we had a male rate and a woman's rate ... my job was to eradicate the differences.

By the time of his retirement Pete Allen had fought eighteen equal value cases for female members of the TGWU. He won seventeen of them.

An equal value ruling can cost an employer huge sums of money, both in terms of back pay and pay going forward. So whatever their personal ethics, their opinions on the true value of their female workforce or the legal merits of the case, employers have a strong financial incentive to resist for as long as possible.

I was shocked to read of the epic legal battles that public sector employers often waged to defend their discriminatory pay structures. Imagine an employer so intransigent that it repeatedly rejected its own job evaluations and lodged eleven appeals against court decisions over the course of a decade. That was the British Prison Service in the 1990s, trying to preserve a big pay gap between male prison officers and female administrative staff.

It took fifteen years for speech therapists in the National Health Service. They claimed equal value with the predominantly male professions of clinical psychology and pharmacy, but the government instructed individual NHS trusts not to settle and instead spent millions of pounds fighting women through nearly thirty court appearances, culminating in the European Court of Justice.

Claimants like the senior speech therapist Pam Enderby showed enormous grit. They also had solid financial support and coordination from their unions, and backing from the then regulator, the Equal Opportunities Commission.

The speech therapist case ground on from 1986 to 2000 and the Manufacturing, Science and Finance union was nearly bankrupted by legal costs. Eventually it secured equal pay for fifteen hundred women, helped establish an important point in law, and contributed to pressure for an overhaul of grading across the National Health Service. Until the NHS Agenda for Change was introduced in 2004, it wasn't just speech therapists who earned less than clinical psychologists. Female floor washers and cooks earned less than male wall washers and plumbers. Nurses earned far less than carpenters despite higher qualifications and greater responsibilities. Many women who work in the NHS today have cause to be grateful to Pam Enderby and the other pioneers of this fight.

Reading these cases, I felt moved. In the first twenty-five years after the Equal Pay Act, the UK's full-time gender pay gap halved from 36 to 18 per cent. Of course, other factors were involved: the growing availability of contraception, which allowed women to control their fertility; the shift away from manual labour; the feminist movement. But the patient struggle by working women, unionists and regulators had surely helped.

In the 1980s, the UK had its first female Prime Minister, but Margaret Thatcher did not champion equal pay. Her objective was to tackle what she saw as the undue power of the trade unions and to reduce wage costs for employers through deregulation and competitive tendering. Many of the service jobs that women typically did were contracted out and women often found they had few male colleagues with whom they could compare themselves in an equal pay claim. Neither in the public nor in the private sector was there an attempt to assess the discrimination baked into decades of pay habits and to conduct a thorough, gender-neutral re-evaluation of women's contribution at work.

In the last decade of the twentieth century and first decade of the twenty-first, progress towards equality slowed. Patchy enforcement of the law seemed to be a factor. The union movement had always had a chequered record on equal pay. The hard truth is that in most real-world workplaces, pay budgets rarely grow. More for women often means less for men. Measured short term and on money alone, the fight for equal pay can look to men like a zero-sum game in which they are losers. By now all unions endorsed the principle of equal pay, but when it came to bargaining processes, some found it hard to reconcile the competing interests of male and female members. At the same time, the power of the unions had been eroded by Thatcherite deregulation of labour markets, and then came under further pressure from the forces of globalisation and the gig economy. Just as women were pulling equal with men on education and skills, and arriving in the workforce with greater expectations of equality, the unions they joined were struggling to defend existing pay bargaining arrangements. The decade after the global financial crash saw a steep decline in real wages, particularly for men, and a steady reduction in the share of the economy covered by collective bargaining. A fitfully resolute equal pay fight found its limits.

The UK regulator seemed less effective too. The Equal Opportunities Commission had one focus, tackling sex discrimination in the workplace, but in 2007 it was replaced by an Equality and Human Rights Commission that was spread thin across diverse agendas including gender, race, ethnicity, disability and religion. It then lost much of its budget in the public spending squeeze that followed the financial crash.

The gap left by unions and regulator was partially filled by a private sector model, the no win no fee lawyer. In the UK, the most famous of these was Stefan Cross. The son of a cleaner, Cross had been a trade union activist in his youth and for sixteen years he'd worked for the union solicitors Thompsons. But what he saw convinced him that the unions were not doing enough for their female members: 'The number one priority was to protect the pay of those who were already getting the higher pay; the men essentially. A study done in 1999 by local government showed that 80 per cent of men's jobs were getting bonuses while only 1.2 per cent of women's jobs were. What's more shocking is that the unions and the employers already knew.'

Stefan Cross fought equal pay cases against local government employers on behalf of thousands of female cleaners, canteen staff and care workers. He even won a case against a union for discriminating against its own female members. Cross became a hero to some and a hate figure to others. When he won a case worth over £1 billion against Birmingham City Council, the city was forced to sell its National Exhibition Centre. In 2017, he was waging another epic battle for female council workers in Glasgow. Despite being deemed of equal value, the council's female-dominated jobs such as catering and cleaning were paid less than 'male' jobs such as refuse collection and gravedigging because of a complex pay system which penalised those working split shifts and irregular hours.

Another legal firm, Leigh Day, deployed the no win no fee model to mount the largest equal pay action in the UK private sector, representing more than thirty thousand mostly female store workers who claimed that their work for the UK's big supermarkets was of equal value to the mostly male warehouse staff.

The supermarket Asda said: 'Pay rates in stores differ from pay rates in distribution centres because the demands of the jobs in stores and the jobs in distribution centres are very different; they operate in different market sectors and we pay the market rate in those sectors regardless of gender.'

The Employment Tribunal ruled against Asda in October 2016, saying checkout workers and shelf-stackers could compare themselves with warehouse staff. Asda appealed, and in August 2017 the Employment Appeal Tribunal ruled against the company again. Asda then took its case to the Court of Appeal.

Comparing one job with another is only the first stage of the process. If the supermarkets appeal at every stage, this legal action is likely to last a decade.

For large groups of women with almost identical jobs, the no win no fee model may be slow but at least it limits cost and risk, and gives women a mechanism for enforcing the law on equal pay. It does not help women in workplaces with individualised contracts, wide job bands and pay secrecy. As far as I can make out, women in these circumstances have almost no means of enforcing the law.

Break financial rules or safety rules, and employers might face a hefty fine or a trading suspension. But on equality legislation, it looks as if they can get away with asserting that they are paying all their men and women equally and wait for an individual employee to prove them wrong.

Proving them wrong is inconceivable, except for women who are supremely stubborn, rich enough to bear the legal costs of lodging a claim at tribunal – or both.

The unequal fight

Pursuing an equal pay claim against an employer is enormously time-consuming. It can cost a woman her career, her mental health and, if she pays for legal advice, her financial security. Without safety in numbers there is a risk of victimisation. The law says victimisation is illegal, but then the law also says pay discrimination is illegal, so that makes two laws a woman now has to enforce.

Even the few women who are rich or stubborn enough to litigate on equal pay tend to settle their cases on the threshold of an employment tribunal and submit to a gagging clause rather than fight all the way to a public hearing. Which means their female colleagues remain unaware of the discrimination risk, the employer is spared any pressure to change and the public is none the wiser. As for low-paid women without union support, they can't afford lawyers. They seem to have no legal redress unless they conduct their own case. In a cost-cutting move after the financial crisis, the government removed legal aid for employment advice. It even imposed fees for lodging claims at an employment tribunal. In 2017, the Law Society warned that together these moves 'create a huge barrier to access to justice for workers seeking to enforce their legal rights'.

When I learned this, I was dismayed. Lone women were already expected to enforce the law themselves, fighting battles that might last years against employers who controlled their careers and enjoyed an overwhelming advantage in resources and information. Now the government wanted to charge women even for access to the battlefield.

I had to get up from my desk, step out onto the balcony of my thirtieth-floor Beijing apartment and take a few deep breaths of polluted night air. Living in China and reporting on its many injustices, I knew all about countries where the law is what powerful people say it is. I didn't expect the UK to be one of them.

When I read on, I was relieved to learn that a trade union, UNISON, had sued the British government over tribunal fees, and in 2017 the UK Supreme Court declared such fees unlawful, adding that higher fees in discrimination cases were in themselves discriminatory against women.

But by this point in my reading, I was almost surprised the UK's gender pay gap wasn't worse.

So I looked at the record in other countries. It's hard to make global comparisons. There is no standard international gender pay gap measure and there are underlying differences in female participation in the paid labour market. But in 2017 the US saw a gender pay gap of 18 per cent, Australia's was 15.2 per cent and New Zealand's 9.4 per cent. Many countries showed progress slowing, fluctuating or stalling. The US gap was little improved in the past fifteen years and according to a 2017 survey by the Pew Research Center, one in four women in employment said they had earned less than a man doing the same job. Four in ten said they had experienced gender discrimination at work, including being treated as if they were not competent, experiencing repeated small slights, receiving less support from senior leaders and being passed over for important assignments.

The most famous American equal pay case was *Ledbetter v. Goodyear Tire & Rubber Co.* In 1998, after nineteen years at Goodyear and just as she was preparing to retire from her job as an area manager, Lilly Ledbetter discovered by accident that she was being paid much less than her male peers. She sued the company and won, but Goodyear fought back on a technicality, claiming she should have filed her case within 180 days of the alleged act of discrimination. In 2007, the case eventually reached the US Supreme Court, which at the time had eight men and only one woman on the bench. The Court ruled five to four against Ledbetter; Justice Ruth Bader Ginsburg delivered a famously withering dissent, accusing some of the justices she sat alongside of wilful blindness: 'In our view, the Court does not comprehend or is indifferent to the insidious way in which women can be victims of pay discrimination.'

'The Court's insistence on immediate contest overlooks common characteristics of pay discrimination,' she wrote. 'Pay disparities often occur, as they did in Ledbetter's case, in small increments; cause to suspect that discrimination is at work develops over time. Comparative pay information, moreover, is often hidden from the employee's view.'

She urged Congress to amend the law, and two years later, President Obama's first piece of legislation was the Lilly Ledbetter Fair Pay Act, which relaxed time limits to allow such cases. Equal pay campaigners were ecstatic, but reading about it nearly a decade later, I was underwhelmed. Is permission to sue really the best that governments can do for women in the twenty-first century? It seemed like poverty of ambition. Despite a decade-long legal fight, Lilly Ledbetter never won equal pay. Goodyear never put right the underlying injustice. Nor did it face the kind of consumer backlash that occasionally forces companies to do the right thing. I resolved never to buy a Goodyear tyre.

By this stage my brain was fried. I was reporting on the North Korean nuclear crisis and China's Communist Party Congress. That meant trying to make films, radio features and online reports about two of the most secretive organisations in the world, both instinctively hostile to BBC reporters and both flexing their muscle in different ways. And after a twelve- or fourteen-hour day at work, I was putting in a regular night shift on my equal pay research.

But the more I read, the more I was struck by just how much unpaid time and energy women had always sunk into trying to enforce the law. Already undervalued through years of unequal pay, their long slog to put it right went entirely unpaid.

I definitely wasn't looking for another long slog. The point of my argument was that my work had value. I didn't now want to spend years working for nothing to re-fight a battle that the generation before me was supposed to have won. Women already do far more than their share of unpaid work in the world. More of us doing even more unpaid work to 'win' equal pay seemed like history as a bad joke.

Levelling the playing field

It's important to acknowledge that the world women are attempting to get equal in is a world which is increasingly unequal in material wealth. In 2017, 82 per cent of wealth created went to the richest 1 per cent of the global population, while wages in developed economies struggled to match those before the financial crash a decade earlier. Even the pay culture of public service organisations – universities, local government, the BBC – seems afflicted by growing inequality, with value delivered by teams but disproportionately captured by 'stars'.

Why do so many employers indulge what does not advance justice or economic efficiency? Why do governments not insist on fair rules to ensure that these games of 'winner takes all' do not become a racket?

Women will never get equal in an economy where grown boys are conditioned to look at the full sweet jar they're holding and the half jar in the woman's hands, and then say 'Now give me her jar too.' If pay was transparent they might feel ashamed to ask for more, but if the sweet jars are opaque and the conversation private, no one need know.

Some argue that free markets will cure gender inequality. If female workers are cheaper than men while delivering the same value, employers will hire more women and by the law of supply and demand the price of women's labour will rise and soon they will be able to command the same price as men. The same levelling effect should apply to eliminate other forms of discrimination. As the economist Luigi Zingales points out, 'Every good economist should also be a feminist, defending a level playing field for all genders.'

In the real world, we haven't got to the level playing field yet. For labour markets to operate well, they require good information and the freedom to withdraw labour. So it's only on some more perfect planet that they might drive out gender discrimination. In our own flawed world, relative pay is often secret, women often feel unable to move jobs after having children, and a 'motherhood penalty' often hangs over pay negotiations even for women who don't have children. A discount is built into the labour price of all women, due in part to the unconscious bias we've already discussed and in part to the unequal caring duties of many.

There's no escape, even for the few women who make it to the very top. In 2017, 5.4 per cent of the Fortune 500 list of the largest US companies had female CEOs. Research conducted over several decades suggests women CEOs are paid less, have shorter tenures and their companies are punished in the stock market, even when their firms are just as profitable as those run by men.

The hard fact is that even people who exhibit no unconscious bias against women, including many who are themselves women, will take advantage of the bias that prevails elsewhere in the market to pay women less. The 'market' itself is driving unequal pay.

In some markets, outright sexism can often be presented as customer or client 'taste'. If there are customers who don't want to be served by women, employees who don't want to be managed by women or clients who don't want to have meetings with women, then demand for women's labour goes down accordingly and the price of their labour follows. In which case, far from erasing pay discrimination or being a passive mirror of the discrimination that is out there, the market can drive it.

It's worth noting that this kind of 'taste-based discrimination' cannot legally justify a difference in pay between men and women. But most victims will never get as far as a tribunal to point that out.

Whose choice is it anyway?

To labour-market economists, women today look more like men than they used to. They are at least as well-educated, have children later, and until then, show the same commitment to full-time paid work. In the early years of working life the gender pay gap is narrow. But at the point of having children, things change. The difference in earnings widens steadily – over the subsequent twelve-year period, the pay of working mothers falls 33 per cent behind that of men.

Some draw the conclusion that this is a result of the choices women make as parents. But employers are implicated too. Research for the UK's Equality and Human Rights Commission suggests that three in four mothers have a negative or discriminatory experience during pregnancy, maternity leave or on their return from maternity leave. Around one in twenty are made redundant.

That's just the start. Part-time work and periods of unpaid caring work are heavily penalised in pay. Part-time jobs tend to be lower paid than full-time jobs, they are less likely to be permanent or unionised, and part-time experience is often not counted as experience. A work history featuring an interruption for childcare or a period of part-time work can lead to much lower pay for women doing the same work as men, even many years after they have returned to full-time work.

The mirror image of the 'motherhood penalty' is the fatherhood premium. Overwork itself carries a premium, particularly in professions like finance, law and consulting. And if one parent has to be on call at work then the other often has to be on call at home, so that even parents who start off with equal career and earning potential take on increasingly unequal roles. Usually it is men who reap the overwork premium. In recent years this has tended to cancel out the effect of women's higher education in narrowing the gender pay gap, particularly among top earners. The American economist Claudia Goldin argues that if they want to deliver gender equality in the workplace, employers must stop penalising flexible working: 'The gender gap in pay would be considerably reduced and might vanish altogether if firms did not have an incentive to disproportionately reward individuals who labored long hours and worked particular hours.'

This is a choice employers can make. Evidence of the damaging long-term effects of long-hours culture is compelling. Even the short-term benefits are in question. One study showed managers could not tell the difference between employees who were working an eighty-hour week and those who were merely pretending to do so. Men pretended more often than women. The latter tended to formally reduce their hours and were marginalised as a consequence.

So when it comes to long-hours culture, employers must look closely at whether 'superman' is actually delivering more value. This point was made neatly in the Pixar animation *Incredibles 2*. The world was, as usual, in danger, and Mr Incredible said 'Heavyweight problems need heavyweight solutions.' But the movie's plotline put superhero recruitment in the hands of a woman. She crunched the numbers on who actually delivered more value and came to the conclusion that Mrs Incredible, aka Elastigirl, was less likely to cause havoc and more likely to get results.

Returning to real-world heroes, sometimes mothers do make an active decision to work part-time or to leave paid work to care for children. But sometimes this is a choice in name only because it is constrained by a lack of flexible working opportunities, shared parental leave, affordable childcare – not to mention the problem of the employer bias that left Elizabeth earning less and progressing more slowly than Mark in the first place. If one parent has to go part-time or give up paid work to look after children, she becomes the cost-effective candidate for that role in the family partnership. We don't know what individual mothers and fathers would choose if they could design parenting and work on a truly equal playing field.

All over the world, women feel frustrated by this. A global survey of professional women found 95 per cent said work/life balance and flexibility were important to them. But as many as

97 per cent of respondents in China and 96 per cent in India also said it was not available in practice and people who worked flexibly were regarded as less committed to the organisation: 'Overall, women ranked lack of flexibility and work/life balance as a top-three reason for wanting to leave their current employer, just behind pay and a lack of opportunities for career progression.'

Suggestions from men

It's hard to imagine women ever getting fully equal at work when the rest of life remains so unequal. As President Obama said in his State of the Union address in 2015, 'It's time we stop treating childcare as a side issue, or a women's issue, and treat it like the national economic priority that it is for all of us.'

Research in the US suggests fathers are more involved in childcare than in the past, almost as likely as mothers to say parenting is extremely important to their identity, and more than half of them feel challenged by juggling work and childcare expectations. Yet the US remains one of the few countries in the world to have no nationally mandated policy on maternity leave, let alone paternity leave. It leaves that to states and employers.

By contrast, the Nordic countries have long made childcare a national economic priority. They have better daycare provision than many other countries, generous maternity leave, and in 1974 Sweden was the first country in the world to introduce shared parental leave. Its neighbours soon followed suit, and after nearly half a century of experimentation in Sweden, Norway, Denmark, Finland and Iceland, some things about paternity leave are clear. Fathers use it when it is well paid, flexible and ringfenced for them. If it's poorly paid, heavily restricted or optional to exchange it for maternity leave, take-up is much lower. As with women's right to equal pay, so with men's right to paternity leave: the right only feels meaningful if it feels realistic to exercise it.

Even with a high degree of flexibility built into these policies, women's take-up remains much higher than men's. Cultural norms about nurturing mothers and breadwinning fathers remain strong and it is women who bear children and give birth to them. But it is now commonplace for Scandinavian fathers to take some parental leave and that brings clear benefits for families in many ways, including women's pay. One Swedish study found that when fathers care more, women earn more. For the first year of childrearing, 'each month that the father stays on parental leave increases maternal earnings by 6.7 per cent, which is an even larger effect than the mother's own leave'.

Most of the world lags far behind. In Australia only 2 per cent of heterosexual fathers take up parental leave. Dr Marian Baird, Professor of Gender and Employment Relations at the University of Sydney, says 'paternity leave in Australia is almost a token policy'.

Likewise the UK. It introduced shared parental leave in 2015, but three years later less than 2 per cent of eligible fathers seemed to be taking advantage of it. Entitlement to leave pay rather than just leave time is crucial but employers are under no obligation to enhance shared parental pay to the same level as enhanced maternity pay. Those who do offer more report a dramatic increase in take-up. The insurance giant Aviva introduced an equal parental leave policy in 2017, promising mothers and fathers twenty-six weeks at full pay. The year before, new fathers had taken only two weeks of paternity leave. In the first year of equal entitlement 95 per cent of new fathers took more than two weeks and 67 per cent took six months off work.

Duncan Fisher of the Family Initiative, a charity that supports parenting, says governments and employers should treat parents equally when it comes to leave entitlements: 'If fathers were to be offered the same as mothers are offered – allowing parents to choose absolutely freely on a level playing field – fathers would take leave in huge numbers. It really is that simple.'

If you're a male reader, are you resisting long-hours culture, pressing your employer to make flexible working the default and asking for gender equality on parental leave? Are you sharing childcare in a way that allows your partner to continue her career? If you're an employer, are you making these choices real for employees?

In some ways I'm optimistic about this. Gender and family stereotypes have changed dramatically even in the years I've been a parent, and that has begun to break down stereotypes at work. The good news is that the human herd can change its habits and expectations. Not long ago it was common for people in the UK to smoke in restaurants and smack their children. Now it is rare. The bad news is that habits and expectations are most stubborn where they deliver power, status and money to privileged groups. For women to be equal, men will need to value equality or reframe their own self-interest to include it.

Change comes fastest when it comes from the top. Which brings it back to men and unconscious bias. Some of us only really hear something when a man says it, as per the famous cartoon of a boardroom in which the chairman observes, 'That's an excellent suggestion, Miss Triggs. Perhaps one of the men here would like to make it.'

For the same reasons, equal pay is a suggestion men must make. The unforced renunciation of privilege that the Norwegian boys demonstrated with their sweets is even more powerful when replicated by adult men with money.

When it emerged that the Hollywood actor Mark Wahlberg had been paid fifteen hundred times more than his co-star Michelle Williams for re-shooting scenes for the film *All the*

Money in the World, he donated his $1.5 million fee to the Time's Up legal defence fund established in the aftermath of the #MeToo scandal.

Interviewed about her portrayal of the tennis star Billie Jean King in the movie *Battle of the Sexes*, the actress Emma Stone explained that equal pay was not just at the heart of that film but a recurring challenge for her male peers. 'In my career so far, I've needed my male co-stars to take a pay cut so that I may have parity with them. And that's something they do for me because they feel it's what's right and fair ... our getting equal pay is going to require people to selflessly say, "That's what's fair."'

What's fair will come about faster if those who have privilege use that privilege to dismantle it. This is a big ask. Most of us, including me, are often too lazy, busy, self-interested, conservative and conformist to try to correct the great injustices around us. Sometimes the wealthier we are, the less compassion we show. According to one University of California Berkeley study, even fake money can make people behave with less regard for others. When researchers paired students to play the board game Monopoly and gave one much more money than the other, the 'wealthier' player expressed initial discomfort, but then went on to take up more space, move pieces loudly and taunt the player with less money. Another study, at the University of Utah, found participants were more likely to lie or behave immorally after being exposed to money-related words. 'Thinking about money leads people to think "business", and it's this framing of a situation as a business one that leads to unethical behaviors, such as lying, cheating and acting in one's self-interest without regard to others.'

Exploiting gender privilege in pay negotiations. Add that to the list.

In many workplaces a meaningful effort to level the playing field might cost men opportunities and money, and it might force them to change their expectations and behaviour. Yes, women need to be proactive in asserting their value and will face worse discrimination if they're not. Yes, women's choices may account for some of the gender pay gap. But choice does not explain why the gap for full-time work is in favour of men even in occupations such as nursing which are dominated by women. Choice does not explain why men dominate all highly paid occupations. Nor does it explain why the occupations dominated by men are where pay gaps are largest or why pay gaps are widest of all for highly skilled women in their fifties. Or why pay declines in occupations which become saturated by women. When it comes to explaining the gender pay gap in the modern world, the choices of women are dwarfed by the choices of lawmakers, employers, male colleagues and fathers.

It is not a choice for British Pakistani women to earn seventy-four pence to the average man's pound. It is not a choice for black American women to earn sixty-three cents to the average man's dollar. It was not a choice for me to earn less than sixty pence for every pound my male peer earned.

By now I was feeling dizzy from following all the threads of such a complex weave. But behind the complexity I felt I'd grasped something simple. History and habit conspired to put a thumb on the scale against women at work, and when they tried to put it right, male colleagues and employers were not doing enough to help. If men and women do the same work it's really not hard to pay them equally. Employers must just do it rather than find excuses not to do it. In workplaces where discrimination is deeply embedded in recruitment and promotion decisions as well as pay, it can be very difficult to tease out its subtle cumulative effects, even for employers who are trying; if employers are not trying, women have no hope. And to tackle occupations and industries where discrimination is systemic, we need superheroes.

All this reading and thinking only made me more impatient about my own workplace. The BBC had said it would try to resolve my case by the end of September 2017, but September had come and gone with no response to my equal pay complaint, let alone a resolution. A journalist's job is to ask the questions that matter. I'd asked them. Now I wanted to change the answers.

3

GET MAD

=

Did you know that monkeys can get mad when they are not paid equally? Primatologists at Emory University in Atlanta, Georgia, paired female capuchin monkeys and gave them rewards for completing a task. The capuchins were happy to pass their handlers pebbles in return for cucumber wedges for as long as their partners were paid in cucumber too. But when a capuchin saw the monkey in the next cage get grapes, all hell broke loose.

I watched the video footage and recognised myself in that capuchin monkey. First she was puzzled. She inspected her pebble to check there was nothing wrong with it. Having decided it was as good as her neighbour's, she threw her cucumber wedge at the handler and pounded the table in protest. It's a good job the handler was wearing gloves and a visor.

In a subsequent paper, the researchers wrote that monkeys refused to play the game if they saw a neighbour get a more attractive reward for equal effort, 'an effect amplified if the partner received such a reward without any effort at all. These reactions support an early evolutionary origin of inequity aversion.'

It's not obviously 'rational' for a capuchin monkey to throw her food away. She was perfectly happy with cucumber until she saw the grapes. Then she got mad and now she's going to go hungry.

Behavioural experiments show that humans also punish unfairness in others at a cost to ourselves. As the primatologists reflect, 'During the evolution of cooperation it may have become critical for individuals to compare their own efforts and pay-offs with those of others. Negative reactions may occur when expectations are violated.'

Expectations are crucial. The capuchin was indignant about inequality because she previously enjoyed equality. It was cucumber for all until it was grapes for the privileged. The same was perhaps true of the Norwegian boys and their sweet jars.

This is not the situation for most women in the workplace. They have never enjoyed equality. Being valued at less is the norm for so many of us. Some see clearly that the man next door gets grapes where they get cucumber, but then they shrug that it was ever thus so why protest today? Others cannot see what their neighbour gets paid, but they can hear the warning note in the employer's voice when insisting everyone is rewarded according to the value of their work. In long-term working relationships it takes a lot for women to spit out their food and fling it at the boss.

I was like the capuchin in expecting equality, but that was because I had insisted it was a condition of performing the task in question. The equal pay complaint I submitted in August 2017 was my version of throwing the cucumber at my handlers when I saw them give my neighbour grapes.

Advice from the Advisory, Conciliation and Arbitration Service (Acas) to UK employers facing an equal pay complaint is that they should 'reply in a reasonable time either agreeing that there is pay discrimination and taking steps to put this right, or to challenge the selection of comparator or provide some material reason which would be a justification of why the questioner's pay and benefits are different'.

The BBC finally responded to my complaint on 10 October

2017. I had asked for a written reply, but I got a phone call instead. I was puzzled by that until a friend who led an HR department for a large private sector firm told me employers often feel that what they commit to writing needs to be checked by their lawyers as it might be used as evidence in an employment tribunal. Oral communication is more deniable.

The time difference meant it was already late afternoon in the Beijing bureau. The team was working hard on editing TV and radio reports on the impending Communist Party Congress. China doesn't have a presidential election cycle as it's a one-party state. It has a Communist Party Congress cycle instead. Xi Jinping had been China's top leader since the previous Congress, in 2012. Now, five years on, he intended to use this moment to signal his own firm grip on China and China's growing grip on the world.

The BBC Beijing bureau is open plan, so for the sake of privacy I took the phone call from London in our radio studio. The cheap ceiling lights cast a lemon pall, asthmatic air purifiers chugged and a smoggy twilight shrouded the Beijing skyscrapers beyond.

I felt nervous. Pay is a power relationship and an employee can't help but go into a pay conversation feeling conscious of an immense asymmetry. Your employer controls your job, your income, your professional reputation. It has all the information, the experience and the lawyers. It knows how to play this game.

The omens were not good. In the three months since the original protest letter from BBC Women, managers had avoided the expression 'equal pay' and talked instead of 'fair pay'. Equal pay is a legal right, fair pay is not. A handful of women had seen their pay 'revised' upward, but not a single case of unequal pay had been acknowledged.

The BBC had just announced a gender pay gap of 9.3 per cent. The Director-General pointed out that with the national gap at 18 per cent, the BBC was 'in a better place than many organisations'. Of course it's possible to have a yawning gender pay gap while being scrupulous about equal pay and, vice versa, to have a narrow gender pay gap while still discriminating against many individual women. But Tony Hall tackled that point by publishing – alongside the gender pay gap – an equal pay audit that said there was 'no evidence of "systemic discrimination against women" at the BBC'. The audit was conducted by the consultancy firm PwC and the legal firm Eversheds, and had been reviewed by former Court of Appeal judge Sir Patrick Elias. He explained that the BBC's pay gap was down to 'an under-representation of women in the more senior jobs'. That explanation raised wider questions about the progression problems facing women at the BBC. But there were more immediate questions. The equal pay audit left out entirely the very group who had complained about pay discrimination in the first place – all the women who had signed the protest letter of 23 July were excluded, alongside nearly a thousand other on-air staff.

Sir Patrick wrote that the audit 'does not, and could not, categorically establish that there is no discrimination in relation to groups or individuals'. Nor did he give the BBC's pay structure an entirely clean bill of health. He identified failings in record keeping and consistency, noting: 'A lack of consistency or transparency in the application of the principles for determining pay understandably breeds suspicion about the process and generates a sense of unfairness which in some cases may be justified.'

BBC Women were suspicious. Having been denied access to data that might answer residual questions, and having learned that the makers of BBC Radio 4's statistics programme *More or Less* had likewise been denied access, we distrusted the audit's findings.

The Director-General naturally welcomed the findings of

both the gender pay gap report and the equal pay audit. He repeated his pledge to close the pay gap by 2020 and said fairness in pay was vital: 'While today's reports show that we are in a better place than many organisations, I want a BBC that is an exemplar not just in the media but in the country.'

The next day Lewis Carnie, the Controller of BBC Radio 2, still seemed confused about the distinction between a gender pay gap and pay discrimination, but in answering questions about the pay gap between top male and female presenters, his chief point was to reject any charge of gender bias: 'The idea that gender in any way would reflect what anyone is paid here at Radio 2 is ludicrous ... What's important is the talent, and they're paid according to that ... Revealing everybody's pay is one of the most unhelpful things that has ever happened. It's a lose-lose situation. Because there's no gender pay issue here at all, it really hasn't helped us. I mean, what is the point of it?'

Since July's pay disclosures his reading list had clearly been different from mine. In fact, there was no evidence that my bosses had done any of the reading and thinking that I'd done since the summer. Or if they had, they'd come to different conclusions.

'An inadvertent oversight'

So on 10 October there was nothing to soothe my nerves as the phone rang from London. On the line were a senior BBC manager I knew well and an HR director I'd never met.

The manager began by apologising for taking so long to come back with answers. He said I should have had a pay rise at the beginning of that financial year, 6 April 2017. But due to an 'inadvertent oversight' I'd been left off. He said he now wanted to raise my salary by £45,000 to bring it to £180,000.

That was a huge sum. I explained again that I wasn't seeking more money, but equality. I asked if my male peers had been invited to volunteer a pay cut to enable me to be equal at my existing salary.

Most pay discrimination is put right by paying women more, and my unease about taking a pay rise may seem strange. But this was public money, BBC budgets were shrinking and I was already very highly paid. Working hard on the other side of the studio glass were talented colleagues who earned a fraction of my salary. I didn't want my bosses to fix inequality for rich women like me at the expense of all the women – and men – who already earned less. I had concluded that our problem of pay discrimination was systemic. However complex and slow it would be to reboot the BBC pay structure, that's what was required. A thorough solution was what the BBC had been promising ever since July.

Now I met unwillingness to discuss the pay of other members of staff. But because of the publication of high pay in the summer, I knew the North America Editor was earning between £200,000 and £250,000. Which meant, even if the BBC raised my salary to £180,000, I would still not be equal.

The manager explained that some people have higher profile or expertise and that North America was worth more than China because it involved a higher volume of breaking news and live analysis, a unique global leadership role and a story of particular interest to domestic audiences.

These points were all just as true of the Europe Editor covering Brexit. But since 2014, Katya Adler, like me, had been paid far less. Besides, my managers knew as well as I did that breaking news and live analysis were the easiest parts of the job because they only involved talking. Making news films, by contrast, involved long and laborious filming trips followed by long and laborious days of editing. If analysing presidential tweets in front of a live TV camera was now going to be judged the valuable bit of the international editor's job, China would always be the poor relation as President Xi does not tweet.

The previous North America Editor (a man) had earned roughly the same as both me and the Europe Editor. A change of incumbent hadn't changed the role. At one level, it all seemed fairly simple. North America was a higher-profile job than China and China was a harder job than North America. Like Ginger Rogers, I did everything the North America Editor did except backwards and in high heels – in this case not literally, but in Mandarin and with a police state at my back.

Only two years earlier the Head of Newsgathering had said the BBC's hiring and promoting culture had worked against female reporters in the past. I did not think the BBC could now legally justify paying male reporters more if taste-based discrimination led it to give them higher-profile roles at earlier points in their careers. Besides, it had said the China and North America jobs were 'on a par' and agreed to pay the China Editor the same as the North America Editor at the outset.

I was now a real-life example of Elizabeth the vet, and the BBC was the employer who insists discrimination is not a workplace problem while paying Mark more. In fact, I think the BBC had even less excuse than many veterinary surgeries because it was a huge public sector employer with special responsibilities to reflect the nation. Its HR professionals should have known that, without great vigilance, gender prejudice infects pay structures so that even a small initial bias can have huge cumulative effects over the course of an employee's career.

My summer research on equal pay legislation led me to expect that my employer would either acknowledge discrimination and rectify it, challenge my choice of comparator, or accept the choice of comparator and explain factors that justified the pay difference. But in that phone conversation, the BBC manager sidestepped the language of equal pay by talking about a 'cohort' of international editors.

The other three members of this 'cohort' were the North America Editor Jon Sopel, the Middle East Editor Jeremy Bowen, and the Europe Editor Katya Adler. I suggested that if we were a cohort, the BBC could pay us the same and avoid a lot of time wasted in arguments about whose role was worth more. The answer was no, there must be a pay range. I said in that case, the BBC would need to give the two women a much more detailed explanation of why they were worth so much less than the two men. Otherwise, the suspicion would remain that discrimination lurked in the gap. I asked for job evaluations so that I could be clear what weight had been put on different aspects of the roles. I could no longer take anything on trust.

I knew job evaluations would only clear up part of the confusion. Even when an employer accepts that a man and a woman are doing equal work, it can lawfully pay the man more if the difference is due to a genuine factor that doesn't involve any sex discrimination. It could be a factor related to the role, like unsocial working hours or the difficulty of recruiting people with the necessary skills. Or it could be a factor relating to the individual, such as better qualifications or language skills.

On any list of such factors, impartially applied, I felt I'd probably come out equal, or possibly higher. However, it's hard for people to be impartial about decisions they took years earlier and never expected to have to explain. This is another argument for the transparent, up-front pay criteria that the Equality and Human Rights Commission and employment tribunals repeatedly recommend to all employers. If managers know in advance that they will be held accountable for the way they evaluate others, they are less likely to rely on stereotypes and unconscious bias. Leave accountability until afterwards and decision-makers rationalise their behaviour defensively.

We've taken all factors into account, I was now told.

My problem was that a BBC boss was asking me to trust him on pay, having just admitted an oversight worth a third of my annual salary. By now I had a bias risk of my own and at least I was conscious of it: I didn't trust BBC managers on pay.

I changed tack and asked how the BBC had come to the conclusion that April 2017 was the moment to suddenly raise my pay by £45,000. Nothing about my role had changed at that point.

There are no hard and fast rules about how employers should handle back pay in equal pay complaints. Under UK law an employment tribunal can award up to six years of back pay (five years in Scotland) from the date proceedings are filed with an employment tribunal. But that requires a woman to bring a case to tribunal and then to win it.

The pay gap between BBC international editors went back to 2014. I didn't want to pocket more public money, but I wanted the renunciation of personal interest to be my decision, not one taken for me by a management that appeared intent on covering up its own mistakes. So why a sudden pay rise in April 2017?

This was a 'pragmatic point' from which to start back pay.

A pragmatic point? Pragmatism is in the eye of the beholder. In my view, it would have been better for the BBC to admit that it could not afford its historic liabilities. Just as it would have been better for it to concede that my work as China Editor was equal, but that the pay for some top men had got out of hand and easing it down would be a delicate task. No one's perfect, and as the EHRC says, inequality often arises from 'lack of awareness, not deliberate discrimination'.

Just own up, I thought. They chose denial instead. An hour passed, night fell on Beijing and we talked ourselves to a standstill. The £45,000 was mentioned again. HR was keen to 'action the pay rise'.

'Please don't,' I said. 'I need to think.'

But as I put down the phone, my conditioning kicked in.

Women don't throw food

In the twenty-first century, capuchin monkeys don't swallow inequality without protest, but appearing grateful for less is a skill millions of women bring to work every day. Throughout history we have been conditioned to mistrust our own anger. In Greek mythology the Furies were terrifying goddesses of vengeance with snakes for hair, bloodshot eyes and bats' wings, beleaguering their victims with brass-studded scourges. Today witches, bitches and bunny boilers stalk popular culture.

From early childhood, girls learn to expect less money for more work. A recent US study found teenage girls do more household chores, are paid less for them than their brothers and have smaller allowances. It starts even earlier. A study of twelve-year-olds in sixteen countries across the economic spectrum found that in each of them, girls spent more time on household chores than boys did.

All children learn that expressing anger risks punishment from those who are more powerful, but some research suggests girls internalise negative emotion more. We often learn to blame and doubt ourselves, to disguise anger or direct it at people less powerful. Anaesthetising ourselves to the everyday sexism of the workplace may not be a great strategy in the long term, but at least it keeps us out of a fight we expect to lose.

I started to reason myself out of my anger. After all, my bosses were trying to be conciliatory. £180,000 might not be equal, but it was less unequal. Throwing food is not polite. Perhaps my pebble was worth less than his pebble anyway. My employer had generally valued North America more highly than China and always valued the man now doing that job more highly than it had valued me. It was naive of me to think that I could change either of those givens.

I reasoned that people everywhere tend to take their privileges for granted and attribute their success to personal factors like talent and hard work. As a white middle-class person with a degree from Oxford University, I'd leveraged some privileges in my life. Being male was one I hadn't benefited from. Perhaps I was just blaming my lower pay on gender in order to avoid facing up to my own professional shortcomings.

Moreover, I didn't want to play the Fury. I was heavily invested in being the grown-up woman who gets the other person's point of view, works out quarrels, avoids grudges. I'd gone through a divorce with no lawyers and stayed friends with ex-boyfriends. I liked men. Now I worried that fighting Xi Jinping's censorship machine had turned me into someone whose instinct was to fight everyone and everything.

Change takes time, I reasoned. The BBC workplace is a mirror of the society it serves. In valuing women less, it is just doing what is habitual and commonplace. Insiders like me would achieve more by patient persuasion than by turning ourselves into a food-throwing rabble at the gate.

But the word 'oversight' kept nagging at my mind. The BBC was sending reporters out to hold other organisations to account. It felt shameful to use this kind of language to hide its own failings.

What's more, there was a predictable pattern to the oversights. Women were being paid less, especially older and more senior women. Every pay expert knows this is exactly the demographic group that suffers the widest gender pay gaps. In 2015, a parliamentary inquiry had found that the BBC had an 'informal policy' to discriminate against older women. My managers should have been particularly alert to the risk of underpaying women like me, instead of letting it happen and then shrugging it off as an oversight when I found out. The BBC had always claimed it had rigorous processes to avoid just such oversights. A gap of £100,000 could not be explained away like this. I might not need or want that money, but I knew that women at the bottom of the pay and power scale needed women at the top to insist on fair rules.

I sent two long and careful emails to my managers, explaining my concerns about the risks of discrimination in the BBC's pay structure, drawing attention to relevant points in equality law and asking detailed questions about the concrete factors that explained paying men more. I reminded them that I wasn't asking for more money, but felt I had 'let all women down by not insisting on equality'.

I was trying to be the capuchin who politely asks its handler to study the rules on feeding. I wasn't screaming 'give me my grapes', nor was I in a transaction looking for a mutually acceptable price. I just wanted the BBC to have a transparent and fair pay structure that would treat women equally. I did feel some sympathy for my management, and wrote 'I know sorting this out is a big headache for you. It's a big headache for me too. I find it hard to work out what is the right thing to do. But simply accepting a big sum of money cannot be the answer.'

To this day, I'm not sure whether anyone read my emails, as no one addressed the legal points or answered the questions about measuring value. When we had a second phone conversation ten days after the first, I pressed again on concerns about the BBC's pay structure. The manager said change would take time and joked ruefully that 'proceedings at the Chinese Communist Party Congress are probably a lot simpler than strategic reviews at the BBC'.

It was not a reassuring comparison.

As for my case, the BBC was not prepared to discuss the huge pay gap of the previous three years or to provide a more detailed defence for the continuing disparity. They wanted me to take the pay rise and move on. When I sent my notes of the conversation to my HR friend, he observed, 'You're asking for science and they're offering art. You've broken their argument and they don't have a counter-argument.'

But the immediate problem was mine.

Running-away money?

If you break an opponent's argument, it's not actually a pressing problem for them if you care more about the breakage than they do. I think at that point I did care more than they did about the BBC having a coherent and defensible pay structure that treated women equally. I was now faced with a very difficult choice. I could say thank you and get back to work, I could throw more food, or I could quit the BBC and look for a job with an employer who didn't discriminate.

In February 2017, the former Uber engineer Susan Fowler had written a devastating blog post about combating toxic masculinity at the ridesharing giant. She had resigned in December 2016 after falling foul of company bosses over their mishandling of sexual harassment allegations she had made. Her story went viral, triggering a welter of similar accusations. Eventually the Uber CEO Travis Kalanick was forced to resign and other bosses were fired. It didn't stop there. Fowler's blog post was a wake-up call to HR departments around the world. She ended with the words 'I feel a lot of sadness, but I can't help but laugh at how ridiculous everything was. Such a strange experience. Such a strange year.'

She could laugh because she got out.

Earlier I mentioned Margaret Heffernan's discovery that, as a CEO, she was being paid half as much as her male peers. Heffernan recommends that women save some 'running-away' money: 'As much as I loved my work, I knew that if I could not find a way to fix this problem, I would have to leave. The only thing worse than discrimination would be to collude in it.' Her pay was corrected.

A pay negotiation is like many other transactions in which you are more likely to win what you want if you are able to walk away. This is not to say that you should voice a threat to leave. In some situations that might actually be unhelpful. But humans are acutely sensitive to power. It's hard to save a running-away fund if you are on a low wage and that wage is your family's only income. But if you and your boss both sense that you cannot quit under any circumstances, it leaves you vulnerable. Try to have a plan B.

I knew I could leave the BBC, at least in the sense that I could find another job. But the BBC had employed me for thirty years and I owed it some loyalty. I believed in its mission and wanted to help management find the moral compass I felt they'd mislaid.

The day after this second phone conversation I wrote to refuse the offer of a £45,000 pay rise, appointed a lawyer and lodged a formal grievance.

To escalate or not?

By now I hated almost everything about the equal pay fight. I hated thinking, talking and writing about money. I hated battling the assumption that everyone has their price and so must I. I hated the negativity and conflict. I hated the constant self-interrogation of where personal interest should end and public interest begin. I hated having to assert the value of my work in ways that felt undignified and boastful. I hated having to compare myself with the men; I admired their work, and talking myself up felt like talking them down. I hated despising my bosses, mistrusting everything they said on pay and feeling ashamed of them. I hated spending so much time and energy on battling my own side when I had obstacles enough in China to contend with. But as 2017 drew to a close, most of all I hated the grievance process.

The law expects employees to exhaust their employer's internal complaints process before they lodge a claim in an employment tribunal. For many workplaces, this includes a formal grievance and an appeal against a grievance outcome. Employers should complete both stages without unreasonable delay. The BBC interprets that as up to ninety days for each stage. Some employers are much faster.

This internal process makes sense when it gives reasonable people an opportunity to sort out problems for themselves rather than overburdening the courts, but equal pay grievances risk serious abuse. The incentive for employers to resist is just too great. After all, upholding a grievance may have implications for an entire pay structure, including liabilities for historic underpayment and a higher pay bill going forward. It's tempting to use control of the process to defeat a challenge rather than to investigate it in good faith.

I have asked many employment lawyers their views on grievances. One wrote, 'Grievances do more harm than good ... Everyone is defending their position and focusing on what has gone wrong, usually with one eye on the tribunal, and this inevitably entrenches positions rather than enabling an employee to resolve any problems with their employer. The employer will not open itself up to a potential claim ... I can count on one hand the number of clients who I have seen where their grievance has been upheld in a meaningful way that isn't just about "oversights".'

For claimants this is a disaster. They are already battling the low worth their employer has put on their work. In raising a grievance they risk antagonising the very bosses who wield so much power over their lives. Women may expend much time, effort, money and trust on an exercise that was always a foregone conclusion.

That's why my advice is to avoid a formal grievance except under one or more of the following four conditions:

1. You know that your employer acts in good faith and uses its grievance process to achieve fair outcomes. Obviously you can only know this in a workplace that is large enough to have colleagues who have used the grievance process and transparent enough that they are prepared to talk about it.
2. You are mounting a strategic exit. You have secured a recent performance evaluation and possibly your next job. You are not over-investing in the grievance process but playing out moves in the equal pay game by well-understood rules to maximise your own financial advantage. You intend to extract a settlement and go quietly.
3. You have low expectations of the grievance process but intend to lodge an equal pay claim at an employment tribunal and need to work through the internal process before doing so.
4. You and other women are challenging gender bias across your organisation and intend to use formal grievances as a way of making bosses more accountable for the way they measure the value of women's work.

If you are not confident about your employer's grievance process, if you don't want to leave or litigate and if you don't feel able to join with other women in challenging gender bias across your organisation, I suggest you avoid raising a formal grievance. Go back instead to the patient, constructive conversation I discussed in Chapter 1. And start thinking about a plan B. Consider your long-term options.

But at the outset, my formal grievance didn't seem hard. I think that's partly because I didn't write it. Back in the summer I had been uneasy about getting lawyers involved in what I saw as a BBC family dispute, but other BBC Women argued that our bosses would not do the right thing just because we'd made a cogent argument. A powerful law firm would be harder to ignore. Three months on I was beginning to see their point.

My long-time friend, the news presenter Kate Silverton, introduced me to Jennifer Millins, an employment partner at Mishcon de Reya. Jennifer and Mishcon had decided to undertake some pro bono work for BBC Women. I was already privileged in having able and determined female colleagues, and now I was privileged in having access to a fine lawyer. Jennifer and her team drafted and submitted my formal grievance.

The Acas code of practice on workplace disputes advises UK employers to schedule a grievance hearing without unreasonable delay. In early November 2017, as soon as I'd finished reporting on Xi Jinping's triumphal Congress and Donald Trump's state visit to China, I flew back to London for mine.

On the morning of the grievance hearing, I met Jennifer for the first time. The Mishcon de Reya office was a striking contrast with the BBC's Beijing bureau. Its entrance had big gilt gates and a grand arch complete with lions couchant. Jennifer herself looked the very Beyoncé of lawyering, elegant and effortlessly authoritative, flanked by a backing band of female junior lawyers. I was too distracted by all the art and chic furniture in her office to pay close attention to her warning that grievance processes are tough and undermining.

'When a man and a woman are doing like work, one of the most obvious ways an employer can prove the woman's work is of less value is by belittling her performance,' she said.

'But I eat Chinese communists for breakfast,' I joked. 'I'm not going to be intimidated by a few men in chinos.'

I was to pay for that arrogance – but not quite yet, as I went from a first meeting with one powerful woman to a reunion with another. According to the Acas code, an employee can take a companion to a grievance hearing. That person may be a colleague or a union representative. I chose Martine Croxall, as she was both. Martine and I had known each other for years because we'd both been presenters on the BBC News Channel before I went to China. In the early months of the equal pay fight, my affection and admiration for her had only grown.

Equal pay is all about relativities, and information denial is a key weapon for an employer determined to resist equal pay claims. Through her experience as a rep for the National Union of Journalists and her tireless attention to detail, Martine had mapped the weak points in the BBC's fortifications. She was also unflappable, unafraid, generous with her time ... and funny. She was the kind of BBC journalist you want in your corner when you are reminding the bosses what BBC values look like.

So on 16 November 2017, Martine and I met for coffee and then made our way to a small basement room below a central London hotel. Across the narrow table was a male senior manager I'd never met before, a female case manager from HR and a note-taker. I didn't want to hurt the note-taker's professional pride, but Martine had warned that hearing notes could often be very poor. It seemed odd not to make an audio recording. Audio recordings are all in a day's work at the world's leading broadcaster. I asked whether I could at least record the hearing on my phone as a back-up to the official notes.

'Audio recordings of grievance hearings are not BBC policy,' said the HR executive.

I had written a lengthy statement, and for the next ninety minutes I ploughed through it, pausing only to deal with questions from the hearing manager. My statement confronted the bedrock problem that my employer had made a promise on pay and broken it, while withholding the transparency that would allow me and other women to protect ourselves:

> The BBC now acknowledges that I have been underpaid. Left to the BBC, I would have been underpaid for many years more and gone to my grave ignorant of the fact. How can this happen? The BBC says, 'Completely inadvertently we left you behind.' But the BBC claims that it reviews all employees' pay in line with peers to identify discrepancies and that where there is a gap of more than 5 per cent, an action plan is put in place to address it.

I turned to a new problem, or rather an old problem newly discovered. A former manager had just alerted me to a conversation he'd had with the Deputy Director of News, Fran Unsworth, at a BBC alumni event just after the high-pay list had been published in July. He told me he'd been puzzled by why both female international editors were absent from the list, and pointed out to Fran, who was the most senior woman in BBC News, that both Katya Adler and I delivered a high volume of high-quality work. As I now told the hearing, Fran answered his question 'in a way that permitted her questioner to understand that Carrie Gracie is a "part-time" China Editor. Fran now says this is clearly a misunderstanding. But she did not say, "Yes Carrie's great, that gap is something we need to look into." The defence of an indefensible status quo makes me despair.'

I listed the range of my work, from daily news output to documentaries, podcast series and immersive long reads on the website. I pointed out that my bosses had urged me to stay in post for as long as I could, acknowledging that they could not replicate my expertise on the China story.

I would like to know how the BBC has weighted intimidation, harassment, surveillance, detentions, poor air quality, time difference necessitating night work, access difficulties, constant travel, editorial complexity, exile from home I did not choose, the absence of any other candidate for the post, Chinese language skills, related academic qualifications, thirty years' experience in specialism.

I'd never previously spent much time or energy boasting about my work or complaining about the difficulty of getting it done. The grievance process forced me to do both.

If you raise a grievance over unequal pay you will have to go over the same ground in relation to your own work. Some BBC Women delivered a file encompassing relevant career history: job descriptions, performance appraisals, training completed, additional projects undertaken, management emails acknowledging their contribution. Others turned that into a grid to make it easy for a hearing manager to see the boxes they ticked compared to their male comparators. I do think it's worth preparing a statement for a grievance hearing and then being firm about delivering it. Otherwise questions from a hearing manager may lead you down a time-consuming dead end. My statement began with a question: How can I trust you to be impartial?

Five pages later it finished with a demand for pay parity, or robust benchmarks and job evaluations to explain pay disparities. And a warning that I would not return to China with this dispute dragging into 2018.

Thank heavens I had prepared that statement. A week later I received the hearing notes. They had been 'finalised', one of many HR expressions I soon came to dread. Too often I had allowed the hearing manager to interrupt my statement, and my evidence had become ten barely recognisable pages littered with errors, omissions and additions.

No BBC reporter's career would have survived such a document, but when I told Jennifer Millins that it should be binned, she said these notes might constitute evidence if my case ever came to tribunal and I must correct them. I had no audio recording, so how could I correct them? The battle for equal pay had stopped being a reasoned discussion about value. It now felt like an assault on my sanity.

This made me very angry. I could make some allowances for a Dickensian pay structure. After all, that is the past all of humanity is struggling from. I could not forgive such gross misreporting. Nor could I forgive a set of notes that presented me as incoherent and rambling. Clear communication is my job, after all.

You may feel this is pedantic. A lawyer friend told me everyone hears what they want to hear at a hearing. If everyone hears what they want to hear, it only makes a stronger case for an audio recording and a transcript. Accurate reporting is what sets the BBC apart from fake news. This was a new low.

Hopelessness has a profound physical effect on me. For two days I couldn't get out of bed. Strange images passed through my mind: a wall of rabbit hutches; Bertha Rochester locked away in *Jane Eyre*; the handmaids in Margaret Atwood's dystopian novel; Bluebeard's cupboard. I thought about the many petitioners I'd met over my years in China. A tradition begun under the emperors, petitioning continued under communism with little change. It was an appeal to the wisdom of the ruler in a system where the rules and the ruler are one and the same.

The petitioners I knew started full of confidence and resolve, but over months and years of failing to get redress they often descended into hollow-eyed inarticulate wrecks who no longer belonged in their former lives and had become enemies of the state.

Not eating communists or anyone else for breakfast now, I reflected in my clearer moments. How much worse the experience must be for women who don't have a support network of colleagues or the advice of a union and a powerful law firm.

In an attempt to spare women such distressing and unequal battles, the National Union of Journalists had attempted to organise a group grievance on equal pay but management refused to accept it. Their strategy seemed to be divide and rule, each woman obliged to raise an individual grievance and to fight the system alone.

To have any hope of getting equal, you do have to get mad. But to get mad enough for action you have to risk the other kind of madness. It is hard to sit with anger long enough to let it crystallise.

Eventually I roused myself and tried to correct the hearing notes using the statement I had read out and Martine's handwritten notes. Correcting my employer's notes took me two days and it made me sick at heart and ashamed of the BBC. I wrote to the grievance manager and HR executive explaining how dismayed I felt to see my own evidence returned as gibberish.

HR offered counselling. Counselling is not wrong, and I was certainly experiencing stress, but as it was the BBC's failure to uphold its own values that was causing my stress, the offer felt like another black joke. In China I'd seen plenty of quasi-judicial processes with predetermined outcomes, and I knew they sometimes worked by convincing the sane that they were mad.

At times, the BBC's approach to the equal pay crisis and

the grievance process even felt to me like gaslighting, a form of manipulation that psychologists describe as intended to sow doubt in an individual by making them question their own memory, perceptions and sanity.*

Withholding information, discounting contradictory information, trivialising or ignoring any counter-narrative, and then wearing down a victim's defences with draining delays and distractions ... these are all tactics from the gaslighter's manual.

If you've never been through an internal complaints process in a powerful and hierarchical organisation, this may sound extreme. It would certainly have sounded extreme to me until my own experience. But when my fight later became public, people from many walks of life wrote to me describing similar ordeals. In the twenty-first-century workplace, openly intimidating troublesome employees is inconsistent with the employer's contractual duty of care. A process that persuades them to doubt their own memory and perceptions is a more subtle alternative.

Even in democracies with a commitment to freedom of information, we often don't know much about the way organisations deal with their internal problems, because the bigger the problem, the greater the temptation to hide it.

In *Private Government: How Employers Rule Our Lives (And Why We Don't Talk About It)* the American philosopher Elizabeth Anderson discusses the paradox that citizens in Western societies are obsessed by freedom and wary of government intrusion, but allow themselves to be tyrannised by bosses at work. She argues that our workplaces are private governments

---

* The origin of the term gaslighting is the 1938 play *Gas Light*, by Patrick Hamilton. A murderer attempts to convince his wife that she is going mad by making her doubt her sanity, including her observation of the dimming of gas lights throughout the building whenever he goes to search the flat of his murder victim for jewels.

with sweeping authoritarian power over our lives. Many employers control information, censor speech and intimidate employees.

Loyal critics are often persuaded by a combination of threats and inducements to shut up and go away. Paradoxically, organisations whose mission statements commit them to truth-telling – universities, charities, health services, churches, news providers – sometimes find it particularly hard to match private practice to public rhetoric when the truth is so uncomfortable to hear.

The BBC had already been forced to confront the failings of its workplace culture as a result of the Jimmy Savile scandal. Savile was a star presenter, famous for his entertainment shows and widely praised for his charitable work, but after his death in 2011 it emerged that he was also a serial sex offender. In 2016 an independent review found that the BBC had missed opportunities to stop his crimes, and those of another serial sexual predator, the presenter Stuart Hall, because of a culture of fear. The review was led by Dame Janet Smith, who said the BBC was a 'deeply deferential' workplace in which it was difficult 'to rock the boat' and celebrities were 'virtually untouchable'. She noted that one employee who complained to her supervisor that she had been sexually assaulted by Savile was told, 'Keep your mouth shut, he is a VIP.'

In response to Dame Janet's report, the Director-General apologised to victims: 'A serial rapist and a predatory sexual abuser both hid in plain sight at the BBC for decades. What this terrible episode teaches us is that fame is power, a very strong form of power and like any form of power it must be held to account . . . and it wasn't.'

The chairwoman of the BBC Trust, Rona Fairhead, said the Corporation had 'turned a blind eye, where it should have shone a light'.

In the immediate aftermath of the Savile scandal, the BBC overhauled its bullying and harassment policy and promised to improve its grievance processes. But in 2016 Dame Janet said she had been told 'an atmosphere of fear still exists today in the BBC'. And in 2017 I was dismayed by a grievance process that I felt was still turning a blind eye to problems raised by staff rather than shining a light.

This is not a challenge particular to the BBC. It is universal. I tell the Savile story only to make the point that even an organisation committed to truth-telling and whistle-blowing will in practice find it hard to confront a problem raised by an employee when that problem is potentially expensive or reputationally damaging. Without leadership that relentlessly shines the light, even righteous organisations protect the powerful and the status quo.

Gaslighting works by isolating the victim. And psychologists say the victim's resistance to it depends on access to independent sources of information, an ability to trust one's own judgement and a firm counter-narrative. My resolve would have died at this point if I had been alone. But I was not alone and the grievance process had made me 'mad'. I felt everything I held dear about the BBC was at stake, and the front line I needed to be on was here in the UK, not in China. Besides, after the fiasco of the hearing notes, I felt sure the grievance process would not find my work equal – and I was not prepared to continue in that very challenging job as less than an equal.

On 6 December I gave a month's notice and resigned my post as China Editor. I intended to return to my substantive role as a presenter on the News Channel and lean into the equal pay fight. I half expected my bosses to change course when they received my resignation letter; after all, they'd said I was irre-placeable. But my Foreign Editor never wrote to me again and the next day a different manager phoned to discuss my return to London. He said he was sorry it had come to this. When he asked how we should break the news to the Beijing bureau, I felt a sharp stab of grief.

Outside the military or emergency services, there is prob-ably nothing quite like the bond of a great BBC team on the road. The Beijing team was small and I loved every person in it. We often shared twenty-four-hour working days and taxing journeys across the vastness of China on every form of uncomfortable transport. We shared beds, clothes, police custody, overnight edits and lifts home at 5 a.m. on the back of a pushbike. We shared fear, boredom, arguments, jokes, judge-ment calls, editorial dilemmas, birthdays and bereavements.

The Chinese president, Xi Jinping, brought us even closer. We were trying to tell the stories that mattered, in the face of his crackdown on freedom of speech and his formidable surveillance and censorship machine. TV journalism is the hardest in these circumstances because it demands pictures and on-camera interviews. A TV crew is unavoidably conspicu-ous. The only way to achieve anything was to work very hard and pull together. We shared exhilarating highs and crushing lows.

The Beijing team was dominated by brilliant and dedicated Chinese women. Two of them were not much older than Rachel and Daniel. The price of my protest resignation was abandon-ing them and abandoning the huge story we'd worked to tell together. In BBC bureaux around the world, pay for local-hire employees is often more opaque and unequal than for those pro-tected by UK employment legislation. I knew my team would understand that the pay fight was ultimately for them as much as for me. But when the manager on the other end of the line started talking about breaking the news of my departure, I was racked by a sudden and piercing pain.

This was no time to dwell on my losses. One strangled sob aside, I held myself together. Towards the end of the conversation, he said he was surprised by my decision to quit as China Editor.

'I can't imagine why,' I retorted. 'I couldn't have been clearer that if you didn't pay me equally I would resign. You don't intend to pay me equally. So I'm resigning. What's so surprising?'

He didn't answer, so I went on.

'I'm surprised that you haven't made the top men take pay cuts so that women can be equal without breaking the budget.'

He said the BBC couldn't do that or it would end up in court against constructive dismissal claims.

'Well the way you're going, you're going to be in court anyway. Who would you rather be up against, overpaid men or underpaid women?'

My manager didn't answer, but it was a lightbulb moment for me. It seemed our bosses were placing a bet that women were the weaker enemy. Whatever the rights and wrongs of the equal pay question, they were not going to confront powerful men. They'd gamed it out and thought cucumber would still be mostly OK for women if the handlers just put on protective clothing before approaching their cages.

That was how it looked to this capuchin anyway.

As my handler and I said goodbye, neither of us guessed that the monkeys were now mad enough to climb out.

4

SISTER UP

=

I talk too much. Worse, I ramble. And worst of all, I get impatient when others do the same. At least once I rudely interrupted Martine Croxall during a phone call in which she was not even rambling, but trying to report what she'd said in a meeting with management.

'Stop there,' I barked. 'I can guess what you said. Tell me what *they* said!'

Martine later teased me about my impatience. Luckily we could laugh about it. But humans are still human in an equal pay fight. Building and sustaining sisterhood is not easy.

As our BBC Women group gathered members and momentum in the autumn of 2017, Jane Garvey said, 'If I've learnt anything: women need to get together, stick together, speak up for each other. Or nothing will change.'

Jane is right. Solidarity is essential when fighting for equality. Whether you work in an office, teach in a school or present a programme called *Woman's Hour*, solidarity allows you to resist the belittling and gaslighting which an unscrupulous employer may deploy against you. Solidarity undermines the information monopoly that is the employer's chief defence. It gives you strength in numbers and allies who know exactly what you're up against. Sometimes it can produce decisive action. Solidarity doesn't level the playing field but it puts you in the game.

This chapter is about a group of women at the BBC. But in other contexts building workplace solidarity is just as relevant to men, and the journey to collective action that I describe may even be a cautionary tale for other employers.

In 1975 Icelandic women went on strike to protest unequal pay. An estimated 90 per cent of the adult female population took part in a nationwide 'day off'. They did no paid work and no unpaid housework or childcare either. This act of solidarity allowed them to observe their own strength. The following year, Parliament passed a law guaranteeing equal pay, and within five years Iceland had the world's first democratically elected female president. It now has the world's smallest gender pay gap, and in 2018 it became the first country to enforce equal pay for women.

Another example: just weeks before the 2017 Women's Ice Hockey World Championships, the American team threatened to boycott the tournament. It was a high-stakes gamble in their fight for better pay and conditions. Captain Meghan Duggan said it was frightening and 'ultimately it could have led to none of us playing on the national team again'.

The solidarity of the players made it impossible for USA Hockey to field an alternative team. Three days before the tournament was due to begin on home ice in Plymouth, Michigan, the US governing body agreed a new four-year deal on pay and benefits. It still wasn't equal pay with the men's team, but it was a huge advance on the previous low status of the women's team. Duggan said, 'We always found ways to stick together and support each other and stay united throughout the whole process. And that was, without question, the reason why we were able to accomplish what we did.'

The team went on to win gold at the World Championships.

It's hard to give advice on this. You may be surrounded by female colleagues and supported by a flourishing women's network; you may be a small band of watchful rivals; you may be the only woman in a roomful of men. I also can't tell you every inside detail of the BBC Women story. I don't want to put careers and livelihoods at risk. But I am going to share much of what we did and hope that some of it may prove useful, however different your own workplace.

No going back

Of course, women have been grappling with collective action for a very long time. The solidarity of first-wave feminists won some of us the vote and rights in marriage, parenting and ownership of property. My own small effort at challenging a stubborn status quo filled me with awe at their achievements. As *Time* magazine said when it named Emmeline Pankhurst one of the hundred most important people of the twentieth century, 'she shook society into a new pattern from which there could be no going back'.

'The personal is political,' declared second-wave feminists as they battled for contraception and equal pay legislation early in the second half of the twentieth century. Simone de Beauvoir anatomised the social construction of gender and Betty Friedan challenged what she called the Feminine Mystique in a ground-breaking book by the same name, insisting that not all women are fulfilled by marriage and motherhood.

The third wave, which began in the 1990s, addressed the ways in which women of colour, disabled women or working-class women had felt excluded from the feminist movement. It tackled the relationships between sexism, racism and other forms of discrimination, with Kimberlé Crenshaw coining the term 'intersectional theory' to draw attention to the way over-lapping systems of oppression worked. 'Originally articulated on behalf of black women, the term brought to light the invisibility of many constituents within groups that claim them as members, but often fail to represent them.'

Crenshaw pointed out that the experience of black, poor or disabled women was different from that of white middle-class women. The latter could not make the assumption that they spoke for the former. She wrote that when feminism does not explicitly oppose racism, and when anti-racism does not oppose patriarchy, both lose. 'It takes a lot of work to consistently challenge ourselves to be attentive to aspects of power that we don't ourselves experience.'

LGBTQ activists make the same point about intersectionality and the feminist movement today. Change is often a battle for priorities.

A wake-up call

I wish I'd paid more attention to feminist history sooner. I wasn't an active feminist at university, perhaps because after my mother died in 1980, my teenage sisters and I were close but argumentative: the feminist movement was already famous for its factions and I wasn't looking for more sisterhood wars. Besides, what struggle? I was white and middle class in the era of Margaret Thatcher and Madonna. When I joined the workforce in the 1980s, powerful high-profile women seemed to bestride the world. They didn't operate through identity politics and it wasn't obvious to me why I should either. I was just a person.

In 1987, at the age of twenty-five, I became a journalist at the BBC. Its professional rules barred the expression of personal views on politics. That made it easy to avoid inconvenient or messy engagement. I simply assumed that I and every other woman of my generation would be treated as equal. When I married, it was to a Chinese rock drummer with no money, which meant I never had the chance to become financially dependent on a man even if I'd wanted to.

Parenting changed my worldview. While Jin was a loving father and did his best to contribute financially, we didn't manage to share the burdens of our family life equally. Rachel, Daniel and I had returned from Beijing to London in 1999, but Jin spent two-thirds of every year making music in China while I did most of the parenting, earning and household chores. Rachel had barely recovered from two and a half years of treatment for childhood leukaemia when I had my first episode of breast cancer and discovered that I had the BRCA1 genetic mutation, which predisposes for both ovarian and breast cancer. Our marriage foundered the following year. To be fair to Jin, he didn't have a great model of family life himself, as the chaos of the Cultural Revolution had often deprived him of his parents. They had divorced and he had been largely brought up by his grandparents.

In the years after our own divorce, Jin and I got into a pattern whereby he would take sole charge of the home and the children for three or four weeks a year to allow me to make a reporting trip to China. Other than that, he dropped in from Beijing when he could while I kept steady hours at work as a news presenter and did my best at home. I felt lucky to have a good salary and a predictable schedule. Like many mothers of my generation in the paid workforce I felt defensive about media messages suggesting I was neglecting my children when I went out to work. All these years later it's interesting to read that having a mother who works outside the home has some positive impacts: 'In the employment sphere, adult daughters, but not sons, of employed mothers are more likely to be employed and, if employed, are more likely to hold supervisory responsibility, work more hours and earn higher incomes than their peers whose mothers were not employed. In the domestic sphere, sons raised by employed mothers spend more time caring for family members and daughters spend less time on housework.'

Another study found that seeing fathers do household tasks is a key predictor for the attitudes of young adults about how to allocate housework. When Jin visited, Rachel and Daniel often saw him clean the house, wash clothes and cook dinner. We were all glad of that. Jin is an excellent cook.

Over these years I was pleased to see other women advance at work. In 2004 the BBC appointed Helen Boaden as its first female Director of News. The following year she appointed Fran Unsworth as Head of Newsgathering. But it was a female manager who dropped Miriam O'Reilly from *Countryfile* when she hit fifty. And it was Fran who later explained to a parliamentary inquiry, 'There is no question at the BBC but that people are appointed on merit,' but then when pressed on why BBC TV had several male presenters in their seventies and no female ones, she admitted that the BBC simply made an assumption that audiences preferred to see younger women: 'This is a subject that we have only woken up to, in that respect, in the last few years. We assumed, as broadcasters, that this was an audience preference without ever properly exploring that.'

That House of Lords inquiry concluded that the BBC had an informal policy to discriminate against older female presenters, coercing them to leave and covering that up with confidentiality agreements. Miriam O'Reilly had told the inquiry: 'The men continue to function as normal, permitted to be ugly, grizzly, fat, old, and peculiar.'

Perhaps it is unrealistic to expect a sprinkling of women to turn around an entrenched culture. But it's also important to acknowledge that bias against women operates in the minds of women just as in the minds of men. In the vet study, two-thirds of the employers who discriminated against Elizabeth were men but that left a third who were women. Madeleine Albright, the first female US Secretary of State, said, 'There's a special place in hell for women who don't help each other.' But she also said, 'I'm not a person who thinks the world would be entirely different if it was run by women. If you think that, you've forgotten what high school was like.'

First used by psychologists in the 1970s, the term queen bee syndrome refers to women in positions of authority in male-dominated environments who are more demanding and critical towards female subordinates than male ones. It's a controversial term among academics and among women. England's first female Chief Medical Officer, Professor Dame Sally Davies, identified it as a problem in her career, complaining of 'queen bees preening and enjoying being the only woman'. But Sheryl Sandberg, Facebook's chief operating officer, said, 'Women aren't any meaner to women than men are to one another. Women are just expected to be nicer.'

Wherever the truth lies, a century on from the suffragettes I reached my mid-fifties with a growing realisation that getting a few women into positions of leadership was not enough to transform the workplace for women. Although we had made enormous strides and now served as soldiers, judges, journalists, firefighters and astronauts, that was not quite the same as equal opportunity, equal pay or equal respect.

Battle lines

In November 2016, Donald Trump was elected US president despite audio tape in which he bragged about his own sexual harassment of women. The day after his inauguration, millions of women marched in the US and around the world to remind him that women's rights are human rights. But that didn't stop him reversing his predecessor's efforts on gender pay, including a rule requiring large employers to submit pay data to the Equal Employment Opportunity Commission. His administration cited privacy concerns and bureaucracy. Nine months after Trump took office, the #MeToo story exploded. The online dictionary Merriam-Webster said 'feminism' was the most-looked-up word of 2017. American actress Meghan Markle got engaged to Prince Harry and made clear that becoming a member of the British royal family would not mean going quiet: 'Right now with so many campaigns like Me Too and Time's Up there's no better time to continue to shine a light on women feeling empowered and people supporting them.'

#MeToo saw a surge of solidarity in which women identified their suffering as women's suffering, named sexism as the root problem and demanded an end to it. If women in so many different circumstances had experienced the same problem, then clearly the problem was not of their individual making or solving. It was systemic and needed a systemic solution. In this too, #MeToo resonated with the equal pay struggle.

#MeToo could not have happened without the 'silence breakers', the women who broke the terms of non-disclosure agreements and risked civil lawsuits and hostile scrutiny to reveal abuse. The global conversation about the misuse of non-disclosure agreements, or NDAs, resonated with BBC Women. Given their very nature, it was hard for us to establish all the facts, but NDAs are used in many workplaces to silence victims of discrimination and had certainly been used at the BBC in the past. For example, Miriam O'Reilly was offered a large out of court settlement shortly before her employment tribunal hearing, but the settlement was offered subject to a gagging clause which she refused to sign: 'It was wrong. If I walked away, the BBC would get away with discrimination and they could say – still say – "We have a clean record on ageism". I had to dig my heels in.'

#MeToo challenged women as well as men. By conditioning ourselves to ignore or tolerate sexual harassment, had we been complicit in perpetuating it? At the BBC, we faced the same question in relation to unequal pay.

Whatever the past, we were determined not to let it dictate the future. Conviction is a form of energy, as any military, religious or political leader knows. BBC Women knew we were making an equal contribution and felt duty bound to demand equal pay, both for ourselves and for the women to follow. Only by sistering up and fighting together could we have any hope of beating the odds.

Reluctant rebels

On the face of it, the women who came together at the BBC were unpromising material for a protest movement. Time-poor career journalists, we had a big stake in the system and many of us had children to bring up and households to run. Our membership stretched from the top to the bottom of the pay scale and cut across lines of class and race. We were scattered around the UK and some were in foreign news bureaux around the world. With a twenty-four-hour news cycle and a multiplicity of different programmes, even women who worked in the BBC's London headquarters often didn't know each other well. We were frequently rivals for the same scarce opportunities and we didn't have a habit of talking openly about pay. What's more, as employees of a public service broadcaster, we were barred from expressing personal views in public. Not your obvious pay protesters, and not your obvious sisterhood either.

In the autumn of 2017, BBC Women as a group started

to work out who we were and what we were for. Without conscious design, we turned ourselves into a hive mind and mapped the patterns underlying our pay culture. It was about so much more than pay. There were women overlooked in favour of male colleagues with fewer skills and less experience; women overlooked in favour of men brought in from outside without a transparent appointment process; women told their roles had gone within days of announcing a pregnancy; women who never recovered their post after maternity leave; women who were told they could either be a great reporter or a great mother but not both. The individual stories that BBC Women later submitted to Parliament give an idea of the picture that was building:

I lead a BBC sports team in a big city with Premier League teams in our patch. There are few women in equivalent jobs, none in a big city ... Four men doing the same job have confirmed their salary is higher by up to £10,000.

In 2017 I submitted an equal pay claim after finding out that a male colleague was being paid £7000 more for doing the same job. I made little progress, so I began a formal grievance. A few days before the hearing I was called in and offered £4500 extra a year. I was told it was not because they thought I had an equal pay claim, but a reward for hard work.

In 2017 just before the BBC published pay over £150,000, I was called unexpectedly and offered an immediate pay rise. It became apparent that for nearly three years I had been sitting next to a man doing an identical job who was being paid tens of thousands of pounds more.

I have co-presented with a male colleague for many years.

Despite working fewer hours than me, he earns more. Pro-rata, I estimate he's paid around double what I earn for doing the same job. I raised the equal pay issue many times over the years, but nothing was done.

Our bosses knew all of this. For years the unions had flagged up concerns, as had an internal women's network. To no avail. The only thing that might make things different this time was solidarity and coordinated action.

We moved beyond information sharing to practical support. We exchanged advice on how to handle equal pay complaints. We attended pay hearings with each other. We followed each other's cases with serious attention and boosted each other's morale at low points. We protected each other from internalising the belittling of our work. Margaret Heffernan, who has written extensively on workplace culture, told me: 'Women usually have no idea how good they are.'

That's why it's so important for them to unite. Solidarity has a multiplier effect. We may not see our own value clearly but we can see each other's. As I later told the *New Yorker* magazine: 'If you tell me I'm rubbish, I might believe you, but if you tell me she's rubbish I know it's not true.'

Academic research is divided on whether women are assertive in negotiating for themselves but the evidence is clear that they are strong in negotiating for others. Having seen BBC Women battle for each other in pay hearings, I wholeheartedly agree. Journalists have to be determined, articulate and resourceful as individuals, and together our group was a formidable force multiplier. On any level playing field we would have wiped the floor with our management.

But current equal pay law is not a level playing field. So we kept our spirits up by discussing ideas to make the BBC a better workplace: transparency on pay, but also flexible working, unconscious bias training, an end to discrimination against women who were pregnant or had recently given birth.

We shared news stories about female role models in sport, entertainment, politics, science. We celebrated each other's work, both within the group and on social media. Men have had role models, mentors and sponsors for centuries. We were making up for lost time. We became more conscious of fighting a workplace culture in which women's ideas were often ignored, marginalised or credited to men. It became second nature to repeat good points made by women and give credit to those who made them. In the US, Aminatou Sow and Ann Friedman, presenters of the *Call Your Girlfriend* podcast, called this 'shine theory'. The term was picked up by senior women in the Obama White House, and the habit was picked up by us in the BBC.

It helped to think positive. But I don't think any of us could have predicted that this support network would become such a powerful antidote to the narrative of low self-esteem that many women had internalised in long careers at the BBC. Confidence-building and consciousness-raising just seemed to emerge from nowhere as we went along.

Each of us had supportive friends and family, but only other women living through these ordeals could fully understand the mix of anxiety, humiliation and resolve that comes from fighting for equal pay.

We had our own niche sense of humour too. One woman described how a boss had rung her to cancel a meeting he hadn't even invited her to, promised to call back and re-arrange but never did. 'He'll be Director-General by Easter,' quipped another.

And when managers repeated the mantra 'Our gender pay gap is primarily about the different balance of men and women at different levels,' we joked, 'Get rid of the women. Problem solved.'

Little of this was done face to face. Exchanging information and advice, sharing observations, laughing over everyday sexism, offering support – it all took place on a messaging app. The rules were firm: daily delete and no sharing outside the group. By sharing with you I am breaking the rules. I hope my sisterhood will feel this account is in the public interest and forgive me on this occasion.

But I'd be misleading you if I said sistering up was always easy.

No catfights but …

The first problem was denial and disbelief. Not only do most humans have gender bias, they also have authority bias. We tend to believe what our 'authority figures' tell us, whether priests, headteachers, celebrities or employers. I think most women who joined our group over those early months struggled to come to terms with the disorientating realisation that they could not trust management assertions.

Fear was the next challenge. Many were cautious about being seen as troublemakers. Some were afraid to lodge an equal pay complaint, let alone a grievance, for fear of the career consequences.

Exhaustion and hopelessness were ever-present risks. The campaign often felt like a second full-time job and we all got tired and dispirited at times. Solidarity demanded a commitment that was hard to sustain against all the other demands of life.

But the biggest headaches of all for the group were leadership and direction. On leadership, the senior women who had organised the July 2017 open letter felt that they could use their profile to speak up for others. They were right in thinking bosses would be prepared to talk to them, and at the start everyone had high hopes of those meetings on the executive floor. But as the weeks and months drifted by with no progress, frustration grew. Those with lower profiles and lower pay wanted a voice.

Direction was another challenge. What exactly did we want and how did we intend to get it? It was easy to say BBC Women wanted equal pay, but were we going to wear down the fortress wall with a slow trickle of grievances or blast through it with a test case at an employment tribunal?

The last female journalist to bring a high-profile public case against the BBC for discrimination was Miriam O'Reilly. I felt Miriam's victory had forced management to put more older women on screen. Some argued the culture change was cosmetic.

Money was another big discussion. BBC people like to think of themselves as loyal and responsible. If there was one workforce that could change to an equal-pay culture without huge liabilities for back pay, we were it. At the start, many of us simply wanted our bosses to acknowledge the problem and fix it going forward. Instead they squandered that goodwill.

I worried that management would settle cases for high-profile women at the expense of just about everyone else. Some members of the group felt all BBC pay should be published and all salaries should be capped at £150,000. Others countered that it was not our role to consider the knock-on implications of equal pay, that none of us knew enough about BBC finances to re-design the pay structure, and that the BBC was clearly not short of money when it came to paying top lawyers and consultants to fight us.

These were all good points. We discussed the pros and cons

of using equal pay settlements to set up bursaries for less advantaged female journalists. I joked that we were spending a lot of time worrying about how to spend money that our bosses had no intention of giving us.

It was right to debate these questions. Where we were able to disagree with each other candidly, we built trust. And we disagreed about so many things. Here are three more at random:

Allies in management: Who is making the problem worse and who is trying to resolve it?

Tone: How much venting is the right amount of venting in a sisterhood group?

Trust: Can we trust each other not to share sensitive information outside the group?

That last became a priority when someone leaked an exchange over the status of trans women to another news organisation. And that wasn't our only intersectional challenge. The BBC had an ethnicity pay gap as well as a gender one. BAME women in our group felt enormously frustrated by a workplace culture that disadvantaged them twice over. One wrote: 'If as a white woman you sometimes feel less favourably treated compared to your male colleagues multiply that a hundred times and you might get an idea of what it's like to be a BAME woman at the BBC.'

Then there was regional and socioeconomic background. British journalism is not just dominated by white men, but by elite white men. A report by the Social Mobility Commission found that only 11 per cent of British journalists were from working-class backgrounds. Most senior editors, columnists and reporters went to independent schools in a country where less than 10 per cent of the public are privately educated.

When the *Sunday Times* asked the white, Middlesbrough-born BBC business presenter Steph McGovern about pay, she said pay gaps were partly about class. In a longer statement shared via Twitter, she wrote, 'We talk a lot in the BBC about how to be better at ethnic diversity, which is important because we're not good enough at it. However, we never talk about class.'

I thought Steph made a valid point. But often different perspectives or priorities among women are demeaned as 'catfights' by those who want to see female solidarity fail. Several newspapers ran Steph's comments under the headline 'posh women are paid a hell of a lot more than me'. Some in the group were acutely sensitive to a sneering media narrative that preyed on any hint of division. Actually we didn't have catfights. What we had was diverse experience, complex challenges and different approaches to tackling them.

Do you think men would have handled any of this better?

There were many moments when I envied the men their freedom from the 'minefield'. Because of the BBC rules barring staff from political engagement, it was a late lesson for many of us in the exhausting give-and-take of collective action, and tensions were inevitable. Women often train themselves to be good listeners but are conditioned to compare themselves and to judge each other. As we worked through many unfamiliar challenges, we had to listen out for the critical voice in our own heads.

I am as quick to jealousy and judgement as the next person. A psychotherapist friend advised me that if I was finding one of my BBC sisters difficult, I should pause to think which of my biological sisters she reminded me of. Once I started being honest about it, most difficult things reminded me of myself. Belonging to this BBC sisterhood gradually made me more aware of my own unconscious biases about women, and more aware of how impatient I could get with people I expected to think or behave like me but who stubbornly insisted on being themselves.

It's hard to build a sisterhood if your workplace is tiny, has hardly any women or has a very competitive culture. But it's worth trying, even if that means reaching out to women who work for your employer in a different location or for a different employer but in the same occupation or industry. You could think about joining a union if you haven't already. Women will struggle to resolve unequal pay without collective action. If you're under one roof, solidarity can be more organic. You could start by endorsing the ideas of a female colleague in a meeting or by volunteering pay information that you'd normally guard, and see how that makes you feel. Or you could do as we did: start an equal pay group on a messaging app with clear rules to keep it safe, legal and polite.

I'm grateful for what my sisterhood taught me about building a coalition. I think I did get better at curbing my ego for the sake of something bigger and listening for the lesson buried in disagreement rather than bearing a grudge. Together we also learned to shrug off self-doubt and negative spin.

Nothing to see here

This was lucky, because there were plenty of people ready to spin against us without us doing the job for them. BBC Women were told that we had been caricatured in a management meeting as 'women on £400,000 asking for a pay rise'. We also heard that bosses would grimace or roll their eyes when certain names were mentioned. There were hints about senior female journalists being flaky or difficult. Some editors turned colleagues against us by warning that equal pay settlements would have to come from journalism budgets and programmes would suffer. It felt as if hostility and disapproval were being pumped out through the air conditioning and we were fighting both the original problem of unequal pay and a management determined to dig in and defend it with the help of expensive lawyers and consultants. What a waste. In those early months, very small sums of money, or simply an apology and commitment to equal pay in future, would have satisfied most of the women involved.

But on 7 November 2017, the Director-General told a routine parliamentary hearing that the BBC had no equal pay problem. He cited the equal pay audit that had been published a month earlier and that found no evidence of systemic discrimination against women.

Three days later, the National Union of Journalists published its own survey on equal pay, reporting that 'almost eight out of ten women journalists at the BBC believe they are paid less than a male colleague doing the same work, similar work or work of equal value'. Michelle Stanistreet, the general secretary of the NUJ, said: 'Men are often paid more than women because of outright discrimination, dated recruitment practices and inflexible working practices which make it difficult for women to juggle work and family life. Then there are the cases where women are not being paid the same even when they are doing the same job as their male colleague.'

She was speaking on Equal Pay Day, the date in the calendar on which the average woman in the UK stops earning relative to the average man. BBC Women marked the moment by sharing selfies with male colleagues alongside a white placard with two black bars, an equals sign.

This was all before my resignation as China Editor and I was in Beijing. Given the eight-hour time difference, we were up before London. In fact I was up at 4.30 a.m., preparing for a live interview on *News at Ten* to mark the end of President Trump's China summit. As producer Kathy Long, cameraman Matthew Goddard and I waited for our programme slot, we took our Equal Pay Day selfies to pass the time and then watched as BBC colleagues around the world joined in. Sarah Montague posted a photo of herself presenting the Today Programme in a T-shirt with an equals sign on it. DJ Jo Whiley posted one of herself with Greg James of Radio 1; Martine Croxall with fellow news presenter Ben Brown. Some of the highest-paid men stayed away, but we had enough solidarity from others to show that this was not a zero-sum battle of the sexes.

Equal Pay Day over, BBC Women went back to the trenches. By December 2017 the mix of anger and hope with which we started our campaign had curdled to bitter frustration. Denied the chance to help solve the problem, we were forced into a dogged fight just to insist that it was real. Here are the variety of reasons management gave for refusing to accept women's equal pay complaints. If you're an employer or a female employee, you may recognise some of them:

It's irrelevant what he gets paid.
He has more experience.
He has a specialism.
He has more skill.
He has more profile.
Your job is slightly different.
This is due to old increments.
His is a legacy payment we can't do anything about.
We can't raise your pay without raising everyone else's.
He has a family to support.

Managers and HR did not use the language of equal pay law. And I know of no case in which they responded to an equal pay complaint by saying, 'You're right. Your work is equal and you will be paid equally.'

One BBC woman commented bitterly, 'When women are cheap, bosses like us; when we ask for equal treatment, they don't like us any more.'

Mansplained again

The mood was darkening. And then on 15 December 2017, Director of News James Harding was interviewed on one of his own news programmes, *Newswatch*. Asked when women at the BBC would get equal pay, he gave a completely unqualified and unequivocal reply: 'We have equal pay. If you look, we did a full equal pay audit which showed there is equal pay across the BBC.'

BBC Women saw this as gaslighting on a grand scale. Why would so many busy professional people invest untold time and energy in attempting to solve a problem that didn't exist? Were women stupid? Were we liars? Were we mad? The equality regulator specifically warns employers not to make overall conclusions about equal pay on the basis of a partial audit.

We could see no evidence that James and our other, mostly male, managers had considered the possibility that they might be wrong. Instead, we felt they had delivered a blunt message about power. They were not listening to women because they did not feel the need. We might as well have belonged to another species. I reflected again that clever, powerful, alpha people often underestimate their adversaries.

I would advise other employers to avoid casually antagonising their female workforce. By the end of 2017, BBC Women felt they had been backed into a corner. We had joined enough dots to have a good map of our pay structure. We had thrashed out a lot of the arguments and honed our talents as negotiators, drafters, strategists and administrators. I don't want to exaggerate. We were still over-stretched and anxious public service broadcasters rather than a swarm of battle-ready ninjas. Even now, all of us would much rather have worked with our bosses than against. But adversity had forged tight the bonds of sisterhood and management had crossed the line marked truth.

George Bernard Shaw once wrote, 'The reasonable man adapts himself to the world: the unreasonable one persists in trying to adapt the world to himself. Therefore all progress depends on the unreasonable man.' This is even truer of the unreasonable woman and her unequal workplace.

Facing down demons

James Harding's interview was a tipping point for me. He had begged me to go to China and now he seemed to be denying a truth for which I'd resigned that role. Life is short. I'm impatient. I want women to win equal pay in my lifetime. My mother died at forty-two because the medical researchers who were trying to solve the problem of ovarian cancer didn't solve it in time. My daughter and I are alive because researchers did solve problems relating to childhood leukaemia and breast cancer. These people didn't waste time, energy and money finding reasons to avoid acknowledging that there was a problem. They saved our lives, they didn't squander them.

Now I wanted my bosses to solve the problem of unequal pay rather than cause more damage by denying its existence. Like many generations of women before me, I arrived at the conclusion that polite persuasion didn't work. Escalation began to feel like a personal duty. My resolve grew like a crystal in a saucer of salt water. All I could do was watch.

Perhaps the Chinese zodiac had James Harding and me right after all. Roosters sometimes lack persistence and tigers risk recklessness in their will to win. While James Harding left the BBC to launch an independent news project, I spent Christmas obsessively drafting and re-drafting a protest letter addressed to the BBC audience. I drew on wise counsel from several BBC Women including household names like Clare Balding, Fiona Bruce, Jane Garvey, Mishal Husain, Sarah Montague, Kirsty Wark.

On 31 December I mis-timed the journey between one New Year's Eve party and another and saw in 2018 alone, under the sobering lights of an almost empty carriage on the London Underground. Suspended between one year and the next, I asked my reflection in the dark train window, 'Are you really going to go over the top?'

I already knew the answer. But I was afraid, tormented by nightmares and self-doubt. I feared the BBC would sack me and use its mighty media machine to incinerate my message at the point of delivery. I feared audiences would misunderstand me and I feared my colleagues would revile me for washing our dirty linen in public. Many of those around me shared these fears. Friends worried a public letter would destroy my career. BBC veterans warned that the bosses would find a way to destroy my reputation.

But what choice did I have? At this point in my life I could not allow my own fear or greed to rule. I owed audiences the truth. My kids were grown up and my finances sound. However unpleasant and however frightening, I must face these risks.

I promised *The Times* my open letter for 8 January. It would be my first working day since resigning the China post and I would be presenting the *Today* Programme. In the week running up to publication I leaned on a great support team. Several BBC Women helped me polish my letter. For everything else

I relied on Martine Croxall and Kate Silverton. Kate was a brilliant communicator and strategist. She recruited two professional media advisers from beyond our struggle who gave us their wisdom pro bono because they believed in equal pay. And by now I had an ice-cool lawyer, Jennifer Millins, who was never far from her email.

Luckily, I had two great distractions. The first was building a website of my best China work so that audiences could make up their own minds about its value. Poring over four years of news films, radio features, written pieces and photos was a reminder of the joy of doing good journalism with colleagues you love. It was also a way to say goodbye to my China life.

The week's second big distraction was the *Today* Programme. This was a strange irony. The last time I'd attempted to break into this sanctum was nearly a decade earlier, after the then editor told a listener who wanted to hear more women presenting the programme that it was 'too tough an environment for novices'.

At the time I didn't see myself as a novice. I was presenting three hours of live TV news a day and I asked the *Today* editor to give me a week as a stand-in presenter, suggesting that it would be a win-win for him. If I was good he could say he was trying out women, and if I was bad I'd be proving him right, that we weren't up to it. He said no.

Come the summer of 2017, I discovered that many other BBC women had similar stories of rejection. By this point, the *Today* Programme did have two regular female presenters, but they were still outnumbered by men, and the male presenters dominated the big interviews. Four more men and no women then appeared as summer holiday stand-ins.

BBC Women gritted their teeth and pointed out that editors couldn't know that men were better if they didn't give women the chance to try.

To cut a long story short, several women, me among them, were offered shifts over Christmas and New Year. Which is why I happened to be presenting the *Today* Programme in the first two weeks of January 2018.

This distraction turned out to be a blessing. After all, whether the story was Trump threatening Iran, winter pressures on the NHS or sexual harassment at Westminster, it was still journalism. It was my core skill set.

Five days before the planned publication of my protest letter, I met Michelle Stanistreet and Roy Mincoff of the National Union of Journalists. They were very kind, and concerned about the risk of disciplinary action against me. They urged me to wait for the outcome of my grievance. In early December, the BBC had promised to expedite the grievance process and said I might get the outcome before Christmas. But now HR were warning it would take more time. I felt I could no longer allow bosses to control the agenda and the timetable. The story was that I'd resigned my China post over unequal pay and the time to tell that story was now.

The hardest decision is the one to jump. I'd listened to all the advice and weighed it carefully. I'd spent six months sistering up and shared a strong sense of purpose with other BBC Women. But in the end, on something as personally momentous as this, only you can decide and you must step up and own your decision.

Jump

It was hard to tell how my protest letter would play in the world beyond the BBC bubble. Many firms were beginning the year by reporting their gender pay gaps, as required by new government legislation. With the fashion chain Phase Eight and airline easyJet reporting gender pay gaps above 50 per cent, one of the sisterhood observed, 'The BBC looks like a paragon of virtue in comparison.'

Friday 5 January was officially my last day as BBC China Editor, a sad moment for me. But few others knew until two days later, when I sent my open letter to BBC Women. I told them that it would appear in the first edition of Monday's *Times*. I then alerted Jon Sopel and Jeremy Bowen because my letter mentioned them. I also got in touch with Sarah Sands, the editor of the *Today* Programme. It seemed only fair to give her time to switch presenters for the following morning if she felt that was necessary. By 6 p.m., 134 BBC Women had endorsed a statement that read,

> Statement in support of Carrie Gracie from #BBCWomen, a group of more than 130 broadcasters and producers:
>
> It is hugely regrettable that an outstanding and award-winning journalist like Carrie Gracie feels she has no option but to resign from her post as China Editor because the BBC has not valued her equally with her male counterparts. We wholeheartedly support her and call on the BBC to resolve her case and others without delay, and to urgently address pay inequality across the corporation. Up to 200 women that we know of in various grades and roles across the BBC have made pay complaints. The NUJ alone is involved in more than 120 of these cases.

Privately, BBC Women wrote me messages that crackled with anger, admiration and resolve. My own emotions were confused: relief that I'd pitched the letter right, gratitude that so many fine colleagues were ready to stand alongside me, dismay that we were about to inflict damage on an organisation we loved, grief as it hit me again that my China life was over, and a strange weightlessness. I'd jumped far out into the void and it was now a long way down.

Mixed with all these emotions, I felt pride and wonder that after months of feeling so belittled and beaten down, this band of sisters was striking back.

SPEAK YOUR TRUTH

=

I t is vital to speak your truth. Whether you speak it to your boss, your colleagues, your friends, your family – or in the pages of a national newspaper – is a secondary question. The first challenge is to speak your truth. Get it out of your own head and into the world. This was how I spoke mine.

Dear BBC Audience,

My name is Carrie Gracie and I have been a BBC journalist for three decades. With great regret, I have left my post as China Editor to speak out publicly on a crisis of trust at the BBC.

The BBC belongs to you, the licence fee payer. I believe you have a right to know that it is breaking equality law and resisting pressure for a fair and transparent pay structure.

In thirty years at the BBC, I have never sought to make myself the story and never publicly criticised the organisation I love. I am not asking for more money. I believe I am very well paid already – especially as someone working for a publicly funded organisation. I simply want the BBC to abide by the law and value men and women equally.

On pay, the BBC is not living up to its stated values of trust, honesty and accountability. Salary disclosures the BBC was forced to make six months ago revealed not only unacceptably high pay for top presenters and managers but also an indefensible pay gap between men and women doing equal work. These revelations damaged the trust of BBC staff. For the first time, women saw hard evidence of what they'd long suspected, that they are not being valued equally.

Many have since sought pay equality through internal negotiation but managers still deny there is a problem. This bunker mentality is likely to end in a disastrous legal defeat for the BBC and an exodus of female talent at every level.

Mine is just one story of inequality among many, but I hope it will help you understand why I feel obliged to speak out.

I am a China specialist, fluent in Mandarin and with nearly three decades of reporting the story. Four years ago, the BBC urged me to take the newly created post of China Editor.

I knew the job would demand sacrifices and resilience. I would have to work 5000 miles from my teenage children, and in a heavily censored one-party state I would face surveillance, police harassment and official intimidation.

I accepted the challenges while stressing to my bosses that I must be paid equally with my male peers. Like many other BBC women, I had long suspected that I was routinely paid less, and at this point in my career, I was determined not to let it happen again. Believing that I had secured pay parity with men in equivalent roles, I set off for Beijing.

In the past four years, the BBC has had four international editors – two men and two women. The Equality Act 2010 states that men and women doing equal work must receive equal pay. But last July I learned that in the previous financial year, the two men earned at least 50% more than the two women.

Despite the BBC's public insistence that my appointment demonstrated its commitment to gender equality, and despite my own insistence that equality was a condition of taking up the post, my managers had yet again judged that women's work was worth much less than men's.

My bewilderment turned to dismay when I heard the BBC complain of being forced to make these pay disclosures. Without them, I and many other BBC women would never have learned the truth.

I told my bosses the only acceptable resolution would be for all the international editors to be paid the same amount. The right amount would be for them to decide, and I made clear I wasn't seeking a pay rise, just equal pay. Instead the BBC offered me a big pay rise which remained far short of equality. It said there were differences between roles which justified the pay gap, but it has refused to explain these differences. Since turning down this unequal pay rise, I have been subjected to a dismayingly incompetent and undermining grievance process which still has no outcome.

Enough is enough. The rise of China is one of the biggest stories of our time and one of the hardest to tell. I cannot do it justice while battling my bosses and a byzantine complaints process. Last week I left my role as China Editor and will now return to my former post in the London newsroom where I expect to be paid equally.

For BBC women this is not just a matter of one year's salary or two. Taking into account disadvantageous contracts and pension entitlements, it is a gulf that will last a lifetime. Many of the women affected are not highly paid 'stars' but hard-working producers on modest salaries. Often women from ethnic minorities suffer wider pay gaps than the rest.

This is not the gender pay gap that the BBC says it is working on. It is not men earning more because they do more of the jobs which pay better. It is men earning more in the same jobs or jobs of equal value. It is pay discrimination and it is illegal.

On learning the shocking scale of inequality last July, BBC women began to come together to tackle the culture of secrecy that helps perpetuate it. We shared our pay details and asked male colleagues to do the same.

Meanwhile the BBC conducted various reviews. The outgoing Director of News said last month, 'We did a full equal pay audit which showed there is equal pay across the BBC.' But this was not a full audit. It excluded the women with the biggest pay gaps. The BBC has now begun a 'talent review' but the women affected have no confidence in it. Up to two hundred of us have made pay complaints only to be told repeatedly there is no pay discrimination at the BBC. Can we all be wrong? I no longer trust our management to give an honest answer.

In fact, the only BBC women who can be sure they do not suffer pay discrimination are senior managers whose salaries are published. For example, we have a new, female, Director of News who did not have to fight to earn the same as her male predecessor because his £340,000 salary was published and so was hers. Elsewhere, pay secrecy makes BBC women as vulnerable as they are in many other workplaces.

How to put things right?

The BBC must admit the problem, apologise and set in place an equal, fair and transparent pay structure. To avoid wasting your licence fee on an unwinnable court fight against female staff, the BBC should immediately agree to independent arbitration to settle individual cases.

Patience and good will are running out. In the six months since July's revelations, the BBC has attempted a botched solution based on divide and rule. It has offered some women pay 'revisions' which do not guarantee equality, while locking down other women in a protracted complaints process.

We have felt trapped. Speaking out carries the risk of disciplinary measures or even dismissal; litigation can destroy careers and be financially ruinous. What's more the BBC often settles cases out of court and demands non-disclosure agreements, a habit unworthy of an organisation committed to truth, and one which does nothing to resolve the systemic problem.

None of this is an indictment of individual managers. I am grateful for their personal support and for their editorial integrity in the face of censorship pressure in China. But for far too long, a secretive and illegal BBC pay culture has inflicted dishonourable choices on those who enforce it. This must change.

Meanwhile we are by no means the only workplace with hidden pay discrimination and the pressure for transparency is only growing. I hope rival news organisations will not use this letter as a stick with which to beat the BBC, but instead reflect on their own equality issues.

It is painful to leave my China post abruptly and to say goodbye to the team in the BBC's Beijing bureau. But most of them are brilliant young women. I don't want their generation to have to fight this battle in the future because my generation failed to win it now.

To women of any age in any workplace who are confronting pay discrimination, I wish you the solidarity of a strong sisterhood and the support of male colleagues.

It is a century since women first won the right to vote in Britain. Let us honour that brave generation by making this the year we win equal pay.

6

FIGHT TO WIN

=

'You'd better be prepared to smash their heads on the pavement before they kill you' – the warning from a normally non-violent BBC Woman on reading my open letter.

I hope you never feel you have to fight your employer. But if you do, you must fight to win. Or you will lose. When the powerful feel attacked, they often seek to punish.

The Chinese military strategist Sun Zi gave good advice two and a half thousand years ago in *The Art of War*: 'Let your plans be dark and impenetrable as night, and when you move, fall like a thunderbolt.'

I faced an enormous power asymmetry and I had to maximise both surprise and solidarity. Of the two, solidarity came more easily. For months, I'd thought aloud in the sisterhood group about our strategic options. I'd been open about the progress of my own case. I'd built trust.

'The quality of decision is like the well-timed swoop of a falcon,' wrote Sun Zi.

Surprise comes much harder to me. I'm an open book, one of life's over-sharers. It was only when trying to protect vulnerable sources and interviewees in China that I'd learned to accept that concealment is sometimes necessary, and when necessary, should be done properly.

Concealment here was necessary. If BBC bosses had learned

of my plan to publish a whistle-blowing letter they would have tried to stop me. So until 7 January 2018, I kept that letter to a tight circle. But that evening I was scooped on my own story. I received an email from Mark Di Stefano, a media reporter from the news website BuzzFeed who wrote that someone had leaked my letter to him and he intended to publish it. I pleaded with him to wait for my carefully planned rollout, but he refused. All's fair in love, war and journalism, I guess.

My first reaction was panic. I was no longer in control. But I reminded myself that no plan survives contact with reality. After many months trapped in the BBC game of cat's cradle, followed by weeks drafting my letter and planning its launch, it was a relief to let go. As the news story broke, I even felt detached about where the pieces would land. I knew that even if I had control of nothing else, I did still have control of my own behaviour.

It's an obvious point, but being true to yourself and the things you care about gives you core strength. I also knew it was both a privilege and a responsibility to have a public platform for my message. I was just doing the job of the BBC reporter by other means. #keepcalmandcarrieon, advised one colleague.

I hope you never have to share this experience. But if you do, I hope you too will follow your inner compass and that this will help combat the terror that comes from loss of control.

If you are a male colleague, do your best to help. If you are an employer, start listening. If you are a woman going up over the top for equal pay, protect yourself and fight to win.

I've talked about the importance of sistering up. You also need legal advice (see pages 243–6). You need supportive friends and family who will help shoulder some of life's other burdens so that you can focus on the fight. You need to look after every aspect of your health and wellbeing so that you can stay calm, true to your purpose and alert to what matters on the battlefield.

Remember to guard the element of surprise, and fight only in the time and place of your choosing with the weapon of your choice.

After BuzzFeed published my protest letter, I was immediately deluged with emails and text messages from journalists seeking confirmation that it was genuine. Luckily, Kate Silverton fielded the media storm on my behalf and made a better job of it than I could ever have done. By chance, Martine Croxall was the presenter on the BBC News Channel that evening. No viewer would have guessed from her professional demeanour that the Martine explaining that the BBC's China Editor had resigned her post to protest against what she had called a 'secretive and illegal pay culture' was the same Martine who, as union rep and equal pay campaigner, had attended the China Editor's grievance hearing and supported many other women in pay hearings over the preceding six months. On-air impartiality is second nature to BBC journalists.

Messages of support soon began to come in, some from BBC Women worrying about the pressure ahead:

> Waking up at 3 a.m. or whatever time it is to do the Today programme is hard at the best of times. We are all holding your hand and we're with you.

Some messages were from female colleagues beyond the group:

> I wish we could win this fight another way but believe the BBC will never face up to the scale of this unless we women a) act together and b) go public.

Friends worried about the fate of the whistle-blower:

> Hope it's not too chilly out there above the parapet.

Jeremy Heywood, my friend at the head of the Civil Service, had predicted that the BBC would sack me for breach of contract. With the Prime Minister planning a Cabinet reshuffle for Monday morning, he now joked with typical gallows humour that if I was axed from the *Today* Programme and from the BBC altogether, I might end up being the biggest reshuffle story of the day.

It must have been a difficult evening for BBC bosses as the army at my back grew larger and louder. Moreover, my timing posed an editorial dilemma, and a strategic one. No BBC journalist is allowed to report on a news story about themselves. But the *Today* Programme has two presenters so this impartiality dilemma was not insurmountable. The strategic dilemma was trickier: if management let me go ahead and present the *Today* Programme, it would be hard to dismiss me as a rambling troublemaker. But if they took me off air, critics would cry victimisation. If they sacked me, they might face a full-scale revolt.

I had considered these possible moves in advance and timed the letter to coincide with presenting the *Today* Programme to give my message impact and myself protection. I felt uncomfortable about being cunning. It wasn't part of my self-image. But this is what I mean when I say you must fight to win. I hadn't picked this fight and I hadn't set the rules for it, but I was in it and I had to do my best to win. Chairman Mao once said, 'A revolution is not a dinner party, or writing an essay, or painting a picture, or doing embroidery.'

He said revolution was instead an act of violence by which one class overthrows another. His revolution then descended into a savage tragedy. The ends don't always justify the means. I knew there were ethical lines I would not cross, weapons I would not use. However, in any human group, insisting that the rich and powerful change the rules by which they amass their wealth and power is not going to be a dinner party. I had to toughen up.

When my friend and colleague had told me I'd better be ready to 'smash their heads on the pavement', I think this is what she meant. The biblical story of Judith floated through my mind. Judith saves her town from destruction by tricking the besieging Assyrian general Holofernes, cutting off his head and displaying it on a spike. His army flees and the siege is over.

My battle involved no violence, but it did demand steeliness and forward planning. As Judith showed and Sun Zi wrote, 'The general who wins a battle makes many calculations in his temple ere the battle is fought.'

That night I didn't sleep. At 2 a.m. I started reading up on the other news stories of the day. At 3.30 a.m. I got into a car bound for Broadcasting House and saw my picture on the front pages of the newspapers. At 4 a.m. I walked past the waiting photographers and TV cameras.

Who would want to be a whistle-blower?

Research suggests most people who come across something seriously illegal or unethical at work will try once or twice to raise their concerns and then give up if the employer does not respond. Those who persevere tend to be highly educated, perform well in their jobs and believe something can be done about the problem. Employers: it's a pity that many of you find it so hard to respond to constructive criticism from within. As Margaret Heffernan has pointed out in her book *Beyond Measure: The Big Impact of Small Changes*, 'Just cultures aim specifically at ensuring that conflict and ideas come out where they can be seen, explored, and confronted safely.'

She writes that employers should welcome disagreements as a sign that employees care. They should create safe environments to explore different ideas and practise creative conflict. In return, employees owe a duty of loyalty and confidentiality to their employer. Public whistle-blowing can only be justified on the basis of a higher duty to the public good, and this is reflected in the law.

Unfortunately, employers who feel threatened by criticism often perceive this higher duty as a form of treachery, a betrayal of the group. Many whistle-blowers are sacked for breaching confidentiality. If they don't follow correct whistle-blowing procedures, with a clear paper trail to prove that they did so, they may be dismissed by an employer who denies that whistle-blowing had anything to do with it. Those who then stay at the same workplace often report bullying, isolation and character assassination. They, rather than their allegations, become the story, with their motives, credibility and competence all questioned. Mistakes are repeated, integrity lost and culture corrupted, in a cycle worthy of Greek tragedy. Employers: a moment for self-reflection. Is this your workplace?

However, I calculated that as free speech was part of the BBC's credo it would be hard to sack me. What's more, I'd made it difficult for critics to claim I was mad and marginal as I was about to present the BBC's flagship morning news programme, my protest was on the front pages of the national papers, I had the support of my union, and I spoke for many women who I knew would defend me fiercely on social media. Sun Zi would have been proud.

Then I just got lucky. Do you ever feel that you throw yourself at the universe and it catches you? That morning the universe caught me. The news scheduler in the sky was on my side and almost every story resonated with mine. The BBC's top headline was the Prime Minister's Cabinet reshuffle to freshen up what had become 'male, pale and stale'. The second story was the Golden Globe awards, with stars dressed in black to mark #MeToo. On the *Today* Programme's news bulletin, my resignation over unequal pay was the third headline, followed by a health story about how women were three times more likely than men to die in the year after a heart attack. The reason? They received less medical treatment.

Resonant in a different way was the presenter line-up. My co-presenter was John Humphrys, one of the highest-paid men in BBC News. Just after 4 a.m., he walked into the open-plan office on the third floor of Broadcasting House, threw his pile of newspapers down on the desk and declared that my protest letter was either idiocy or a stroke of genius.

He then did some harrumphing that it would be uncollegiate of me to repeat. I bit my tongue, got on with writing scripts and when John disappeared to do a pre-recorded interview with Jon Sopel in Washington DC, I was grateful for a few minutes of peace.

Soon the deputy editor arrived to talk to the team about how to handle the problem I'd posed: a presenter who was also one of the top news stories of the morning, having accused the organisation for which we all worked of breaking the law. He and the rest of the production team were professional throughout. I felt sorry for causing anxiety and trouble to hard-working innocent parties.

At 5.55 a.m. John Humphrys and I sat down side by side in the studio, and as we logged into computers and organised scripts and newspapers, I asked whether he'd read my open letter. He said he hadn't had time. When the microphone lights went on five minutes later, I faced three hours of live broadcasting to the nation and felt small and afraid. Then suddenly, I heard Oprah Winfrey's resonant voice as the news bulletin played a clip from the Golden Globes ceremony.

'Speaking your truth is the most powerful tool we all have . . . For too long, women have not been heard or believed if they dare speak the truth to the power of those men. But their time is up,' she said.

Oprah, thank you for reminding me, I thought.

A word about Oprah and equal pay. In 1980, she was in her mid-twenties and co-hosting a TV show in Baltimore. She went to her (male) boss to complain that she was being paid less than half the salary of the man she worked alongside. Her boss pointed out that she didn't have children to support. He refused to acknowledge that her work was of equal value.

'I knew he didn't hear nor see me, and that I was not going to get the validation that I needed . . . I decided not to file a suit against it because I knew at the time that I would lose, that no good would come of it.'

It was several years before Oprah quit, but she said she started planning for it the moment she left her boss's office. Later she fought pay discrimination again, this time on behalf of her show's production team against a studio boss who said they were 'only girls'. As she recalls, 'He actually said to me, "They're only girls. They're a bunch of girls – what do they need money for?" I go, "Well, either they're going to get raises, or I'm going to sit down." I will not work unless they get paid. And so they did.'

Oprah confronted unequal pay in an era when the gender pay gap was wider than it is now, and she did it despite the much wider gap for black women. She acted before she wielded the power of being Oprah. We can all do something, and the more small somethings we contribute, the easier it becomes for others to do the same. Many shoulders to the wheel.

At the Golden Globes, Oprah put her shoulder to the wheel with magnificent force. She left no one out, emphasising that the #MeToo story 'transcends any culture, geography, race, religion, politics, or workplace'.

She didn't waste her moment in the spotlight, which reminded me not to waste mine. Her inspirational warm-up act was a happy accident of timing. But academic research suggests that being exposed to a powerful role model measurably boosts women's performance – in the moment, let alone in the lifetime. This is why universities are beginning to hang women's portraits on campuses. Whenever your confidence falters, bring to mind a powerful woman.

For me, it's sometimes Ding Zilin, the Chinese university professor who never lets the Chinese Communist Party forget the hundreds of young people who were killed in the Beijing massacre of 1989. It's also the singer-songwriter Taylor Swift. When a radio DJ groped her in a studio and subsequently got sacked for it, he sued her for millions. She counter-sued for a symbolic $1. In court she stood her ground against the DJ's lawyer, insisting, 'I'm not going to let you or your client make me feel in any way that this is my fault ... I'm being blamed for the unfortunate events of his life that are a product of his decisions – not mine.'

Then there's Rosa Parks, whose refusal to give up her seat for a white bus passenger helped trigger the 1955 Montgomery bus boycott, a civil rights protest so dignified, determined and united that it brought the end of segregation on public transport in the city. Rosa Parks was not the first person to resist bus segregation, but when the National Association for the Advancement of Colored People chose her to see through a court challenge for civil disobedience, she proved a calm and devastatingly effective communicator.

'People always say that I didn't give up my seat because I was tired, but that isn't true. I was not tired physically, or no more tired than I usually was at the end of a working day. No, the only tired I was, was tired of giving in.'

It helps to think about role models who stand their ground. As the British suffragist Millicent Fawcett once said, 'Courage calls to courage everywhere.'

So I got through those three surreal hours of live radio as the news agenda veered from Hollywood to the BBC and back.

Beyond the soundproofed studio, my open letter was met with a huge shout of solidarity on social media. The chorus was led by BBC Women, but many male colleagues joined in and the reverberation spread far beyond our workplace:

Many things in this life are complicated, but the concept of Equal Pay for Equal work isn't one of them. #IStandWithCarrie

Women in every broadcaster, boardroom and office are cheering her on.

At one point, after the review of the morning papers, which covered my resignation and protest letter, John Humphrys turned to me on air. Explaining to the audience that the BBC has rules on impartiality which mean that presenters can't suddenly turn into interviewees on the programmes they are presenting, he asked how I felt about the public response. I said I was moved by the support, which spoke to the hunger of women everywhere for equal, fair and transparent pay. I also said I was touched by how many people mentioned my China work, as I wanted to be remembered as a fine China reporter and not just a woman who complained about money.

'Too late, too late,' John replied.

A horror of losing the rest of one's identity and being labelled as a victim is something many whistle-blowers describe.

'Nobody wants to be the buzzkill,' said Lindsey Reynolds, one of the women who *Time* magazine featured when they named the #MeToo movement their 2017 Person of the Year. Reynolds explained her initial reluctance to call time on sexual harassment at the Besh Restaurant Group in 2017. 'I was nobody. I have no money, no power, no social standing. And they have more power and money than I will ever have. I felt extremely vulnerable and scared.'

Usually whistle-blowers are employees or members of the community on which they're blowing the whistle. They can't control the way they are perceived in those communities afterwards. Their lives are rarely the same.

In these situations, you need someone to protect you from the scrum. When I emerged from the studio, a smiling Kate Silverton had arrived to take charge of the rest of the day. She and I walked out of Broadcasting House for a few words with the waiting reporters from other news organisations. They said pay discrimination afflicted their newsrooms too and they thanked me for speaking up.

Some people called me brave that day. Over three decades of working as a journalist in China, I have seen real courage. Do you remember the famous video of a thin young man with plastic shopping bags standing in front of a column of tanks the morning after the Beijing massacre? 'Tank man' has never been identified, but every day there are individuals in China being punished for acts of enormous self-sacrifice. I was not brave like that.

At the same time, I took some risks and all BBC employees who tweeted #IStandWithCarrie or posted other equal pay messages took risks too. The BBC has strict rules on impartiality which means that its journalists cannot both take sides in a dispute and report upon that dispute. Jane Garvey was barred from interviewing me on *Woman's Hour*. Winifred Robinson was suspended from an edition of the Radio 4 consumer affairs programme *You and Yours* after tweeting 'Superb journalist, great China Editor. What a mess to lose her from that post. @BBCCarrie #equalpay #istandwithcarrie'. Many BBC managers felt the hashtag compromised impartiality and some male presenters and reporters who had used it on social media quickly deleted their posts.

I believe in the BBC's impartiality rules but I don't feel they were impartially applied on this issue. To my mind, expressing a personal view on equal pay didn't seem to be a problem – the problem was expressing the 'wrong' view. I feel our view was rooted in BBC values and if our bosses hadn't put themselves on the wrong side of history by mismanaging pay and then denying it, I think they would have been proud to know us.

It was a time to take sides. Many male colleagues wrote privately to say how sorry they were that I was leaving my China post and how much they agreed with the fight on pay. Their support meant more to me than I can easily put into words. This message was typical:

> You are probably going to get a lot of shit thrown at you in the next few days. But your colleagues are 100% behind you and cheering your bravery in confronting the secretive and self-serving management culture at the BBC.

Management kept its head firmly below the parapet. BBC news programmes were reduced to saying, 'We did ask to speak to the BBC, but no one was available.'

The following day, the drama moved to another big stage, the UK Parliament. MPs, like the public, had long felt star pay was too high at the BBC. Six months earlier they had been concerned to learn that it was not just inflated but unequal too. My open letter now triggered an urgent question in the House of Commons from the SNP's Hannah Bardell. Speaking for the government, the Culture Secretary Matt Hancock agreed that there was strong cross-party feeling on the subject. '[A]s a treasured national institution, the BBC must not only uphold, but be a beacon for, the British values of fairness that this nation holds dear. That includes fair pay and equal pay for equal jobs.'

The chair of the Commons Women and Equalities Committee, Maria Miller, wanted to know why the Equality and

Human Rights Commission had allowed itself to be 'placated by a BBC-funded internal review, which has clearly not tackled the problem'.

Seventy-two MPs joined Labour's Stella Creasy in a letter asking the government to force the BBC to stop silencing women. Thirty also signed a letter demanding answers on the BBC's use of non-disclosure agreements. The Digital, Culture, Media and Sport Committee announced a hearing on equal pay at the BBC. The Equality and Human Rights Commission wrote to the BBC demanding answers.

I'd been so focused on surviving day one of battle that I hadn't thought about what might happen on day two. I certainly could not have foreseen any of these extraordinary developments. Nor did I foresee that my email inbox would overflow with messages from members of the public talking about their own experiences.

This one came from a former academic:

> Your resignation letter rocks and I really hope your actions DO something at last about this pernicious issue, which has dogged me my whole professional life.

From a marketing professional:

> We all need to stand up and fight like you are doing. This pay discrimination is happening up and down the country in private and public organisations. Every one of them needs to be forced to be open and transparent.

Not all the reaction was so positive. On social media, some complained that I was greedy and deluded. Critics said Jon Sopel was obviously more high profile than me and North America was obviously more important than China. As a 'pay martyr' I was a hypocrite because I had resigned my post without resigning from the BBC altogether.

I resisted the temptation to argue. I felt relieved that most of my colleagues and most of the public seemed to have got the point I was making. Moreover, I had not been sacked and nor had anyone else. For the rest of that week I concentrated on doing my job to the best of my ability, and on my last morning on the *Today* Programme, I tweeted a tribute to the BBC:

> What other news organisation would let you call it secretive and illegal on #equalpay, + still let you front flagship show? Despite troubles, #BBC IS GREAT.

It's important to keep things in proportion. You're fighting to win, not to destroy.

Owing to a delayed flight, the *Today* Programme editor Sarah Sands hadn't been in the *Today* studio on the day of my protest letter and when we met later in the week, she asked why I'd written it.

'I'm the BBC's Lord Altrincham,' I joked. John Grigg, Baron Altrincham, was fresh in my memory because his story had featured in season 2 of the Netflix series *The Crown*. In 1957 Altrincham publicly criticised the young Queen Elizabeth II, warning that if she didn't modernise the monarchy, she would put it at risk. In an age of deference, his candour caused a furore. One newspaper accused him of 'daring to pit his infinitely tiny and temporary mind against the accumulated experience of centuries'. Altrincham said constitutional monarchy was too precious an institution to be neglected: 'I regard servile acceptance of its faults as a form of neglect.' Many of his recommendations were later adopted.

'I believe in the BBC. I'm just trying to help it into the twenty-first century,' I told Sarah.

Stand well back

Then the fight took an unforeseen turn. It emerged that when John Humphrys had gone off at 4.30 a.m. on that torrid Monday to record an interview with Jon Sopel about the latest from the Trump White House, they had also discussed my protest letter. Their interview had been recorded and their discussion of my letter had also been recorded. It was later leaked. The conversation went like this:

> JOHN HUMPHRYS: ... the first question will be how much of your salary you are prepared to hand over to Carrie Gracie to keep her and then a few comments about your other colleagues, you know, like our Middle East Editor and the other men who are earning too much ...

> JON SOPEL: I mean, obviously if we are talking about the scope for the greatest redistribution I'll have to come back and say: 'Well yes Mr Humphrys, but ...'

> JOHN HUMPHRYS: And I could save you the trouble as I could volunteer that I've handed over already more than you fucking earn but I'm still left with more than anybody else and that seems to me to be entirely just – something like that would do it?

> JON SOPEL: Don't ...

> JOHN HUMPHRYS: Oh dear God. She's actually suggested that you should lose money; you know that don't you? You've read the thing properly have you?

> JON SOPEL: Yeah, I have. Yep.

JOHN HUMPHRYS: And the idea is that I'm not allowed to
        talk to her about it throughout the whole course of the
        programme. Not a word.

JON SOPEL: I mean … can we have this conversation … I'd
        love to talk to you about it.

JOHN HUMPHRYS: Probably not now, yeah right.

By Friday, the newspapers had got hold of the transcript of this conversation and John was besieged by reporters.

'Silly banter,' he said. 'This was what I thought was an exchange between two old friends who have known each other for 30 years and were taking the mickey out of each other.'

'It was not meant for any other ears than Jon's, although there happened to be a producer in the studio at the time, a woman as it happens, who thought it was very funny.'

Asked for his views, the Director-General said, 'I think two things. One is oh why, why, why? And the second thing is the old rule everyone always tells you, if there's a microphone don't say anything.'

I felt this answer revealed low expectations. The equal pay row had been running for six months and my protest resignation took it to a new level. Tony Hall might have expected some recognition of the seriousness of the crisis from two men whose pay made them key players. He might also have expected senior men to show more respect for a female colleague by representing her argument accurately and acknowledging the risks she ran in making it.

I felt both John and Jon had let me down, let the BBC down and let audiences down. John Humphrys caricatured my argument and Jon Sopel made no attempt to correct him. To be fair to Jon, he was clearly a reluctant participant. I was disappointed when he later said he had been at 'the court of King John'.

As for the 'banter' defence from John Humphrys, I thought it only made matters worse. 'Banter' is how various powerful men, including Donald Trump, have shrugged off criticism of the demeaning way they talked about women or behaved towards them. John is an admirably fierce interviewer and I suspect that if he had been interviewing himself, he'd have made this point – along with a few others.

The BBC tried to close down the story, saying it was deeply unimpressed, but 'this was an ill-advised off-air conversation which the presenter regrets'. John would not be disciplined, nor would he be barred from doing interviews on gender pay. To the charge that yet again impartiality rules were not being applied impartially, the BBC said John had not campaigned on the issue. Any suggestion he was mocking women demanding equal pay was 'an interpretation'.

Friends tried to console me that the world could now see what BBC Women were up against. The week ended with John Humphrys still presenting his programme and yet another female presenter absent from hers. Anita Anand had tweeted about equal pay and was reportedly replaced on Radio 4's *Any Answers* because the programme was expected to feature discussion of the pay row. It almost looked as if only carefully vetted men could present news about equal pay for women.

Where power is entrenched, it takes more to change culture than winning the argument and watching the powerful catch themselves out, red-faced and ridiculous. BBC Women had started the week with a fight to win. We ended it with a farce.

Sun Zi gave me no clear guidance on the art of farce in a twenty-first-century workplace. But in the Bible, the Book of Ecclesiastes advises 'There is a time for everything ... a time to be silent and a time to speak, a time to love and a time to hate, a time for war and a time for peace.'

That weekend was not a time for love or peace, but it was a

time to be silent. I had jumped into the void, fallen through space, hit the ground. One week on, I found I was dazed but alive, and not even seriously injured. When reporters asked me to respond to the Humphrys tape and programmes asked me to come in and be interviewed, I declined. Fight to win, I reminded myself, stay focused. Sometimes winning demands the self-discipline not to fight. You too will have to pick your battles. For me, there was a bigger one coming.

7

LISTEN UP

=

The next battle required me to stop talking and start listening.

On anything important, I try to do a lot of listening. As a workplace habit, this can be misunderstood as indecisive or unconfident, but listening makes the difference between an ill-informed decision and a well-informed one. The right amount of it is common sense. Throughout the equal pay fight I was always keen to hear what others thought. And now my brains trust grew to encompass women and men from around the UK and across the world.

It was an even bigger hive mind than the sisterhood. All the things I'd read about pay secrecy, unconscious bias, imperfect markets and the failures of the law I now learned again through the lived experience of real people.

One fortysomething called to tell of working in a team where all the women with children had been eased out and she, single, childless and from an ethnic minority, was the only woman left. Having discovered she was being paid far less than her male peers despite being the acknowledged expert in her field, she asked politely and repeatedly for equal pay. Her large and reputable employer brushed her off and eventually she felt she had no alternative but to raise a grievance. Immediately her line manager gave her a damning performance evaluation.

Micro-aggressions and exclusion swiftly followed. She told me she was about to embark on legal action.

A retired American city administrator wrote to describe working in 'top policy positions where I was paid less than half of what the men made, for doing at least twice the work ... my pay inequities over the years left me with minimal retirement income'. Having eventually sued her employer and won, she had the satisfaction of seeing the next generation of administrators better paid.

Broadcasters, banks, universities, public bodies, multinationals, charities ... I was shocked by how many big-name organisations were cited as discriminators by members of their female workforce. It didn't chime with the good intentions about diversity that many were publishing alongside their gender pay gap reporting.

Along with the BBC equal pay story, the gender pay gap was concentrating reporters' minds that spring. From pay transparency to job evaluations, pregnancy discrimination, board diversity and shared parenting, all dimensions of gender and pay were suddenly mainstream news.

For the BBC, pay scrutiny was also growing. The day after my open letter, the parliamentary committee that describes itself as the BBC's 'only line of accountability to licence fee payers' announced a hearing on equal pay. MPs knew from their own experience of the expenses scandal a decade earlier that people behave to a higher standard when observed. Under the chairmanship of Damian Collins, the Digital, Culture, Media and Sport Committee had just conducted an inquiry into sport governance, shining a light on racism and bullying at the Football Association. Later in 2018, it would investigate the problem of fake news, accusing Facebook of 'intentionally and knowingly' violating data privacy law. Facebook denied any illegality.

In January 2018, the Committee invited the Director-General

and me to give evidence on equal pay at the BBC. This would be the first such airing of the issue in the court of public opinion. I hoped it would help women in other workplaces.

I wanted to communicate with men and employers too, and that required listening to men and employers. I'd already benefited enormously from the wisdom of many. I started with old friends like Jeremy Heywood, who as head of the Civil Service commanded a workforce ten times as large as the BBC's, and who could help me see the world from an employer's point of view. Another friend from university days was a private-sector employer in the hotel industry, and a third had a career in corporate HR and could read a pay negotiation or complaints process better than I ever would. Beyond my friendship group, other men helped because they believed in the cause.

There seem to be many factors that decide whether a man will step into the struggle for gender equality. One may be the gender of his children. In the US, judges with daughters are more likely to support women's causes than those who only have sons, and in Denmark there is a positive correlation between male CEOs who have a first-born daughter and higher female pay in the companies they run.

I suspect mothers who work outside the home are also an influence. Jeremy's mother, Brenda Swinbank, had been one of the first female professional archaeologists in the UK. Another friend of mine regularly checked the payroll of his engineering firm to monitor for discrimination – he was brought up by a single working mother. And the accountant John Brebner, who took it upon himself to organise a public petition in support of equal pay for women at the BBC, told me his mother, Celia, had been one of Scotland's first female child psychiatrists.

But I also wanted to listen to men who could help me understand the BBC machine as I wanted to learn how best we might nudge it towards progress. As I prepared for the parliamentary hearing, I sought out BBC veterans. One told me that in crisis conditions, the BBC power structure was a 'paralysed matrix' without effective decision-making. Another warned that however urbane the image BBC bosses cultivated, they would 'press the destruct button' on BBC Women if we threatened them. 'Prisoners don't run prisons' and we should not offer solutions, but keep pointing out that bosses must make the system fair. 'They have the tools. They just need the will and the sense of urgency. They have to be doers, not just signers.'

A third former insider said bosses would paint me as a conspirator who didn't have the BBC's best interests at heart. They would punish me by exclusion. On a leafless January afternoon he and I paced round St James's Park while he warned, 'The pressures are such that people soon fade away from this kind of movement.'

BBC Women should consolidate their leadership, he said, force greater scrutiny of management, commission academic research, find allies in other organisations. In short, we must fight hard or face defeat. 'The only way is up. Inflate the story. Intensify the pressure.'

As twilight descended on the wintry lake, I watched the moorhens paddling in pointless circles and felt daunted by his advice. BBC Women were already over-stretched, with full-time jobs and families. On top, they had equal pay claims to fight and each other to support. I myself was weary. I felt confident that I could communicate my own story and be a voice for women too vulnerable to speak. I could frame the wider narrative, but that was the limit of my capacity.

A friend who led a large company warned that I was wasting my time if I imagined that BBC bosses would ever acknowledge the scale of their equal pay problem. The potential liabilities in terms of back pay and pension restitution would be crippling. 'The truth is unaffordable,' he said.

I went back to see Jeremy Heywood. He'd given evidence to many parliamentary committee hearings over the years, and as we'd known each other since we were teenagers, I knew he'd be blunt with his advice. He warned that I mustn't sound 'like a leftie feminist in charge of the sisterhood'.

'Don't be threatening to men. Just point out that this is public money and that even for those who might want to keep an open mind on the strength of a case like yours, it's very clear there are serious anomalies. Acknowledge that if you were in charge perhaps you too would worry about a tsunami of claims for back pay. Then remind the MPs that you and the rest of the BBC Women have repeatedly said the last thing any of you want to do is threaten the BBC's future.'

Spin and distraction

In the week before the parliamentary hearing, my careful listening exercise designed to understand the workings of the BBC machine was drowned out by engine noise from the machine itself.

First, the BBC announced that six top men would take pay cuts. The men were John Humphrys, Jon Sopel, Jeremy Vine, Huw Edwards, Nicky Campbell and Nick Robinson. They were just six out of nearly twenty thousand members of staff, but they happened to be among the most high profile and highly paid, and so the news story made headlines.

Was it true? Had male stars agreed specific cuts, cuts in principle, or merely to take part in 'discussions' on cuts? It was hard to tell, as even the BBC's own account of the story kept being rewritten. But if the facts were murky, the motive was easier to read. 'BBC slashes pay for star men' was a useful headline to take into a grilling on pay discrimination against women.

BBC Women didn't want the equal pay issue turned into a gender war. The group issued a calm statement reminding media and public that adjusting the pay of six men was not an adequate answer to the problem:

> For the last six months we have been calling for a transparent and systematic mechanism to address pay inequality for women at all levels, especially those working in less well-paid off-air roles. BBC management should now focus on a comprehensive strategy to correct all unequal pay decisions it has made for decades, rather than on a few high-profile individuals.

The BBC was not in listening mode. Instead it issued a statement saying it was very grateful to the star men: 'These are great journalists and presenters, who have a real connection with the audience. We are proud to have them working at the BBC.'

At no point had the BBC said it was grateful to any of the women who had been underpaid for years and patiently asking for the problem to be fixed. Some now considered tweeting under the sarcastic hashtag #verygrateful. The fear of victimisation held them back. One producer described how her manager had suddenly appeared beside her desk and whispered that she should give up her equal pay claim because job cuts were coming. Another said she'd been offered a pay rise on condition she abandon her claim. #IStandWithCarrie had not been forgotten. Some presenters were still barred from conducting interviews on the subject of equal pay.

In any case, #verygrateful was soon overtaken by another loud intervention from the BBC. On the day before the parliamentary hearing, the BBC finally published its much-delayed review of pay for on-air staff. Despite repeated requests, BBC Women had not been allowed a role in designing the review's terms of reference nor had we been allowed to give evidence.

The review was another paper exercise by auditors PwC based on evidence provided by management. Just like the equal pay audit of three months earlier, it found no evidence of gender bias in pay decision-making. Where pay differences existed between male and female employees in similar roles, the review found these were 'typically driven by material and justifiable factors unrelated to gender'.

It said: 'In all sampled cases, non-gender related reasons for the pay differentials were provided by the BBC. In some examples, the evidence to support these reasons was very strong, whereas in others the objectively verifiable evidence available was more limited. However, we did not see anything which indicated that pay decisions had been subject to gender bias.'

BBC Women felt this was like conducting a trial without hearing the prosecution evidence. After six months of mapping and sharing, we knew far more about the 'material and justifiable factors' than PwC did. We knew that many pay decisions had been taken without any clear reasoning at all. The BBC's defence of them had no consistency. We knew that factors cited to explain a pay difference between man A and woman B were often turned on their head to justify a pay difference between man C and woman D. It was hard to see how auditors could feel confident that factors contributing to pay differences were justifiable and gender neutral. They were inconsistent and frequently resulted in lower pay for women doing equal work.

Soon this would be demonstrated in the course of individual equal pay battles as women demolished such justifications line by line. Even at the very point of publishing its on-air review, the BBC seemed to lose faith in some of the 'justifiable factors' by suddenly cutting the pay of top men.

BBC Women felt that lazy habits, unconscious bias and a lack of scrutiny had resulted in a clear pattern of discrimination and that BBC management knew this but did not want to face the financial risks of admitting it. In his response to the on-air review, the Director-General gave what we thought was a misleading defence: 'I don't believe there has been illegality in the BBC to the point where someone said: "You're a woman therefore you're going to be paid less."'

No one had made this accusation. It's not necessary to talk like a cartoon misogynist to practise pay discrimination. As my lawyer Jennifer Millins drily pointed out in a background briefing note for MPs, 'It is rare for unequal pay to be deliberate, but if the end result is that a woman is paid less than a man for doing equal work, that is still unlawful.'

Having cleared the BBC of gender bias, the PwC review rapped it over the knuckles for 'lack of clarity and openness about the basis for pay decisions' in an approach that was 'far from perfect'. It said too many pay decisions had been made at local levels and 'a period of significant pay restraint' had meant a slower rate of pay progression for both men and women over the past decade. The BBC admitted 'a complex and bureaucratic system which was unclear to everyone, difficult to operate and hard to measure against the external market'.

Given all of this, along with the problems of bias and market I discussed in Chapter 2, it would have been nothing short of a miracle if the BBC had not been incubating multiple problems with pay discrimination. As I read this pay review, I realised that a miracle is what the BBC now claimed. Without even trying, and in the midst of chaos, the BBC had still succeeded in meeting its equal pay obligations. Any evidence we brought to the contrary was merely an anomaly.

Harriet Harman tweeted, 'Paying men more than women @BBC is systemic discrimination not an "anomaly". PWC report pointless. Numbers speak for themselves.'

BBC Women rejected the review. Jane Garvey spoke for all of us when she observed, 'It's really hard to not reach the conclusion that they commissioned the report they wanted and it's provided the result that they wanted.'

Some senior, and highly paid, BBC men expressed frustration over coverage of the story. Andrew Neil tweeted: 'The BBC has led every radio news bulletin I've listened [to] today with its pay problems. It's a story, needs to be covered and wrongs need to be righted. But is it really the most important story of the day for British people'. The *News at Ten* presenter Huw Edwards retweeted Neil's tweet.

Journalists are always arguing over what should be the top story but I think Andrew and Huw were wrong on this one. Just over half the British public are female. They pay their licence fee just like men and equal pay speaks to core British values of justice, human dignity and equality before the law. Many men feel equally passionate about it. In fact, news stories about inequality should probably lead bulletins more often. And this one raised questions about truth-telling and trust at the national broadcaster.

The BBC's third loud engine rev ahead of the parliamentary hearing was for my ears only. My grievance outcome. I'd almost given up expecting it. It seemed a lifetime ago that I'd admired Jennifer's Mishcon office and boasted casually that I ate communists for breakfast. Since then, the grievance hearing notes had rocked my trust in my employer, I had resigned my China post and published my open letter. Now, on day eighty-nine of the ninety the BBC gives itself for a grievance process, my outcome finally arrived.

Nailing jelly to the wall

This document said I had misunderstood Fran Unsworth in the original discussion about my salary as China Editor. She was thinking of the current pay of those doing the Europe and North America roles while I took the conversation to mean a commitment for the duration of the role. There had been no intention to mislead.

The grievance outcome did make some concessions. It acknowledged for the first time that I had been underpaid in all of the years that I served as China Editor. But at the same time it said 'growth and development' accounted for much of the disparity and so my revised pay would still be at a very significant discount to the men.

The BBC had never mentioned 'growth and development' during the years I served as China Editor. Instead I had one glowing appraisal, one contract renewal, a stream of praise from management and multiple nominations for awards in TV, podcast and online work. None of my male peers was at a 'growth and development' discount. In 2015, the Director-General himself had told the public that it was the expertise of reporters like Nick Robinson, Robert Peston and Carrie Gracie that made the licence fee worth paying for. My radio and podcast series *Murder in the Lucky Holiday Hotel* had been singled out as a 'must-listen' in the BBC 2016/17 Annual Report. 'Growth and development' seemed like another cynical retrofit excuse, bosses belittling my work to avoid liability for back pay. The alternative interpretation, that they actually believed what they'd written, was even worse.

In the fourth year of my China posting, at the point when the BBC now said I had grown into my role, the grievance outcome said I was still not equal to the male international editors. Instead, Jon Sopel's profile helped to justify a pay disparity of up to £70,000. This claim was supported by one audience-recognition survey conducted a month earlier. It was hard to see how a survey at the end of 2017 could explain a pay decision taken in 2014, and hard to be sure the profile belonged to the reporter rather than the story he happened to be covering. If roles had been swapped and I had been fronting the Trump election campaign and presidency, I would have had the profile. It was not even clear which audience was involved, as the BBC had many different audiences in the UK and globally. At no point did the BBC consider the audience-recognition evidence I offered to submit.

Besides, the BBC had never used profile in a consistent manner to determine salaries. It had reporters with a high profile whose pay was relatively low and vice versa. 'Profile' was a particular bugbear for BBC Women, as the group's written evidence to Parliament explained: 'In effect, the BBC is saying they selected men for the positions, they are on air and therefore exposed to the BBC's audiences and are now recognised by those audiences so should be paid more.'

'Material factor' defences will differ from role to role and workplace to workplace, but employers who want to pay men and women differently for equal work have to find some such defence and show that it is consistently applied and non-discriminatory to defend against an equal pay claim. The incoherence of the BBC's pay structure would have made that hard.

Returning to the grievance outcome, the other justification the BBC offered for the 2017 pay gap between my male comparator and me was that Jon had more experience. In fact, our career history was broadly similar. We were roughly the same age and had both served as correspondents and presenters, anchoring news channels and other programmes. Jon had more of some kinds of experience, I had more of others. In terms of experience relevant to the role, I had a degree in Mandarin Chinese and three decades of reporting on the ground in China.

By labouring all of this I do not mean to diminish Jon's work in any way. Jon's reporting was and is excellent, but when

I accepted the China post, managers had led me to expect pay parity with the North America Editor. Several months later they appointed Jon at a much higher pay rate than his predecessor and thereby broke their promise to me. I accept that this was an inadvertent oversight at the time of Jon's appointment. But now they were determined to defend a large pay disparity partly on the grounds that one role was worth more than the other, and partly on the grounds that this man was worth more than that woman.

I think employers often hope women will give up in horror at how personal this becomes. If you can bear it, you should stand your ground and meet the assertion 'he's worth more than you' with the reply 'prove it'. Everyone has choices here. The employer can choose to pay the woman equally for equal work. The man can choose to say 'she is my equal'. The woman can choose to give up.

Because my fight was public, I also had to put up with some spin. MPs and media reporters were told I had 'family issues' and 'ulterior motives', that I was 'to a certain extent part-time'. Identical briefing lines made it sound like a coordinated effort. In fact, I had no ulterior motives. The explanation for my actions was simple: I resigned my post because I wasn't being treated equally.

The part-time line angered me because it was very far from the truth. My failing was exactly the opposite. As China Editor I had worked too hard. I always felt I had to read everything and consider every perspective before I could allow myself to take an editorial line. Impostor syndrome, the fear of not being good enough and being found out for it, is a common problem for women and men at work, but particularly for women who advance into male-dominated fields. Even the former US First Lady Michelle Obama, best-selling author, lawyer, graduate of Princeton University and Harvard Law School, told a group of schoolgirls in London, 'I still have a little impostor syndrome . . . It doesn't go away, that feeling that you shouldn't take me that seriously. What do I know?'

What's more, I had imposed sacrifices on my children in order to serve as BBC China Editor. The previous year I had spent 214 days away from home and I had worked overtime all year round. It was wrong that I, as a woman, became fair game for this kind of belittling, unlike male international editors who lived in London and were never called 'to a certain extent part-time'. As for family issues, we had no more than any other family and I wondered where this line was coming from. Rachel was by now a second-year student at Newcastle University and Daniel was working in Canada.

Four years earlier I'd said I would only do the job if I was paid equally and in the six months since discovering I wasn't, I'd repeatedly warned I would resign if that wasn't put right. How complicated was it? I was just a capuchin throwing food at my handler because I wasn't being treated equally. Now it seems laughable to me that anyone could find a statement of self-respect so dangerous. I couldn't laugh at the time, but at least I didn't waste energy on chasing down shadows to identify who was behind the spin.

Nor did I allow myself to feel distress about the resulting media coverage in which commentators short of a coherent argument resorted to personal abuse. Some attacked my motives or called me a nonentity. Others said I sounded like 'a stricken trawler that's lost its catch' or found me guilty of 'flouncing out'. Overall, some sections of the media were supportive to BBC Women, some were neutral, but others resorted to a mix of misinformation and downright sexism. We were 'whinge-ing', 'greedy witches', our campaign for equal pay 'feminist drivel'. We belonged to a 'shrieking culture of victimhood', 'self-righteous lynch mobs', a scary new world of 'grievance-seeking betrayal'. In some versions of the BBC equal pay story, star men were the chief victims.

If you ever challenge on equal pay, I hope you won't have to face this kind of public scrutiny, but you will inevitably have to filter out some of the undermining things that will be said and written about you in the course of your case. Many employers fight by seeking to undermine the professional credibility of the claimant, just as the defence team in a rape case attempts to undermine the personal credibility of the victim. Remind yourself that if a boss suddenly damns your performance or finds you 'in development', it is because you have dared to ask for equality. Listen with a cool ear.

It helped that I had done my job to the best of my ability. It also helped that I had a clean employment record and good allies. We often get judged by the company we keep and I had the strong, steady and vocal support of some of the BBC's most trusted journalists. With the help of my sisterhood and my brains trust, I avoided wasting energy on self-doubt or Twitter spats.

Then three days before the parliamentary hearing, my uncle died. I was grief-stricken, overwhelmed. I had to lie down and turn my face to the wall. But soon anger got me up again. I knew my uncle would have wanted me up. I was a hard-working fifty-five-year-old professional broadcaster at the top of my game with a thirty-year track record on China. No one could have been a better BBC China Editor. I was not in development and I had to turn my anger into effective action in the hope that future generations of women might escape these insults.

You too. You may not want to reinvent the suffragette movement for the twenty-first century, play gladiator games in an employment tribunal or speak your truth in a parliamentary hearing. You shouldn't do more in this fight than feels right, but once you've staked your ground, you should try to hold it.

On 31 January I went to Parliament to give my evidence. On the same day, the Prime Minister was in Beijing, on her first official visit to China. It all seemed so topsy-turvy. What's more, I had spent my career holding others to account on behalf of the BBC. Now I was reliant on others holding the BBC to account for me. I felt sad about that.

My children helped me get through it. Daniel had come home for a few days from Canada, Rachel from Newcastle. They both knew how hard I'd worked as China Editor and believed the fight was right. For them, it wasn't about the money. Having grown up around many of my BBC friends who earned less, they didn't feel I should take more. They understood the point of public service. As we sat on the Underground on the way to Westminster, Daniel watched me feverishly stapling my jumbled notes together and, not for the first time, said: 'It's not the biggest mountain you've climbed, Mum.'

Rachel snatched the stapler from me and laughed at my hair standing on end. They hadn't seen each other for months and their carefree conversation about friends and music was soothing.

Many of the BBC's women converged on Parliament that day. Martine Croxall and Kate Silverton were there. Louise Minchin and Naga Munchetty, the presenters of *BBC Breakfast*. Razia Iqbal from BBC World Service, Philippa Thomas from BBC World News, Sonja McLaughlan from BBC Sport, the arts presenter Mariella Frostrup, the veteran war reporter Kate Adie, and the presenter who won her ageism case against the BBC, Miriam O'Reilly. The committee room could not hold all the BBC Women who wanted to show solidarity; many had delivered powerful written testimony instead. Others had worked hard to collate evidence and organise the group. They were the same tireless producers the BBC relies on to keep it on air day in day out, with the most tireless Cinderella-in-chief the

World Service producer Kriszta Satori. And in offices across the country and across the world, BBC colleagues watched live TV coverage of the hearing.

Just before I sat down to give evidence, I found a moment of solitude. Standing at the mirror in the ladies' toilet, I tamed my hair, straightened my blouse, looked myself in the eye and willed myself calm. I had never given evidence in a parliamentary hearing before, while the other side were old hands. The Director-General was himself a member of the House of Lords.

But I reminded myself I was lucky. Even today, employers don't get challenged enough on equal pay, much less in the national spotlight. Most women have to face years of expense, hard work and stress to get to tribunal for an impartial hearing of their individual case. Now BBC Women had challenged an entire pay structure, and in doing so we had challenged the power structure. I knew how precious was the scrutiny enshrined in British parliamentary democracy. I didn't want to let anyone down.

Equal pay lawyers say one of the reasons women often give up and accept settlements worth far less than the equality to which they're entitled is that they are afraid of having to give evidence in public. If they can only be persuaded to overcome that fear, they usually give compelling evidence because they simply tell the truth. All I needed to do was to tell the truth.

Some day it will be your turn. It doesn't matter whether the stage is a parliamentary hearing, an employment tribunal, a formal grievance or a friendly coffee with the boss. You are simply asking for a fair hearing of the facts and you should feel proud of giving the world that nudge towards equality. As Oprah said, you're doing something for women everywhere.

I took my seat beside Michelle Stanistreet, the general secretary of the National Union of Journalists. While I answered questions about my own case and the experience of BBC Women, Michelle amplified with the wider context.

She told MPs that NUJ surveys had repeatedly highlighted women's concerns over pay equality at the BBC, but instead of listening, wilful blindness had prevailed, with secrecy and managerial discretion helping to normalise a 'discriminatory and unlawful approach to pay'. She confirmed that the union had lodged a collective grievance on behalf of 121 members of staff, with more women joining subsequently. These were women complaining not just of gender discrimination, but of discrimination on grounds of race, maternity, part-time and flexible working.

I won't repeat my evidence. You can imagine much of it by now. However, my grievance outcome was new to everyone present, including the BBC Women behind me, and the lines about 'growth and development' brought gasps of incredulity. I said, 'It is unacceptable to talk to your senior women like that. I would never have gone to China on those terms.' I recounted how James Harding and I had walked back across Portland Place from meeting the Chinese ambassador shortly after my appointment and James had turned to me afterwards and said, 'You're it. You're in charge. I will have your back.'

The Conservative MP Rebecca Pow now asked whether I felt humiliated. I said I didn't: 'If you try to humiliate me, I feel angry and I am determined to fix it. Hence my grievance outcome is entirely self-defeating because anyone who tells me I was in development for three years in China is going to lose.'

Michelle Stanistreet expanded the point to include the many other BBC Women facing the same management narrative: 'When you have this notion of women in perpetual progression or development, always lagging behind blokes doing the same work, you cannot understand how insulting that is to individuals who are hugely experienced and have spent their careers doing this job.'

It felt raw to answer personal questions from strangers for two hours and to know that around the country and across the world, people watching the live broadcast would be forming judgements about me. But it was also cathartic to explain the facts to an audience that was actually listening to the evidence with an open mind.

In the brief break that followed my testimony, I sprinted to the toilet down a corridor full of BBC Women, and collided with the Director-General and his team coming in the opposite direction. To me, they looked like a papal delegation. To them, we must have looked like a rebel army.

Tony Hall stopped to offer a strained but civil greeting. His retinue braked behind him. BBC Women looked on. It was a strange moment. They were 'the BBC'. They could make or break the career of every woman in that corridor. But by caring about the truth and taking risks to tell it, we were more BBC than they were, in command of the moral high ground for this brief moment in which that ground mattered.

When I got back into the committee room, the BBC's top brass were preparing to give evidence. I took a seat between Rachel and Daniel, just behind the Chairman of the BBC Board Sir David Clementi, Director-General Tony Hall, Deputy Director-General Anne Bulford and Director of News Fran Unsworth.

The Labour MP Julie Elliott tried to get to the bottom of who was responsible for 'looking at the equity across people's pay'.

'I think that would have been done within News,' hazarded Fran Unsworth. A moment later she'd changed her mind.

'We are accepting that it was not done within the News team.'

Fran had been the Head of Newsgathering who negotiated my contract to go to China in 2013. She had then served as James Harding's deputy, and now that he'd left she was Director of News. In her first month in post came my protest letter, a near-mutiny of senior female staff, and now this.

It's hard to shut down empathy. It felt shockingly intimate to sit directly behind my bosses as the questioning grew fierce. I noticed small details including the Deputy Director-General's handbag tucked beside her neatly aligned feet, as if precision over posture and accessories might make up for any want of precision in answers. But the body language of all four was uncomfortable, and with the controlled anger of my own moment in the spotlight over, I now found it hard not to feel sorry for them.

For six months our bosses had presented the pay crisis as a little local difficulty in the monkey lab. Somehow the monkeys had now climbed out of their cages, wrenched the drama onto the national stage and explained it as lawbreaking on a newsworthy scale. Handlers were in the dock. I started to take notes to fool my fight-or-flight response that this was just another reporting task and not a major insurrection for which I would later pay. When MPs urged the Chairman of the BBC Board to apologise to me, we were close enough for his gaze to scorch.

I scorched back. It was 2018 after all, exactly a century since some British women had first won the vote, and almost half a century since the Equal Pay Act. The Palace of Westminster had witnessed enormous sacrifices by women of earlier generations to achieve those landmarks. BBC Women in the audience behind me, the female MPs asking the questions, and I myself were all beneficiaries of those sacrifices. Until recently, the make-up of this parliamentary committee had been entirely male. Even in 2018 only three out of its eleven members were women. They had pressed for this hearing and now they made their presence count. Julie Elliott kept up the pressure on why no one was responsible for keeping the BBC inside the law on equal pay.

'I think that is the point that we are making here, which is an oversight, which is why we are putting the framework in place,' said Fran Unsworth.

'It is a little bit more than an oversight,' shot back Julie Elliott. 'I think there is an illegal pay structure going on in this organisation.'

For months, BBC managers had been brushing off my pay disparity and many others as oversights and I'd grown numb to their language. MPs seemed as incredulous as I had once been. It was also interesting to hear them challenge the use of talent agents. In my grievance hearing I'd pointed out that salaries are unlikely to be equal if some employees negotiate their own and others hire agents to boost their perceived value. Fran Unsworth told the Committee that Jon Sopel had negotiated his own salary but later the BBC corrected the record to say he had used an agent. Anne Bulford said Jon went to Washington without a pay rise. This too was later corrected to acknowledge that he had received a pay rise of 3 per cent. The Director-General said the BBC should have been more upfront about a 'pecking order' between international editors. Certainly a pecking order was news to me. No one had mentioned it four years earlier when I said I wouldn't go to China unless I was equal. The job had been advertised as 'on a par' with North America.

In response to sustained interrogation, the witnesses now admitted decision-making on BBC pay had been less than ideal, but blurred the narrative on whose decision-making that might be. To nail the facts would have required forensic cross-examination by fully briefed barristers – in other words, a tribunal or a courtroom.

The MPs moved on to questions about the PwC pay review published the day before. Julian Knight called it 'the worst get out of jail free card I have ever seen in history'. Jo Stevens asked whether auditors had talked to any of the staff doing the jobs whose pay was under review. Three times the Director of News offered an evasion; the Deputy Director-General then offered a fourth, and only at the fifth time of asking did she finally concede, 'We dealt largely through the editors, the managers who deal with these jobs.'

In future the BBC's pay structure would be great, according to the Director-General. 'Management is constantly about learning and it is about listening and it is about acting on what you hear.'

On equal pay, I felt he had not listened to staff, unions or the House of Lords Communications Committee that warned the BBC had an informal policy to discriminate against older women. As I listened now, I could not feel confident that the BBC's future would be different from the past. I feared managers would continue to insist that women were worth less than men by whatever convenient fudge of 'justifiable factors' came to hand.

I wished BBC staff member 9889 had still been alive to cover proceedings. George Orwell might have called out his old employer for 'doublethink': a BBC that admitted operating without clear rules on pay but was nonetheless quite sure the absence of rules had not resulted in abuses. As a woman fighting pay discrimination, I felt angry. As a BBC journalist, I felt ashamed. I had many colleagues who risked their lives to uphold BBC values. Their bosses let them down.

Would yours have fared better? If your workplace is vigilant for bias and has clear rules on pay and full transparency around those rules, perhaps. If your workplace is wilfully blind to bias and pay is opaque and subject to much managerial discretion, then possibly not. How much do employers have to care about this? Beyond looking incompetent and evasive in the court of parliamentary and public opinion, paying women less for equal work still carried no costs for mine.

I was grateful to the MPs for trying. For five hours they

laboured through the slippery entrails of BBC pay, until interrupted by a shrill division bell that sent them rushing to the Commons chamber to vote on some other pressing issue of the day. As Tony Hall and Anne Bulford stood up to leave, they said a polite goodbye to Rachel, Daniel and me. David Clementi and Fran Unsworth ignored us. Many BBC Women came over to give me a hug. They said I'd made them proud and gave me a silver pendant engraved #ISTANDWITHCARRIE. I've worn it every day since.

Later, there were hundreds of messages from women who'd been watching. A sixteen-year-old who said my stand had given her courage to tackle sexism at her local football club; a victim of sexual assault; a university teacher forced to leave her job after a 'grievance charade'; a corporate executive who said I had made her feel less lonely; a mother who recorded the hearing for her newborn daughter to watch when she was older; a Girlguiding leader who'd sat her troop down in front of the live broadcast. Women bringing grievances wrote that I'd voiced their ordeal; women waiting for tribunal hearings said I'd stiffened their resolve. Linda Wong, one of the Leigh Day lawyers representing supermarket workers in the biggest private-sector equal pay case in British history, wrote to say that I had helped give some of her clients the confidence to speak up: 'Seeing you step forward, but more so, realising that the hurt, anger and need for equality is the same no matter the background.'

From the other side of the world, a friend wrote, 'I think you have chosen the battle worth fighting and I am ashamed of my earlier pleadings that you take the money . . . I think I have that mix of vulnerability and cynicism that creates the mindset that it is not possible to change things, one will always be fucked over somehow, so keep the head down and run.'

Fight or flight? The age-old dilemma. I felt she and I were both right.

When we stopped for dinner on the way home, Rachel said I looked more worried than on the way in.

'I've only just realised how much trouble we're in,' I replied. By 'we' I still meant the BBC.

I'd listened hard. Behind the evasions, euphemisms and circumlocutions, I'd heard the cunning and complacency at the heart of the machine. Parliamentary scrutiny wasn't going to be enough to transform our pay culture. 'And whatever the strength of the evidence,' I told Rachel and Daniel, 'I'm the one who comes out of today with "in development" branded on my forehead.'

Daniel said, 'You've got to admit that's funny.'

It was. For you too, there'll be moments when you just have to laugh.

8

LAUGH, ENDURE AND DARE TO HOPE

=

'There was no evidence of gender bias at the BBC. It was just that the men were really super.'

The panel of comedians on the BBC's *News Quiz* were having fun at the BBC's own expense.

'You know, China . . . once you've seen *Kung Fu Panda 1* and *2* you've pretty much got the hang of it. Whereas America! All right, in China there's a different language, but in America they say sidewalk. You could be confused for months!'

The first weekend in February 2018 I caught up on the comedy podcasts. I was sitting in my Beijing flat, dazed and jetlagged, surrounded by open suitcases and a chaos of clothes, recording equipment, reporter's notebooks, and maps from every town and city in China I'd filmed in. The day before, I'd been in London, waving Daniel and Rachel off to Canada and Newcastle respectively before climbing on an overnight economy-class flight to Beijing. In a week's time I was due back on air in London in my old/new role as a TV news presenter. So I had five days to empty my Beijing flat, complete Chinese tax and visa formalities and say goodbye.

'If you were troubled by this issue don't worry, we have got our best white men on the case,' chirruped the *News Quiz*.

Thank God for comedy. As Margaret Heffernan later observed, 'Fun disables fear. It makes people feel braver.' My laughter now ricocheted off the bare walls of my flat. Totalitarians hate being laughed at, so satire is underground in China. You can go to jail for comparing President Xi Jinping to a steamed bun. Any mention of Winnie-the-Pooh is likewise a no-no. Dictators demand dignity.

So too do many employers and some are vindictive, as I'd learned from the stories of women writing to me and stopping me in the street. The *News Quiz* reminded me of things to like about my employer. At least BBC reporters were trained to ask tough questions and its comedy shows were permitted to poke fun. To distract myself from packing, I surfed for more entertaining nuggets and discovered that in the very week of my protest letter, the BBC had tweeted, 'Back at work and feeling undervalued? Not being paid what you're worth? Why not start the year by asking for a pay rise? Here are some tips on how to negotiate one.'

The Twitterati merrily drew attention to the comic timing and the BBC deleted its tweet on the grounds that it might be 'open to misinterpretation'.

The transcription software that generates subtitles for TV News did not disappoint. Because of the random nonsense it sometimes hears in place of human speech, this software had provided a long-running gag line in *W1A*, the comedy series about BBC management. Now a friend sent a TV clip of me looking fierce and insisting I could not collude in pay discrimination while the subtitle beneath explained that I could not collude in 'papal rumination'.

A friend who'd watched the committee hearing emailed: 'I still can't understand how they were so dumb as to think they could buy you off, after you went on air with no hair.' That too made me roar with laughter. In her eyes, the most badass thing

I'd done was back in 2012 when I returned to TV news presenting bald headed after cancer treatment.

The comic lines from the wider equal pay fight were legion.
One of my favourites was when one woman was told she
couldn't have details of what the BBC owed her 'for reasons of
confidentiality'.

Can your workplace beat mine for laughs? You must find the
humour where you can. BBC Women survived by laughing at
our bosses, the men and each other wherever possible.

Laughing certainly helped me through those bittersweet
days in Beijing. The bureau team had made me a leaving video,
a spoof on how China coverage might suffer without me but
at least the producers would get a lie-in. We had lunch at our
favourite dumpling restaurant and an evening of alcohol-fuelled
reminiscing.

I said goodbye to old Beijing friends and gave a farewell
speech at the Foreign Correspondents' Club. There were many
questions about equal pay from women in other news organisations. That made me reflect on how much harder it is for
women to sister up when they work in isolation or in a small
workplace with few women. At least broadcasting gives you
a team. Scattered around the world, often on local contracts
and passports, lone print journalists were doubly vulnerable to
discrimination. They would need much more pay transparency
to have any hope of getting equal.

I had a walk with Jin in Ritan Park, once the garden of a
sixteenth-century temple, later a family favourite where Rachel
and Daniel played when they were little. A Siberian wind now
shivered the ancient cypresses and a childless merry-go-round
sang plaintively as Jin quizzed me over the pay structure at the
BBC. He couldn't comprehend why there wasn't a set of clear
rules as there would be in China. I challenged him on that.
Certainly Chinese people tend to be much more open about

discussing their pay, but grading is murky in the private sector and even in the public sector, rules are circumvented through all kinds of perks, including the practice of giving 'red envelopes' stuffed with cash.*

'Private companies are different,' Jin conceded. 'And I suppose there are two kinds of red envelopes. The ones you see and the ones you don't.'

I pointed out that on the World Economic Forum's global gender gap ranking, China was at 100 out of 144, that despite experiments with affirmative action and quotas, top-level politics was a virtual no go for women and big business wasn't much better unless a woman had launched the company herself or inherited it from her family.

'Women get the senior posts reserved for women,' said Jin. 'I think they can get equal pay where they can get the jobs, but there are plenty of jobs they just can't get. Traditional mindset ... it's stubborn.'

After our walk, I went to say goodbye to the British ambassador, and the following day I met officials from the Chinese Foreign Ministry. They had been a big thorn in my side and I had been a big thorn in theirs, but over the years we'd spent many, many hours discussing all dimensions of China's domestic and foreign policies and I'd come to know them well. Over lunch they gave me farewell gifts and enquired about my equal pay battle. I said bluntly that four years of defending BBC values against their own efforts at censorship had developed my capacity for defiance. They laughed. They knew it was true.

The following day I left my China life for good.

---

* In Chinese culture, a red envelope is traditionally a gift of money expected at special occasions like weddings or the birth of a baby. In the workplace, red envelopes are now common at Chinese New Year, as a gift from employer to employee.

No more laughs

The date was 8 February 2018, which also happened to be the deadline for submitting an appeal against my grievance outcome. The appeal is the last step of the internal complaints process and should be completed before litigation. The Acas code does not impose a hard and fast timetable on employers but warns against unreasonable delay. The BBC grievance process gives an employee fourteen days to lodge an appeal and then gives itself ninety days to deliver a response. Luckily, while I'd been packing, laughing and eating dumplings, Jennifer Millins and her formidable Mishcon team had drafted the appeal for me. It put the BBC on the spot over several tightly argued pages:

> In circumstances where the BBC appears to have absolutely no records of rationale for its pay decisions, and has admitted that the question of whether its pay structures and decisions are discriminatory is not considered by management, the burden of proof is on the BBC to prove that there was no discrimination in pay decisions.

At this point you may be thinking that a grievance appeal would be daunting without a good lawyer. I agree. Even with a top law firm working pro bono, I'd hated the grievance ordeal and I was about to hate the appeal even more. My best advice is to avoid it except in very limited circumstances. See my list on page 93.

Back in London I tripped over suitcases at home and struggled to adjust at work. I was back on the mother ship and in direct conflict with the commanders on the bridge. The trouble with being George Bernard Shaw's unreasonable woman – trying to adapt the world to herself – is that it is so very uncomfortable. Pushing progress comes at a price.

Do you sometimes take a decision on principle and then feel trapped when the costs of your decision start to bite? Someone has to fight. But does it have to be me? Does it have to be you? As a self-respecting working woman, you should seriously think about moving on if you've flagged up unequal pay and your employer has refused to put it right. If you have the choice, do as Oprah did. Move to a workplace where you are seen and your value appreciated.

If we all do this, the sexist workplace will eventually perish. But in the early twenty-first century there are still not enough of the other kind. You may feel unable to move for personal or financial reasons. And what if your workplace has features you hold dear? I didn't want the BBC to perish because it had failed to adapt. I wanted it to adapt. This was almost as personal as family.

So it was time to endure another hearing, on this occasion the hearing of my appeal against my grievance outcome. Imagine a central London safe house in a John le Carré novel and you'll be close to the soulless anonymity of the room where this hearing was held. This time the hearing manager was even more senior than the one from four months earlier, but still male and still flanked by a female HR manager.

I reflected that in the four years I had served as China Editor all my bosses – Foreign Editor, Head of Newsgathering, Director of News – had been men. At every stage of my equal pay complaint – informal complaint, grievance, grievance appeal – the hearing managers had all been men. When I started the job, I was the BBC's only female on-air editor. None of the hearing managers ever mentioned this. They were determinedly gender blind and I felt that made them blind to the many things that gender still shapes.

At my appeal hearing, there were now two other women in the room: a note-taker and an external employment consultant from a company called Croner, which describes itself as expert in employment law, HR and health and safety. BBC Women had demanded independent adjudication of cases and tried to discuss with management what that independent scrutiny should look like. Management ignored us and appointed Croner without consultation. Croner advertises itself as 'The Business Owners' Choice'.

As Martine Croxall and I sat down and got our notebooks out, I looked at the four people across the table and wondered bitterly how much public money was being spent on going through the motions.

I'm not going to weary you with a detailed account of that appeal hearing. It lasted two hours and began with another long and angry argument over the BBC's refusal to allow an audio recording. Exhaustion, helplessness and rage made me emotional and self-righteous. Martine had to leave halfway through for a presenting shift on the News Channel and I spent the second hour one against four and then went home in a dark and hopeless mood.

If you ever have to endure a grievance appeal over equal pay, I hope you will invest less. If it's a way station on your journey to an employment tribunal, keep your expectations low. This is the last step of the internal process and managers may well be more committed to each other and their collective survival than they are to your equality. In an appeal hearing, you may be up against several factors that made it difficult for your argument to be heard in the first place and which have only hardened since: the unconscious bias underpinning the original pay decision; the financial interests of the employer; the human instinct to want to be right; hostility to you as a stubborn and 'unreasonable' woman; groupthink. The boss who hears your appeal may feel that the boss who made the original pay decision, or the boss who heard the grievance, got it about right.

However, I wasn't wrong to argue about the absence of an audio recording. After my appeal hearing, it took nearly a month to agree a set of hearing notes. BBC HR kept omitting things that had been said. They changed their own record four times. Every time they changed it, I had to spend hours going through the notes again line by line. Many others endured the same. BBC Women *v.* the BBC made me think of Jarndyce *v.* Jarndyce, the interminable case whose futility Dickens sketches so brilliantly in *Bleak House*:

> Jarndyce and Jarndyce drones on. This scarecrow of a suit has, in course of time, become so complicated, that no man alive knows what it means. The parties to it understand it least; but it has been observed that no two Chancery lawyers can talk about it for five minutes, without coming to a total disagreement as to all the premises. Innumerable children have been born into the cause; innumerable young people have married into it; innumerable old people have died out of it ... but Jarndyce and Jarndyce still drags its dreary length before the Court, perennially hopeless.

If BBC Women *v.* the BBC wasn't quite perennial yet, the case of Women *v.* the Workplace was centuries old. It seemed cynical to duck the argument by means of draining delays.

Winter turned to spring. I'd looked down to the first set of my hearing notes under a bright, leafless sky. I looked up from the fourth set to an unfurling symphony of fresh leaves. For the first time in the entire fight I burst into tears; tears of helplessness for myself and shame for the BBC. If we couldn't even agree on what was said at a hearing, how could we ever agree the facts and find a solution to fix this? I needed help, and called Michelle Stanistreet. Acting in her NUJ capacity, she stepped in to put a stop to the game-playing over notes, and when the

BBC announced that in future, staff would be allowed audio recordings of formal pay hearings I chalked it up as one small victory. In March 2018, this was the only small victory BBC Women could point to after eight months of fighting.

If you ever have a grievance or appeal hearing, try to insist on making your own audio recording for note-taking purposes. It is supposed to be your hearing, after all. An accurate record should be in everyone's interests. To avoid argument, some employees secretly record hearings on their mobile phones, but there are employers who explicitly prohibit the practice and consider it to be an act of gross misconduct. Employers, please be reasonable.

The same week as my appeal hearing, BBC Women marked International Women's Day with an equal pay protest. We filled the piazza in front of Broadcasting House with chanting. Plenty of men joined in.

But it was hard to sustain momentum as attention shifted to two huge management initiatives on pay. The first was a new grading and banding structure. It was called Career Path Framework. In conception it was exactly that, a well-meaning attempt to impose order on a sprawling organisation in which all kinds of inconsistencies had taken root over the course of a century. Management billed CPF as the transparent and coherent system that would cure our pay problems. But many BBC Women were unconvinced. Some complained that what CPF called 'job families' didn't map onto the reality of the work they did; others said they had no means of comparing their salaries with men doing equal work, and that bands were mocked by 'outliers' at both ends – at the top typically by men whose salaries were above the band and at the bottom by women who were below it. Far from being a robust pay framework for the future, they grumbled, CPF looked like a flimsy buttress for the status quo.

Hard on the heels of CPF came new terms and conditions for the entire workforce. The BBC said these would be fairer and more consistent, offering a simplified pay and grading structure, and a new approach to balancing organisational flexibility and work/life balance.

The deal was endorsed by the unions and a majority of NUJ members voted in favour. But a significant minority were unhappy, including some of the NUJ reps who also belonged to the BBC Women group. The intention may have been to simplify the pay structure, but I was not alone in finding the proposed changes fiendishly hard to understand. All the uncertainty over CPF and new Ts and Cs also made it very hard to focus on the equal pay campaign.

The BBC also tried hard to change the subject by opening a wider conversation with its female staff. The Director of BBC Scotland, Donalda MacKinnon, was commissioned to lead a report on how to make the BBC 'the best place for women to work'. BBC Studios CEO Tim Davie began a similar project on behalf of BAME staff. The BBC commissioned two wide-ranging reports on pay transparency. This was all valuable work, but it didn't solve the equal pay problem and BBC staff had seen too many reviews on workplace culture for the announcement of several more to restore trust.

I was overstretched. I had a full-time job, a grievance appeal, colleagues to support on equal pay, public campaigning on the subject and a deep reluctance to renounce my expertise on China. When I gave evidence to a House of Lords inquiry on China, I found myself feeling nostalgic for what seemed in retrospect a simpler life of tussling with the one-party state. Then one evening, while I was on the phone to a newspaper reporter sorting out confusion over which presenters had signed a protest letter on pay transparency, a frog jumped into the kitchen, and at the very same moment, my washing machine froze. In the wash was the equals T-shirt *BBC Breakfast* presenter Louise Minchin had given me. I'm not superstitious, but this odd coincidence of small stresses felt like a sign: enduring was taking a toll.

The nudge

That spring it seemed the whole world was grappling with the question of gender pay. Governments everywhere were discussing how to close the gap. The UK was the first major economy to introduce mandatory gender pay gap reporting for all large employers. That this coincided with #MeToo and the BBC equal pay row was an accident of timing, but together all three underlined that women were still far from equal in the workplace.

Companies and public bodies with over 250 employees were required to report the difference in average earnings for men and for women and to express that as a proportion of men's earnings.

The results were stark. More than three-quarters of large UK employers showed gaps in favour of men. Ryanair topped the table for airlines, with a median gender pay gap of 71.8 per cent. That means for every pound the average man earned, the average woman earned just twenty-eight pence. At banks and building societies the gap was 35 per cent but for bank bonuses it was more than 50 per cent. There were yawning gaps in the construction sector, so too in information and communication. My UK publishers Hachette had a pay gap of 20 per cent and bonus gap of 28.5 per cent. The Telegraph Media Group had a pay gap of 35 per cent, with men receiving almost twice as much in bonuses as women. The *Telegraph*'s arts and entertainment editor Anita Singh tweeted, 'As I've spent a lot of time hammering the BBC for its gender pay gap, it would be hypocritical of me not to say that the Telegraph's 35% pay gap is woeful.'

Huge media pay gaps came as no surprise to me. Ever since January, female reporters had been thanking me for highlighting a problem they could not risk bringing up. All the commercial broadcasters had worse gaps than the BBC's 9 per cent. ITN's gap was more than twice as wide, at 19.6 per cent, with a shocking bonus gap of 77 per cent. The BBC had promised to close its gender pay gap by 2020. Now ITN promised to do so by 2025. Women could compare their employer with rivals and ask about a wider gap or slower pace of correction. Writing in the *Telegraph*, the presenter of *Channel 4 News* Cathy Newman said, 'We're employed to ask tough questions: now our own bosses are having to answer some themselves.'

Women make up more than half of union membership in the UK, but gender pay gaps for union staff suggested the movement had not yet escaped the problems of its male-dominated history. The biggest union, Unite, reported a median gender pay gap for their staff of 29.6 per cent. The teachers' union NASUWT was even worse, its women earning an average fifty-seven pence to the men's pound. Meanwhile, in a separate story about union pay, the National Union of Journalists moved to rectify an anomaly that left Michelle Stanistreet paid less than her male deputy.

From an equal pay perspective, gender pay gap reporting is a blunt instrument. To establish whether they are victims of discrimination, women need to know the pay of men doing similar work. Gender pay gap reporting doesn't allow for such individual comparisons. But Harriet Harman, who had championed gender pay gap reporting in the first place, was hopeful. 'We've got the rhetoric very nicely developed. And now suddenly the facts are marching up to the rhetoric and tapping it on the shoulder. And it's going to be: bang! Now it's the day of reckoning.'

The reckoning was reputational. The government hoped

that uncomfortable scrutiny from employees and customers, alongside comparisons with competitors, would provide
a necessary nudge to the boardroom. The Prime Minister
wrote, 'By making this information public, organisations will
no longer have anywhere to hide. We will have established a
baseline from which to hold them to account in the future.
Shareholders and customers will expect to see improvements,
and will be able to hold organisations to account if they fail
to achieve them.'

Yet there were no sanctions for employers with wide gender
pay gaps nor were there league tables by sector or region.
The equality regulator, the EHRC, which was responsible
for overseeing compliance, urged employers to produce their
own 'time-bound and target-driven' action plans for narrowing gender pay gaps. On the sensitive question of equal pay, it
observed, 'The low number of employers conducting or stating
an intention to conduct equal pay audits was surprising given
how many employers claimed in their narrative reports that
their gender pay gap did not reflect any problems with equal pay.
Most claimed that pay gaps were instead driven by other issues,
such as the concentration of men in senior roles. Without an
equal pay audit, it is difficult to see how these assertions could
be evidenced.'

Some employers did design action plans with measurable
targets for progress and with initiatives including unconscious
bias training, gender-balanced recruitment, flexible working
and shared parental leave. If you work for an employer of more
than 250 people, check its action plan and discuss it with your
boss. Look around at the people who thrive in your workplace.
Do they look like you, and if not, does your boss have a credible story on how that might change? Offer ideas. If you're an
employer, invite ideas.

Different things will be appropriate for different workplaces.

For example, in the world of classical music, 'blind' auditions are now often used to recruit orchestral performers. A study published in 2000 found that using a screen to conceal musicians from recruiters during preliminary auditions increased the likelihood that a female musician would advance to the next round by 11 per cent and that during the final round, 'blind' auditions increased the likelihood of female musicians being selected by 30 per cent.

The EHRC has published lots of ideas to make recruitment in other contexts more 'blind', including anonymised application forms and structured interviews. On flexible working, it suggests advertising jobs at all levels as open to flexible working from day one and showcasing examples where it is successful. On childcare, employers can actively promote shared parental leave. Even small things can help to chip away at the motherhood penalty, like keeping in touch with women when they're on maternity leave, rather than closing their email accounts and removing their ID passes.

In the end, a lot comes down to the signals from the top. If CEOs take a keen interest in putting in place unconscious bias training, transparent performance benchmarks, women on promotion shortlists, BAME pay gap reporting, mentoring programmes and software that flags up pay anomalies, that will all filter down the management chain. What gets measured gets managed, after all.

At this point it's too early to tell whether the UK's mandatory gender pay gap reporting is the clever nudge that's needed. According to the behavioural economist Iris Bohnet, for nudges to drive change they must be simple, visible and hard to manipulate. Gender pay gap reporting provides limited transparency, the regulator is overstretched, the media may get bored, employers may lose focus or find ways to game the system. Their day of reckoning may be postponed.

But not yours. Having read your employer's gender pay gap report and action plan, study those of rivals. Is your workplace best in class? Is it committed to doing better? If you feel you have a choice, work for an employer that is.

Reasons to be hopeful

The good news is that more women are voting with their feet on equality and more workplaces are ready to receive them: a virtuous circle that is growing.

I was heartened to read the Salesforce story. The Californian tech company had thirty thousand employees selling customer relations software. In chief of personnel Cindy Robbins it had a senior woman who spoke up. When she first told CEO Marc Benioff they might have an equal pay problem, his response was disbelief: 'We don't play shenanigans paying people – paying people unequally. It's unheard of. It's crazy.'

But he allowed himself to be proved wrong. In 2015, Salesforce started to look hard at its gender pay gap and found problems in every department, every division, every country of operations. In the first year of its equal pay audit, the company spent $3 million on raising the pay of 10 per cent of its female workforce. In the second year, Salesforce found its pay gap had widened again, mainly because it had bought a number of small firms which themselves had problems. The company again spent millions of dollars making pay equal. It also expanded its pay analysis to include bonuses and to identify pay gaps across race and ethnicity as opposed to gender alone. And it addressed some of the structural problems that underpin pay inequality with on-site childcare, flexible working and more family leave. Benioff says he no longer simply focuses on the technology and the product when he's buying a company, but on the culture.

And on equal pay, admitting you have a problem is only the first step. Technology makes it possible to do the rest: 'CEOs, with one button on one computer, can pay every man and every woman equally.'

Cindy Robbins echoes the point: 'No matter the size of your company, you have all the data. There's really no excuse not to look at it.'

Another encouraging story came from the University of Waterloo in Ontario, Canada. In 2016 it acknowledged a 'systemic gender anomaly' across salaries and raised pay for all female faculty. In India, the multinational software company Adobe closed its gender pay gap by paying a set rate for roles rather than asking for employees' previous pay history in setting salary.

Many employers have woken up to the fact that the rules of the traditional workplace were designed by men and that unconscious bias, pay secrecy and the structural inequalities of the labour market will leave women competing on an unlevel playing field unless they are vigilant. Some are interrogating their computer algorithms to weed out the bias baked into employee data, others are overhauling their bonus culture to limit the potential for managerial discretion to succumb to discrimination. An open-minded response should feed into business decisions and make these workplaces more resilient to a turbulent world. If you're just starting out on your career, choose an employer like this. It won't just improve your own chances of equality but will send a 'survival of the fittest' message to rival employers.

Governments too are trying different solutions. Many US states have legislated to ban employers from asking a job candidate about their pay history and then using that to set salary. Iceland has gone further. From 2018, any Icelandic organisation with more than 250 employees has needed certification from an accredited auditor that they are paying an equal salary for work of equal value. Without that certification they face fines.

'The pay gap was hidden behind a lack of transparency,' said Magnea Marinósdóttir of the Icelandic government's equality unit. 'Employers can take into account experience, qualifications – it's just that it now has to be transparent and justified.'

And so Iceland shifted responsibility for enforcing equal pay from individual women to employers. Ideas often start life unthinkable, grow up to sound sensible, mature into policy and end up taken for granted.

Tougher regulation on equal pay might seem unthinkable in many countries now, but this will change. The point was made forcibly to me by an elderly stranger on a train. Having congratulated me on my own equal pay fight and reflected on pay structures in the various businesses he had run, this man then drew a parallel with the airline industry. He told me safety had been improved only by rigorous external investigation of accidents. 'What's key is a willingness to learn from failure,' he said, 'and the same is true on pay. Whenever a problem crops up, employers must bring in job evaluators from outside. Just relying on managers marking each other's homework will never fix it.'

When I got home I checked the air safety figures. There is one fatality for every 287 million passengers carried by UK operators. The Civil Aviation Authority does not put accident investigation in the hands of injured passengers or airlines. Instead it closely regulates all players, from pilots to maintenance teams and air traffic controllers. Airlines are not permitted to hire the accident investigator of their choice. Unsafe airlines are banned from European airspace. All of which makes the point that there's serious regulation and then there's regulation that no one takes seriously.

I'm not suggesting an equal pay equivalent to the Air Accidents Investigation Branch. One case of pay discrimination for every 287 million women in the workforce will not happen in my lifetime, but if we could get the ratio to one in 287 women it would be transformative. My guess is that it's currently closer to one in 2.8 than to one in 28. I would like to see significant penalties. In the spring of 2018, BBC staff were required to do mandatory training on the new EU General Data Protection Regulation, with a stern warning that penalties for mishandling data might cost the BBC twenty million euros or 4 per cent of the BBC's total worldwide turnover. There was no such training on breaches of equality legislation. A cynic might say that was because there was no such penalty.

I also believe in greater pay transparency and regular equal pay audits for employers whose pay and bonus gaps look suspicious, preferably by an auditor who is not beholden to the employer.

Until then, women who go into unequal fights for equal pay must endure much misery in their effort to stand up for what is right and make the workplace safer for the rest of us.

Unsung heroes

Take Kay Collins. Until 2016, Kay worked as a chef in Weston-super-Mare. By chance she learned that a much younger man with less experience was earning more for the same work, despite her own long service and good record. Kay raised a grievance and asked for pay parity. Her employer said the man's job was substantially different. An employment tribunal found the differences to be 'of no practical importance'. Kay won her case. But beyond that vindication, it's hard to say she won anything. As she herself has pointed out, 'I am not in work because I was dismissed during the action, and I am struggling to pay my mortgage. All I wanted was what I was entitled to.'

Kay's employer was the Compass Group, with a workforce of sixty thousand people, and just as her case was coming to tribunal it boasted that its gender pay gap of 12.3 per cent was better than the national average. 'At Compass Group, we are committed to the diversity and inclusion agenda.'

The Co-operative Group is another big employer of women. It said its gender pay gap was 'mainly due to us having more men in senior positions than women ... our Co-op values are built on equality, equity and inclusion'.

In the spring of 2018, the Co-op's former HR director, Sam Walker, got in touch. She had a different story to tell. At the opposite end of the pay spectrum from Kay Collins, she too had been dismissed two years earlier after complaining about unequal pay and was waiting for her case to come to tribunal.

I was no longer surprised by stories like this. Since I published my open letter, women from all walks of life had been telling me of efforts to secure equal pay, efforts which started in hope and ended in wholesale distrust of their employer. Whether firefighters, administrators, charity workers or journalists, they described a tragedy in three acts. Act One: a polite attempt to reason with a line manager. Act Two: an internal complaints process in which they felt treated as vexatious, obsessive, exaggerating conspiracy theorists. Act Three: a slog towards a tribunal hearing, only to be offered an eleventh-hour settlement on condition of signing a confidentiality clause.

Many women told me they felt guilty for settling on these terms, because colleagues would be left ignorant of the risks. Some said they had no choice, as the union or insurer funding legal expenses had threatened to withdraw that funding if they refused to settle. Besides, these claimants were already exhausted and a public hearing would further risk their health, financial security and future work prospects.

Even in the rare stories that ended before a judge, there were no fines for employers and no punitive damages. The most claimants came away with was some back pay, benefits and pension that they should never have had to fight for in the first place, and much of which they now spent on paying their legal team. Women complained of the impact on their mental health, listing sleeping problems, depression and even suicidal tendencies. Some told me they had given up because they just wanted it all to end.

Must women put up with this? Perhaps the answer is yes. A mass petition on women's suffrage was delivered to Parliament in 1866. It took another half-century of campaigning, the life and death struggle of the suffragettes and the war work of millions before any woman won the right to vote.

Occasionally women can short-circuit history – Martina Navratilova, for example, one of the greatest tennis players of all time, winner of eighteen singles grand slams. In spring 2018, the BBC, already embroiled in an equal pay fight with its own staff, managed to trip up in a match against Navratilova as well. The *Panorama* programme reported that the BBC was paying John McEnroe at least ten times as much as her for commentary at Wimbledon. Ever since Billie Jean King set up the Women's Tennis Association and beat Bobby Riggs in the famous Battle of the Sexes match, tennis had been a front line in the fight for equal pay, and here it was again; this time in terms of match commentary. Interviewed on *Panorama*, Navratilova said she was shocked to discover her Wimbledon pay gap and went on to make a wider point: 'It's two weeks of my life, but for the women that work there full-time, maybe the discrepancy is not that large, but it adds up over a life time.'

The BBC said Navratilova and McEnroe were performing

different roles, and 'he is widely considered to be the best expert/commentator in the sport'. But, shamed by public outrage, it then moved swiftly to resolve matters with Navratilova.

Something similar happened when it emerged that for the TV drama, *The Crown*, Claire Foy earned less for playing the Queen than her co-star, Matt Smith, for playing Prince Philip. Foy's role was the lead and the Netflix period drama was all about the obstacles a woman faces in exercising power. The production company apologised and put things right. Foy said the experience was embarrassing but 'opened [her] eyes to a lot'.

Both examples demonstrate that in high-profile one-off cases that don't involve historic liabilities or precedents for a wider pay structure, transparency can solve an equal pay problem in a trice.

For women who are not screen or sporting royalty, there is no convenient short-cut to being equally valued or paid.

Whose cross to bear?

By now it was Easter and I was counting down the ninety days of my grievance appeal and looking ahead to the outcome, which would be the end of the internal process. I no longer had faith in the BBC to give me either pay parity or a clear explanation of why my work was worth less. I expected to face a choice: whether to accept its final verdict on my complaint, resign in protest or pursue the case to tribunal. The time limits for making a claim to an employment tribunal are very strict and affected by various factors. Jennifer warned that in my case the position on time limits was not clear cut. To be absolutely sure that I would be able to bring a claim I would need to act by 4 July 2018, making the early conciliation notification to Acas that is a legal prerequisite to bringing a claim.

A friend who'd spent his career at the BBC warned, 'Do not crucify yourself on a lonely cross.'

That bracing image made me think of Miriam O'Reilly. I wondered whether her tribunal case against the BBC had felt like a lonely cross. I called her to ask. Miriam told me she'd been left with 'blinding anger' but fighting the case had been the right thing to do: 'I would do it again in a heartbeat.'

I feared I lacked Miriam's tenacity. I'd already admired the dogged way some BBC Women fought skirmish after skirmish without losing their sanity or good humour, but I didn't have the patience. Nailing lies made me despise my bosses and arguing about money bored me. What would be the point in enduring this further? I put one question to everyone I could think of: Would a test case on equal pay change BBC pay culture and help to educate the public about the risks?

'No,' said an employment judge, 'litigation is a disaster.'

'No,' said a barrister. 'The BBC will spin it as a grudge match about one anomalous case rather than an education on the wider issue.'

'No,' said a veteran of BBC management. 'The more credible you look on the way to court, the more alone you will become. The BBC will find ways to peel away the support of other women.'

There was also the problem of money. Mishcon had undertaken my grievance and appeal pro bono, but I would have to raise hundreds of thousands of pounds to fight a tribunal case. Relying on my union for funding or on legal expenses cover under household insurance would have taken key decisions on whether, when and on what terms to settle the case out of my hands. An employee's financial constraints are a trump card for employers. The BBC spends public funds on the best lawyers money can buy. I investigated the possibility of crowdfunding my legal fees because I knew there were sections of the public who would want to see the issues aired. But those wise on media strategy warned that crowdfunding would make me vulnerable to charges of greed from enemies of equal pay. They would present me as a woman who was already paid too much public money now expecting cash-strapped audiences to fund her bid to extract yet more money from the public purse. 'You can see it yourself, Carrie, they just don't report it when you say it's about the principle and not about the money.'

Yes, I'd noticed that. I was still preoccupied by how to fund a test case when I met Sam Smethers. Sam is the CEO of the Fawcett Society, the UK's leading charity for women's rights and gender equality, and I wanted to hear her views on women in the workplace. It turned out she was hatching a plan for a strategic litigation fund to finance test cases in the public interest. That made her a problem-solver after my own heart, but her fund would not be ready in time for me.

I don't know about you, but when I've done all my listening, I like to make a clear decision. As April turned into May I waited for clarity to strike.

Lie down, leave or litigate

The mood among BBC Women was bitter and weary. Even after nearly a year of making a strong argument with solidarity and determination, we were not winning. In many cases, we felt that managers continued to cite cosmetic differences in work to justify large discrepancies in pay, cherry-pick 'material factors', deny women's choice of male comparators, ignore inconvenient questions, make assertions without evidence, cite experience and length of service even in disparities lasting many years, and, if all else failed, put pay differences down to men's 'legacy salaries' or women's 'development'.

July 2018 would be the first anniversary of the equal pay fight. In the run-up, BBC Women carried out a survey of our members to assess progress. There was very little progress to report.

'Equal pay is the law but they treat it like a favour,' came one response. 'Management are fighting women every step of the way.'

'Bruising, humiliating, attritional,' wrote another. 'Am considering handing in my resignation.'

Every day I too fantasised about resigning. I'd never liked talking about money or boasting about my work and now I'd spent months doing both in a way that was crowding out the rest of my life. I was becoming rigid in warrior stance, angrier than was healthy. In fact, I found this stage of the equal pay fight harder to endure than my battle with breast cancer. That had been frightening and painful but my prognosis had been good. To get well all I had to do was cooperate with my doctors. Here all was chaos and conflict and the odds against us overwhelming. The daily torrent of judgement calls was framed by an overwhelming sense of powerlessness.

At work, I was afraid of lifts and other confined spaces where I might bump into the growing number of managers implicated in bad decisions around pay. The awkwardness was clearly mutual. Some bosses developed a thousand-yard stare if they glimpsed me across the newsroom. I was scheduled on evening and weekend shifts. I half suspected it was so that they didn't have to endure looking at me on screen or in person.

As I moved through Broadcasting House, I felt like a force field that repels but also attracts. Many colleagues thanked me for speaking up. Some asked for advice on their own cases. Most were women, but men too begged me to fight on. When you're in the fight of your life, everything is heightened. You never forget who steps in to help, who stops to acknowledge your existence and who strides past with eyes averted.

One male colleague asked innocently, 'Is equal pay all you do now?' He was a well-meaning feminist, but his question irked me. All you do, I thought. Isn't it enough for you? Isn't it important enough for you? As I say, I was becoming a brittle warrior.

If you know a colleague who is going through an equal pay fight and you'd like to show support, say something kind about their work, get them a coffee ... or just say hello. Workplace disputes can be very isolating and small acts of kindness are a great balm.

Kindness is a good idea for bosses too. Employers have a legal duty of care to take all steps which are reasonably possible to ensure the health, safety and wellbeing of their employees. Many bosses are already alive to the ways compassion can reduce workplace stress and improve culture. But I suspect kindness has an even more marked effect on employees enduring long-running workplace disputes. I think there are ways for managers to show humanity without compromising the organisation's legal position. Smile. Acknowledge an email. Do something, however small, which shows that you are not blanking your employee and wishing them dead.

Over the edge

It was hard to front several hours of live television news a day while feeling some of my bosses would be glad if I messed up. But I was managing to hold things together until the straw that broke the camel's back: a historic pay review into my salary for the year before I went to China. This was not part of the normal complaints process but a recommendation from January's grievance outcome. I hadn't asked for it. I simply wanted my China work to be valued equally. My pay as a News Channel presenter had been lower than that of male peers for more than a decade and I couldn't see the point of a review for the year 2013 alone.

Whatever the purpose, this review forced me into conflict with my immediate line manager, required me to excavate records, write another submission and appear at yet another hearing. Worse still, I learned that this review would hold up the grievance appeal process beyond the allotted ninety days. Are you glazing over now? Imagine how I felt. For nearly a year, I'd tried to balance doing my job with fighting this battle. Everything else in life was on hold, including my physical and mental health. I was fixated on the appeal outcome and this delay was a blow. I stopped sleeping and started to struggle with depression.

It was hard for me to admit weakness, but eventually I accepted that going to work had begun to make me ill and my doctor signed me off. I now understood why whistle-blowers rarely continue to work for the organisation they call out, often don't work again at all and struggle to recover their trust in people and organisations.

There is no easy advice I can give you on enduring this kind of ordeal. The only thing I would say is what I've now said twice already. Think very hard before you embark on a grievance process, because if you start you will feel you have to endure till the end.

On 1 June 2018, HR finally wrote to alert me that outcomes were imminent for both the grievance appeal and the historic pay review. That same day, the debate which had been raging in my head miraculously stilled. Lie down, leave or litigate? I finally knew the answer.

I would not accept an unequal verdict from a rigged process, but nor would I litigate. I would leave. Back in January, I'd given up my China post to come home and fight. Now that fight had run out of road. Emotionally and physically I was done. I had endured enough.

9

ENLIST GOOD MEN

=

On 2 June 2018, my male comparator Jon Sopel told a national radio audience that I had mugged him. It was an extended joke about how he got mugged three times within a fortnight – first by me with my open letter, then by the John Humphrys tape and third by BBC management with an enforced pay cut. But, he laughed, he could still afford a cup of coffee on his way to the studio.

I didn't laugh. It was day 114 of ninety in my grievance appeal and I was having a sense of humour failure. Moreover, I don't want men to laugh about equal pay, I want them to sign up. It didn't help that, amid the boys' banter on the BBC Radio 4 *Loose Ends* programme, the presenter forgot my name and demoted me from China Editor to correspondent, a post I'd held twenty years earlier. Sloppiness from him or pettiness from me? It didn't really matter.

What did matter was that Jon misrepresented my argument. He said my purpose was a pay rise. This made me first angry and then thoughtful. I was angry because it wasn't true. I felt Jon must have known that writing an open letter calling one's employer 'secretive and illegal' was not the way to a pay rise. If money had been my motive, I would have fought hard behind closed doors, agreed to a confidentiality agreement and banked a bigger salary and several years of back pay in exchange for my silence. If I had single-mindedly pursued my own self-interest, not only would I be much richer, I would still have a flourishing career and I would have avoided an all-consuming and stressful year on the equal pay barricade.

But when I'd stopped feeling angry, I started to think about why Jon would present the story like this. I concluded that his was an account that made him a bystander. If he'd acknowledged that my fight was about equality, he might have been forced to think about how he'd benefited from the original inequality and stood aside from the protracted effort to resolve it. But if my letter to audiences was only ever an eccentric bid for a pay rise, then it wasn't about him at all. In fact, he might see himself as the victim of a stunt. Later that summer he did say in an interview that it had been 'ghastly on a personal level': 'I was quietly minding my own business – I had no idea what other people earned – and then suddenly I was in the spotlight.'

What can women expect from male colleagues? If you're a woman, what can you hope for from yours? And if you're a man, what help can you offer?

In the US, nearly half of men think the gender pay gap has been made up to serve a political purpose. A 2019 global study on attitudes found 50 per cent of men believe too much is expected of their support for women's equality, with the numbers highest in Peru at 62 per cent, Colombia and Mexico at 61 per cent, and Malaysia and India at 60 per cent. But interestingly, three in five men around the world believe women won't achieve equality unless men take action.

To achieve change, women don't need men to lead, but we do need men to identify their privilege and renounce it. That takes an open mind, empathy and courage.

Here's an example from the mid-nineteenth century. Victorian Britain at the height of empire was a confidently masculine society not much given to examining its gender stereotypes.

Which made the questioning, self-educating change-maker John Stuart Mill a rarity.

Mill was a philosopher and political campaigner. He observed that it was not just unthinking herd habit that kept women down but male self-interest. Women were excluded from public life in order to 'maintain their subordination in domestic life, because the generality of the male sex cannot yet tolerate the idea of living with an equal'.

As for the argument that women are by nature more fitted for domestic life, Mill disposed of it with cool reasoning:

> If men had ever been found in society without women, or women without men, or if there had been a society of men and women in which the women were not under the control of the men, something might have been positively known about the mental and moral differences which may be inherent in the nature of each. What is now called the nature of women is an eminently artificial thing – the result of forced repression in some directions, unnatural stimulation in others.

As an MP, John Stuart Mill supported women's suffrage, property rights and education. For three decades, the biggest influence on his thinking was the woman with whom he shared his life, the fellow philosopher and women's rights advocate Harriet Taylor. She influenced him and he influenced the world around them. Hopefully Taylor will get more credit as we all commit to seeing the great women of the past more clearly. But hers was an age in which women needed powerful men to help advance the cause of equality. A century and a half later, so is ours.

In an equal pay battle, the most effective ally for any woman is the male comparator himself. An employer will always find it much harder to argue that a woman's work is worth less than a man's if the man in question firmly insists that it is worth the same.

In the summer of 2018, Elizabeth Rowe, the principal flautist in the Boston Symphony Orchestra, sued her employer over unequal pay, naming John Ferrillo, the BSO's principal oboist, as her male comparator. Rowe's lawsuit stated, 'Both the principal oboe and principal flute are leaders of their woodwind sections, they are seated adjacent to each other, they each play with the Boston Symphony Chamber Players, and are both leaders of the orchestra in similarly demanding artistic roles.'

In a statement to court supporting Rowe's claim, Ferrillo referred to her as his equal and said she was 'every bit my match in skills, if not more so'. He publicly contradicted the Boston Symphony Orchestra's defence that he should earn more because the oboe is harder to play than the flute. 'Ever looked at a flute part? They've got to play a million notes. The technical standards are astounding. Every instrument has its own private hell.'

After long conditioning in workplaces with a divide and rule pay culture, it's hard for men to risk their own immediate self-interest by standing with women. John Ferrillo's very public solidarity with a female peer made him an unusual man – a grown-up version of the Norwegian boy with the sweet jar.

I dare to hope that men in other workplaces will follow suit. Those who give their salary information to female colleagues are already doing something for the principle of equal pay. At the BBC, many men helped in this way. It was generous, and in cases where it risked angering bosses, it was brave.

After being open with information, the next big stride for men is active solidarity.

Actor Benedict Cumberbatch now boycotts projects that do not pay women the same as their male co-stars. 'Equal pay and a place at the table are the central tenets of feminism . . . Look at your quotas. Ask what women are being paid, and say: "If she's not paid the same as the men, I'm not doing it."'

Comedy is also plagued by unequal pay. For example, in 2018 Sandi Toksvig revealed she earned only 40 per cent of Stephen Fry's rate for hosting the BBC panel show *QI*. But the Canadian comedian Katherine Ryan said that when it came to negotiating pay on a series of the stand-up show *Roast Battle*, her co-star Jonathan Ross stepped in to help. 'He approached me and said, "How much are you getting paid for this, because I won't do it if I'm earning more than you." That's the first time a man has ever said this. He took the initiative and I really appreciate it.'

Since the autumn of 2017, BBC Women had been attending each other's pay hearings to take notes and give support. Senior presenters sat alongside junior producers to make the point that no woman was left behind. Having supportive men in the room would have been even more powerful. Men can neutralise an employer's defence of unequal pay. I know of one case at the BBC in which this worked. A woman was accompanied at an informal pay hearing by her male comparator who insisted their work was equal and invited the hearing panel to picture both of them in retirement, him with a far higher quality of life due to decades of the higher pension entitlements that came with his higher salary. Her pay was corrected quickly and painlessly.

In another well-known media company I met a group of men who went further. First, they risked management displeasure to support a female colleague throughout an internal equal pay complaint. Then, as the case moved into litigation, they provided written witness statements and offered to give oral evidence at her employment tribunal hearing. In the end, the company settled just before the case reached tribunal. Those men were heroic team players and they helped win that woman equal pay.

In the same vein, many US business schools now nurture male ally groups whose members make a commitment to help end gender discrimination both through advocacy and through growing awareness of their own attitudes and behaviour. These 'manbassadors' started at the University of California Berkeley's Haas School of Business. The first group was launched in 2015 by classmates Patrick Ford and Mike Matheson. The MBA allies network now offers its members a programme of activities and resources and encourages them to sign up to the following pledge:

Gender inequity is not an issue just for women – it is an issue for everyone – and we will take action to address it.

We men, in partnership with women, have an important role to play in ensuring all women have the same opportunity to succeed professionally as we do. For the good of all people, we pledge to:

- Work to eradicate explicit sexism in all forms
- Identify and mitigate implicit bias in ourselves and our workplaces
- In our homes, engage in dialogue with our female partners about sharing household duties and raising children (for heterosexual men)
- Honour the voices and contributions of women of all backgrounds, cultures, and identities
- Help our companies become more competitive through implementing gender equity best practices and driving cultural shift

We also thank the many generations of women (and men) who have worked so hard for a level playing field – and who continue to do so. We've made incredible progress but still have a lot of work to do.

There will never be gender equality in the workplace until men care about it as much as women. All men can help here, but powerful men can help the most as they can accelerate change, or they can block it. If you're a powerful man in your workplace, please champion a robust and transparent set of gender-neutral rules on pay, and point out to other powerful men that those rules need to be immune to the kind of special pleading that their privilege might give them. Shake the complacent by pointing to the many proud organisations – churches, charities, corporations – that have done untold damage to their brand by permitting some to be above the rules.

At the BBC, even if the powerful men had joined us late they would have been a huge asset. A year in the equal pay trenches taught me the truth of the aphorism 'All that is necessary for the triumph of evil is that good men do nothing.'

GET EQUAL

=

'First they ignore you, then they ridicule you, then they fight you and then you win.'

A line sometimes attributed to Mahatma Gandhi, but also a favourite with Donald Trump. The 'they' in this story had certainly ignored me, ridiculed me and fought me over the course of a year, but when I received my appeal outcome on 4 June 2018 it didn't look as if I would win.

When this document dropped into my email inbox I felt some trepidation about even opening it. Four months earlier, the grievance outcome had used 'growth and development' to justify the pay gap, and although others had laughed at the absurdity of this, I still felt insulted, and ashamed for the BBC. So now I was wary. I opened the appeal outcome and scanned it fast.

My appeal was rejected. The outcome echoed the grievance outcome of four months earlier. I didn't allow myself to feel disappointed. I read the document again more slowly. It concluded with the words, 'Please note that you have now reached the end of the internal procedures and there is no further stage of appeal.'

The outcome of the historic pay review arrived at the same time. I was struck by how little those involved seemed to know about the work they were evaluating. The review was littered with omissions and factual errors. I imagine poor records were once again a factor. I mention this now as a warning to you to keep good records yourself, so that your work can't be forgotten later either by accident or design. But the historic pay review did find that my salary as a news presenter should have been raised by £25,000 back in 2013.

A quick recap of the journey in figures. In October 2017, my employer responded to my initial equal pay complaint by offering me a £45,000 pay rise. In January 2018, the grievance outcome said I was owed £105,000 (which added three years of back pay at the 'development/growth in experience' rate). Now, on 4 June, the historic pay review added more back pay for 2013, and after a page of calculations, said the final figure was £132,792. All of which makes the point that an employer's first offer may not be their last. But even the last offer was much less than equal. Jon Sopel's annual salary for 2017/18 was between £230,000 and £239,999. My 2017/18 salary as China Editor was now calculated at £180,000. And in the previous three years it was still less due to what was now called 'growth in experience'.

If you take this journey, you're likely to reach a moment like this, an appeal outcome in which your employer says, 'Game over. We still judge you less than equal. Your move.'

This is not a moment to get mad or speak your truth. It is a moment to stop and think. If you're anything like me, it is also a moment to listen. I sent all the documents to Jennifer Millins and to the same handful of BBC Women who had read my draft protest letter five months earlier. I also included two letters of apology.

The first was from Fran Unsworth. As BBC Director of News, she apologised for an approach to setting pay that was inadequate and for failings in relation to my pay over an extended period of time. She acknowledged that I had been right to raise these issues, had made personal sacrifices to go to China, had done an exceptional job there, and had not been 'in development'. It was a generous letter.

The other letter was from the HR Director of BBC News. She accepted that note-taking in my case had been seriously substandard and she apologised that this had made an already difficult situation harder for me. She reassured me of her personal commitment 'to address inequality and unfairness wherever it lies'.

My side were unimpressed. 'Sorry, but not sorry,' was the consensus view.

Jennifer noted that saying sorry for the misunderstanding about 'in development' didn't make up for three years of lower pay. As for the remaining pay disparity in my final year as China Editor, a gap of between £50,000 and £60,000, she felt the evidence looked flimsy, and on key points non-existent. She believed we would win a tribunal case unless we were unlucky in the judge, 'But that doesn't mean we should fight it.'

In fact, Jennifer advised me to think carefully about litigating, reminding me again that to sue a big employer which has top lawyers and a powerful spin machine would be a lonely war of attrition.

Among BBC Women there was a split. Some said I'd already done more than my share in the fight. They felt the outcomes and apologies constituted a victory. I should be proud of what I'd achieved, they said, and get back to my career as soon as my health allowed. Others complained that after a year-long battle I was still deemed less than equal with no good explanation.

If this had been about my case alone, I would certainly have drawn a line under it at this point. After all, mistakes had been acknowledged and progress is a journey. But I knew this pay system was costing life-changing amounts of money to women who were less privileged and more vulnerable. It was also putting them through an intolerable ordeal when they tried to put that right. Even at the finish line, my case showed that pay decisions were not robust and nor was the complaints process.

So I felt I couldn't go back to normal service.

If I wasn't going to litigate, the only other form of protest loud enough was to leave the BBC altogether. The day after receiving my appeal outcome, I wrote my resignation letter. It would mean saying goodbye to an organisation I love and embarking on a job hunt, but I felt energised by the prospect of putting all this behind me and breathing clean air again.

You too may get to the end of an internal complaints process and make this decision. I think you should feel proud of having done something for the women who come after you. Even if employers don't admit it, equal pay claims that are pursued through grievance and appeal force them to think about gender bias in their pay structure. If, after leaving, you follow Susan Fowler's example and publish a detailed indictment of a workplace culture, so much the better. Her viral blog post 'Reflecting on one very, very strange year at Uber' alerted women everywhere to danger. Likewise, I'd already sounded the unequal pay alert in January and intended to do so again on my way out of the door.

I didn't make it to the door.

'You'll cast a chill on the whole campaign!' some BBC Women remonstrated. They argued that I might see a protest departure as a victory, but others would see it as defeat. Listening can be so inconvenient. But reluctantly I concluded that they were right. And I had my own nagging doubts about leaving. If others were putting their shoulder to a heavy wheel, how could I remove my own? What would Emmeline Pankhurst think? Or Oprah? Or Miriam O'Reilly? How could the right to equal pay ever become more than rhetoric if even privileged women like me would not fight for it?

So leaving was no longer an option and lying down was unthinkable. Winning was the only thing left to me. This is how I did it.

First I wrote to the Director-General explaining that I could not accept the outcome of my grievance appeal and would now prepare to litigate. I suggested he and I should meet in a last-ditch attempt to find a way out. Even better than fighting to win, is to win without fighting. Sun Zi calls it 'the acme of skill' and it often requires setting out not just the problem and the solution to the problem, but the painful consequences of doing something different. I sent Tony Hall a brief analysis of the weaknesses of the BBC's legal position. I also sent him a two-sentence statement he could deliver to make the problem go away:

> The BBC acknowledges that Carrie's work as China Editor was of equal value to that of her male peers and she was entitled to equal pay. The BBC apologises for underpaying Carrie for several years and has now put this right.

When we met in Tony's office on 18 June, the first thing I did was to ask if conversations there were recorded. People who'd worked at the top of large private-sector organisations had warned that I should insist on talking elsewhere and leaving mobile phones behind. Tony said no, his office wasn't bugged.

I told him that many BBC Women feared their work phones and email might be monitored, which was in itself a measure of how little trust they now had in their management. I said the pay fight was damaging morale: the lies and spin, the charade where a robust complaints process should be. Tony didn't waste time contradicting me. Leading a large organisation cannot be an easy job and calculating when to expend energy on arguing must be a key skill.

He let me finish and then unfolded a piece of paper and passed it to me. A brief statement. After a year of shouting up at the fortress wall, was the drawbridge rattling down?

Perhaps the Director-General calculated that my case was strong, that I was determined to win it and that a battle at tribunal would expose serious failings in the handling of both equal pay and internal complaints. That afternoon we were conducting a negotiation and not a news interview. I didn't ask why he was changing course. Instead I haggled hard over those lines. Within half an hour we'd reached a compromise. But by the time I saw that statement again it had been rewritten. I shouldn't have been surprised. Former BBC managers had warned me abut the 'paralysed matrix' at the top and BBC Women had joked about lawyers in command 'on the bridge of the Death Star'.

For several days, that statement shuttled back and forth. I did my part to help build the Director-General a dignified off-ramp. Off-ramps are so important for leaders of large organisations, and for you and me, winning without fighting should not be about insisting that the other side lose. Once you've embarked on peace negotiations, you have to be constructive. I discussed with Jennifer, BBC Women and others where I could be flexible. Could I give ground on the wording of the statement? Could I offer to refrain from media interviews or from publicising details of the now obsolete grievance appeal outcome? Some BBC Women worried that I might end by conceding too much and become a prisoner of the process.

By the time I went into my second meeting with Tony Hall, he was talking about making a joint statement. The BBC wanted to draw a line under the problem and show we had made progress. But there were hundreds more cases out there, which made it difficult for me to talk about progress. Likewise, I couldn't talk about a difficult year for both sides. BBC Women didn't feel there was any comparison between our difficulties and those of management.

Tony had his chief of staff, Phil Harrold, at that meeting and I was accompanied by one of BBC Women's sharpest negotiators. The four of us argued about everything, right down to the prepositions. From Broadcasting House, I went to visit Jeremy Heywood in hospital. On the way, a woman stopped me in the Underground to tell me she herself had once been a BBC employee but that she had seen her post closed when she was seven months pregnant, only for someone else to be appointed in her place on a full-time staff contract.

Jeremy was as stoic as ever about his ongoing cancer treatment but he was drafting a public statement of his own on his intention to step back from Cabinet duties. He joked that Suzanne, his wife, was doubtful, on the grounds that 'the distraction of running the country' was good for him. We talked about my equal pay fight. Jeremy said I should avoid a tribunal at all costs, take the money, leave the BBC and start somewhere new.

The next morning, I received yet another version of the joint statement, and it seemed that everything had gone backwards again. I felt frustrated, wondering whether it wasn't just my listening habit that might have been misread as weakness but also my negotiating style. When I said 'this is my red line', perhaps others thought I meant 'this is my starting position, feel free to push at it'. I felt not just frustrated but angry. It looked to me as if faceless apparatchiks were making key decisions in defiance even of the Director-General. Or perhaps it was all a mind game, I wondered, in which case that 'prisoner of the process' warning was prescient and winning without fighting a pipe dream.

That evening I took part in a public panel discussion on the gender pay gap. It was at the Mishcon de Reya office and Jennifer was in the chair. The other panellists were Julia

Simpson, Chief of Staff at International Airlines Group, and Stella Creasy, MP. Before we went on stage, Julia mused on how much time men dedicate to networking, managing up and handing out their CVs. She complained that even when she asked for fifty-fifty shortlists from head-hunters they sent back all-male lists. Some blamed it on women, saying they were too busy being perfect at their existing jobs to apply for new ones. Others blamed employers, saying even the ones who asked for fifty-fifty lists would choose a man anyway so there was no point putting women forward.

On the panel, I was gloomy. I pointed to the BBC experience, saying if a year-long campaign by highly organised and well-informed women couldn't fix equal pay in a large organisation that claimed to be driven by its values, the prospects weren't good elsewhere. Gender pay gap reporting was a positive, but not enough. Women cannot fix what they cannot see. And even in cases like mine where they do stumble on the facts, a legal right to equal pay is meaningless if enforcing that right costs their career, health and sanity.

I travelled home with a friend who'd been in the audience, an in-house employment lawyer for a large company. She disagreed with me on transparency, saying lower-paid employees would feel demoralised if pay gaps were exposed. I acknowledged that getting real on pay might be uncomfortable at first and that exposing problems without fixing them wouldn't help much. But I argued that transparency would drive progress in the long term, as employers would be forced to clean up the various 'anomalies' in their pay structures and explain remaining pay disparities to their workforce. Employees would feel more focused and motivated if they could see the rules of the game and understand how to advance. This argument took us all the way back to south-west London, where we bumped into a third friend. Over a nightcap, I told them about my to and fro with the Director-General and said I thought I would have to fight on. The employment lawyer said, 'If you go to tribunal, you don't have to foot the bill for barristers. You can always represent yourself, as you know your case inside out and you can talk. It would be the ultimate David and Goliath. The BBC would hate it.'

The other friend, a businesswoman, said, 'Don't even think of going to tribunal. It's all very well for other women to say they'll be there with you but it'll be two years from now and you'll be on your own by the time you get there.'

The next day, Sam Smethers of the Fawcett Society put the same concern a different way: 'These cases are like a bereavement. Everyone's there for the funeral but then they drift away.'

I was meeting Sam because it was still possible that I would settle my case and I needed a plan for what to do with the back pay. Jennifer and her team at Mishcon had generously worked on my case for no fee, so I had no legal bill to pay and I wanted to help women who were less privileged. Sam and I discussed setting up a service to provide free legal advice for low-paid women who would otherwise have no access to such support. We agreed that the service should be run through the excellent employment lawyers at the legal charity YESS Law.

By now it was Friday. The BBC had sprung a surprise for the weekend, sending a draft settlement agreement to Jennifer with its preferred joint statement attached. I'd never seen a settlement agreement before but Jennifer explained that it is a legally binding contract often used to end a workplace dispute. It waives an individual's rights to make a claim to an employment tribunal or court. The BBC's draft settlement agreement offered me yet more money but still no equality.

That made me angry. I called Tony's office to complain

that this was yet another attempt to buy me off and that I had no intention of signing any legal document. I felt that if the Director-General and I put out a joint statement that should be enough. After all, I believed I had been trustworthy throughout. Jennifer informed the BBC lawyers she had no instructions from her client to settle. In this game of chicken, the action was now frozen for the weekend. But on Saturday I sent another personal email to the Director-General. I have included it here in full as I think it shows how firm you have to be about your objective if you intend to achieve it, and how important it is to frame that win as a victory for your employer too.

Dear Tony,

Apologies for intruding on your weekend but I've been thinking about our win win . . .

After a rather intense week, it might be useful to clarify what the win is for me. It is not a large sum of money . . . I am giving that away. It is not the apology or the admission that I was underpaid for years . . . all of this has been in the public domain for five months. The win for me is the principle of equality, in this case my equality. I realise that the BBC does not acknowledge mine as an equality issue. I respect your sensitivities. But equality is what it means to me. So I can only allow this dispute to be over if the equality point is in the right place in our joint statement and if the money signifies (to me, not to you) parity with my male peers. Without these two points there's no equality and therefore no win for me.

The secondary aspect in which this outcome is a win for me is that it is not a loss. It spares me from the prospect of a long and all-consuming public battle. And it protects the BBC (which I cherish despite everything) from further brand damage. But if this secondary win comes at the expense of my equality, it is a loss in disguise. I am conscious that we are very short of time to get this done. It really has to be next week or a different outcome will gather momentum. My diary is already filling up with appointments with Counsel and EHRC. Being very candid with you to avoid the risk of miscalculations, I have no choice but to notify ACAS in the first week of July and I will feel impelled to announce that publicly along with a full exposition of the reasons why I have felt forced to take this step. My guess is that public pressure will then build and you will want to settle this in the next few weeks. But by then a lot more would have been said about all of this and the win win would look very bruised. Even worse for the BBC, if we go all the way to employment tribunal, this will become the equal pay test case to mark half a century since the Equal Pay Act.

I do understand that it may be difficult to convince everyone involved of the wisdom or necessity of showing greater flexibility. I too have a voice in my head which doesn't want to give an inch. But for the sake of all involved and of the BBC we all serve, it is wise and it is necessary to resolve this. Please give others my assurance that I will handle things in a dignified way. I will avoid opening new wounds or re-opening old ones. But on all matters of substance, I have been as flexible as I can be on a long list of points. Now it's in your hands.

All the best

Carrie

I hoped that, on reading this email, Tony and his legal team would realise that I was mad and bad enough to declare war on them and that I would not give up until I had won. I knew by now that only if they believed the threat of war was real would they make peace.

Being mad and bad is exhausting. That weekend, questions teemed in my head. Where on earth would I find the hundreds of thousands of pounds to fight this to court? Where would I find the energy? In less than a fortnight I'd have to mobilise the sisterhood again and deliver a ringing public battle cry. I had great support from Jennifer and from my close circle of BBC Women, but the weight of a warring future hung heavy.

My dad was worried: 'You didn't ask for my advice, but here it is anyway. Don't take on the BBC,' he warned on the phone.

To take my mind off things, I chatted to Rachel and Daniel, had a drink with a friend, watched a couple of World Cup matches. Monday was quiet until mid-evening, when I got a call to let me know that the Director-General was struggling to get his side to agree to my terms. I'd guessed as much, but I couldn't help him. I had nothing left to concede. As I hung up, I reflected grimly that in this game of chicken I'd now disabled the brakes and jammed the steering. All because I insisted on being equal. Was I absurd? I couldn't tell. At least I'd been consistent and done my best. Now I had to stand back and watch events play out.

At 11:43 on the morning of Tuesday 26 June the other chicken blinked. I got a text message from Phil Harrold. He wanted to come to my house.

First reaction: that's good. No senior executive travels across town in the middle of a working day unless they've got something worth saying. Second reaction ... my house? I looked around. Daniel was sprawled asleep on the settee after a late-night reunion with friends just back from university. The kitchen sink was full of washing-up. The grass hadn't been mown in weeks. Imagine the home of a single parent locked in a long battle with her employer and suffering depression as a result. That's what my house looked like.

In the time it took Phil to travel from central London, I did the bare essentials. I shooed Daniel upstairs, hid the washing-up, straightened cushions, picked up the dog's squeaky toys, swept the front path and turned the sprinkler on. I then sat down and watched as it rhythmically sowed diamonds in the grass, an arc to the right, an arc to the left.

War or peace? The next hour will decide, I thought.

Do you ever have those moments when you hear your fate coming round the corner? A dark car swept up my road and moments later my phone rang.

It was Phil. He was worried that there was a journalist outside my house. I told him if there was, they were nothing to do with me. I thought by now my bosses should have realised that wasn't my style. Phil ventured in. A parody of a parlour game followed in which I gave him a glass of water, my dog gave him a shoe and he gave me a sheet of paper: the latest draft statement from the Director-General.

As soon as I read it, I realised I'd won. The wording still skirted any direct admission that mine was an equal pay case, but the import would be clear to any normal reader. I could live with it. As for the money, the BBC now intended to pay me £373,000. Finally, this was pay parity with the North America Editor. It was a grotesquely large sum for a public service broadcaster to pay any employee and I was relieved to be giving it away. But money can mean different things at different times to different people. To me, at that moment, it meant equality.

Truce transacted, Phil and I talked for a few minutes about the problems of large organisations. As his car swept off, I watched my warring future dissolve. I'd had to make it real for myself in order to believe in it, and now it felt strange to let it go.

The next day was my birthday. I had a third meeting with the Director-General. It's good to be dignified in victory, and having seen how hard Tony Hall had to fight his own side to get this deal through, I did now see it as a win for him as well as for me. It takes courage for any general to climb out of his own trench and cross no man's land to shake hands with a 'partner for peace', who may shoot him on arrival. It takes even more courage if the general in question fears a stray bullet from behind. Tony was overruling all the decision-makers in my complaints process. So, on sitting down in his office, the first thing I said was thank you. Tony replied, 'Carrie, I'm not going to lie, it has been very difficult to get this done. But I'm certain it's the right thing to do.'

We agreed the joint statement would go out two days later. When various people on the executive floor came by to shake my hand, it was an odd feeling. I'd got so used to being a non-person.

From Broadcasting House, I went to Somerset House to meet the brilliant barrister Jane Mulcahy. This was an irony of timing. The BBC is a Goliath that fights with the best legal team money can buy. Playing David may be heroic but it's very risky. Hence meeting Jane. We'd originally intended to talk plans for war but found ourselves celebrating peace instead, and as it was my birthday, we drank pink champagne under magnificent London plane trees on the terrace overlooking the Thames. I liked Jane so much that I almost regretted we weren't going to spend the next two years in a litigation bunker together. I still had a wisp of that warring future in my head. Jane mused, 'Some clients get into fight mode and just don't know how to get out. It's good that you worked out when to stop.'

I told her all I did was doggedly follow the moral compass of a BBC reporter. I showed her my BBC ID pass, which lists our values on the back.

'Trust is the foundation of the BBC: we are independent, impartial and honest,' Jane read aloud, raising her glass to me with a smile.

I then accidentally dropped that pass through a crack in

the terrace decking. Perhaps I shouldn't read more into it than a glass of champagne before lunch, but it seemed like a sign. Shared values lost, trust buried. And as I moved on to a birthday lunch with friends, I imagined my ID pass being dug from the sediment in a few hundred years' time, with curious readers trying to decode a once-mighty civilisation from its stated values. A bitter streak broke through. Why had the BBC put me through a year of hell? Why had it surrendered only at knife-point? Why had it invested untold resources in management time, consultants and lawyers to fight so many good women and prop up so many lies?

'And why won't they accept even now that these are equal pay cases?' I vented at my friends over lunch. Recovery is a crooked journey and all these questions still bubble up to trouble me. But it wasn't the day for it, and my friends just laughed at me for raining on my own parade.

There was still work to do to get this win over the line. I'd always insisted I wouldn't sign a non-disclosure agreement and the BBC didn't ask me to, but Jennifer advised me to sign a standard settlement agreement. Without it the BBC would not have paid up.

So on my birthday afternoon, she sobered me up by going through the nitty-gritty on the phone.

The next day, I focused on my charitable donation. The tax office intended to deduct a few thousand pounds, but there would be £361,000 to get the Equal Pay Advice Service started and contribute to Fawcett's strategic legal work. With my partners in the Fawcett Society and YESS Law, I scrambled to pin down enough of the detail for a press release. Sam Smethers said, 'Women need real pay transparency at work and they need legal advice and support when they believe they have been discriminated against. Our first priority with this money is to help low paid women and those who do not have access to advice.'

For YESS Law, Camilla Palmer, QC, said, 'Our aim at YESS is to try to resolve any disputes without litigation as so many women want to keep their job and maintain their employment relationships whilst also achieving parity. Carrie's donation will assist us and Fawcett in achieving that.'

The only people unhappy about the way I was spending this money seemed to be BBC lawyers.

I could have said, 'It's my money and I'll do what I like with it.'

But winning without fighting is not served by being ungracious. So I reassured Tony's office that I was not planning a vendetta, and in any case most BBC Women had access to legal support via their union. YESS Law were conciliators wherever possible, they did no litigation and had no incentive to push cases towards tribunal. I pointed out that the joint statement attached to the settlement agreement currently carried an outdated version of the Director-General's quote. At the time there was a confetti of different versions flying around the executive ether in W1A and I think this was an honest oversight.

Due to these last-minute alarums, Jennifer was still running circuits with BBC lawyers the following morning, just two hours before the joint statement was due to go out. Then my printer, after uncomplainingly rattling through hundreds of pages of BBC verbiage in the course of this year-long fight, chose to give up just before the signature page of the final settlement agreement. I called Jennifer and she said, 'Don't worry, settlement agreements are always right up to the wire.'

So I crawled out, dust-covered, from under my desk and ran for the bus. On my way into London I sent a flurry of messages to alert those who needed to know what was coming.

My biggest concern was the sisterhood. We now numbered nearly five hundred, and occasional leaks since January had made it impossible to discuss the most sensitive developments with the entire group. We were still good at support, advice and solidarity, but we found it as hard as ever to coordinate strategy. We had hoped that our unions or the regulator would take on that task. But it hadn't happened. I knew everyone would be glad my ordeal was over, but I also knew that as I stepped onto dry land, many were still at sea. Optimists would read my win as a signal that the Director-General wanted equal pay cases resolved. Pessimists would fear the BBC was decapitating the movement by neutralising its ringleaders. I sent the sisterhood a message promising I would not desert the cause just because my personal fight was done.

At 10:50 I careened into Broadcasting House and signed the settlement agreement. At 11 a.m., the BBC published on schedule and without oversights:

Joint statement between Carrie Gracie and Tony Hall, Director-General of the BBC

The BBC and Carrie Gracie have reached an agreement to resolve their differences.

The BBC acknowledges that Carrie was told she would be paid in line with the North America Editor when she took the role of China Editor, and she accepted the role on that understanding. The BBC is committed to the principle of equal pay and acting in accordance with our values. The BBC acknowledges the specific circumstances relating to Carrie's appointment, apologises for underpaying Carrie, and has now put this right. Carrie is donating the full amount received to a charity of her choice.

Carrie has made, and will continue to make, an important contribution to the BBC. During her tenure as China Editor, Carrie delivered reports, analysis and work, that were as valuable as those of the other International Editors in the same period.

Reading these lines again now, I'm reminded how hard I had to battle for the words 'equal pay' and 'as valuable as', not so much with the Director-General but with those who stood behind him in the shadows.

I had one more task to complete. Words to camera. Martine Croxall and Razia Iqbal agreed to stand alongside me. Martine had been with me at all the key moments in my fight, and Razia too was a staunch ally. My advice is always to rehearse words that are deeply felt. I now rehearsed. I was overwrought and on the edge of tears. Razia and Martine heckled me with absurd questions to make me laugh. Eventually it was time to stop clowning. The three of us walked over to the waiting cameras outside the BBC. The statue of George Orwell leaned in to listen, burning cigarette in hand, penetrating gaze. I spoke briefly:

> This is a huge day for me. I love the BBC. It's been my work family for more than thirty years and I want it to be the best. Sometimes families feel the need to shout at each other, but it's always a relief when you can stop shouting.
>
> I'm grateful to the Director-General for helping me resolve this. I do feel he has led from the front today.
>
> In acknowledging the value of my work as China Editor, the BBC has awarded me several years of backdated pay. But for me this was always about the principle and not about the money, so I'm giving all of that money away to help women who need it more than I do.
>
> After all, today at the BBC I can say I am equal. I would like women in workplaces up and down this country to be able to say the same.

The more precious the words you're saying, the more you have to take time to breathe, look your audience in the eye and speak with the conviction you feel. After that, you can walk away and get on with your life.

'All power to you, Carrie. Who's "in development" now?' roared the messages of support from BBC Women. Other colleagues and members of the public joined in on social media:

> Made the BBC a better place.
> Today's suffragette!
> On behalf of women with less power.
> Warrior queen.
> Don't disappear from our screens. We need to be reminded what courage looks like.

Not everyone cheered. Some members of the public were understandably shocked at the amount of public money involved. Others seemed angry that I gave it away. One *Sunday Times* columnist painted me as a tearful, virtue-signalling nonentity.

You can't please all of the people all of the time. It was a gorgeous summer day. I walked down to Covent Garden to give Jennifer a hug. On the way, my dad phoned, struggling through tears of relief. My sister texted to say she and her daughters were proud. I missed my mum.

It had taken a year to get equal. Nothing compared to what Lilly Ledbetter endured at Goodyear Tires in the US, and nothing compared to the ordeal of the Dagenham workers, speech therapists or fish packers in the UK. Barely a blink of the eye set alongside the centuries that women have been struggling for basic rights. But it had been a long enough year in my life and I hoped that playing much of it out in the glare of publicity had helped to alert other women that they must find out the facts on pay, think hard about their value and feel more confident about asserting it.

When I got to Covent Garden, I discovered it was Jennifer's birthday and she was having lunch with her mum. I posted a photo of the three of us, dedicating the equal pay win to 'my mum, Jennifer's mum and mothers and daughters everywhere'.

I went home for a celebratory drink with Rachel and Daniel, and promised myself that after a good night's sleep, I would get grounded again with a day of household chores. On the evening news, the BBC's Media Editor Amol Rajan was asked whether the outcome was 'a victory for Carrie Gracie'.

He said it was both victory and vindication, adding that the significance of my story went far wider than one workplace. 'This victory will give succour and encouragement to other people across the generations and across the gender divide who are also fighting for equality at work.'

I hope so. I got equal in the end only thanks to all the women and men who put their shoulder to the wheel to help me. Together we move the world forward one case at a time: 'Deeds not words.'

EPILOGUE

ARE WE NEARLY THERE YET?

=

2 July 2018

I began six months of unpaid leave and started to write this book. Whenever I felt daunted by the challenges of writing, Rachel and Daniel reminded me that fighting the BBC all the way to employment tribunal would have been worse.

11 July 2018

The BBC published its second annual list of those paid above £150,000. All ten of the highest-paid presenters were men, and only two out of the top twenty high earners were women.

14 July 2018

My lawyer, Jennifer Millins, gave birth to baby Arlo. I'm confident he's going to be a feminist when he's old enough to sign up. After all, he was there throughout.

20 August 2018

New Zealand infrastructure consultancy WSP Opus closed unexplained pay gaps for fifty-five women. Managing Director

Ian Blair said, 'It's 2018 and we should be rewarding people fairly for doing the same work at the same level of performance in like-for-like roles . . . I have two sons and two daughters and cannot imagine living in a world – or being part of a leadership team of an organisation – where I have to tell my daughters that they get paid less than their brothers because of their gender. That's unacceptable.'

5 September 2018

BBC Women submitted a dossier of equal pay cases to the Equality and Human Rights Commission.

11 September 2018

The BBC's Deputy Director-General Anne Bulford told a parliamentary committee that only seven equal pay grievances at the BBC had resulted in an increased pay offer. Nearly seventy grievances remained outstanding, some after more than a year.

24 September 2018

The New Zealand Prime Minister Jacinda Ardern became the first world leader to attend the UN General Assembly with a baby. Her partner, Clarke Gayford, was also there as their child's primary carer.

11 October 2018

The British government launched a consultation on whether to introduce mandatory reporting of ethnicity pay gaps.

23 October 2018

Eight thousand council workers in Glasgow mounted the biggest equal pay strike in UK history after a dispute lasting twelve years.

25 October 2018

The UK Parliament's Digital, Culture, Media and Sport Committee reported that the BBC was failing to live up to its duty under the Equality Act to advance equal opportunities for women. It said evidence suggests women working at the BBC in comparable jobs to men earn far less and the BBC's new pay reforms have serious shortcomings.

BBC Women issued a statement thanking the Committee for 'clearly spelling out the experience of so many women seeking equal pay at the BBC: intractable processes, lack of transparency, evasive tactics and no genuinely independent oversight'.

I was personally grateful to the Committee for noting: 'Ms Gracie deserves great credit for using her protracted and distressing ordeal to make points of principle for other women.'

1 November 2018

Google staff in offices across the world walked out to protest the company's treatment of women.

4 November 2018

My dear friend Jeremy Heywood died. A dedicated feminist to the end and an example to all in public service.

9 November 2018

On the eve of Equal Pay Day, the day in the year when women start to work for free, the Equal Pay Advice Service was launched with my backdated pay and other donations via the Equal Pay Fund. The Service now offers free legal support to low-paid women who face pay discrimination. It is run by the UK's leading gender equality charity, the Fawcett Society, with advice delivered by the legal charity YESS Law.

10 November 2018

Stella Creasy, MP, issued invitations for a party in London to celebrate the closing of the global gender pay gap, with guests asked to save a date in the year 2235.

16 November 2018

The former HR Director of the Co-operative Group, Sam Walker, won her claim for equal pay and unfair dismissal. The Co-op said it would appeal.

7 December 2018

The BBC published an investigation into pay discrimination against BAME academic staff and found that at top universities black teaching staff earn on average 26 per cent less than their white colleagues, and that black teaching staff who were also women fare even worse.

13 December 2018

The Fawcett Society hosted a speech by the President of the UK

Supreme Court, Baroness Hale, to mark the centenary of the Representation of the People Act. Asked what women could do to turn their right to equal pay into reality, Baroness Hale said, 'Women must bring cases.'

16 December 2018

Some of the BBC's highest-paid executives received annual pay rises of up to £75,000, or 30 per cent. The BBC said: 'Where people take on significant extra responsibilities or make an exceptional contribution to the business, it's recognised in their pay, just like at other organisations.'

21 December 2018

I completed the first draft of this book.

7 January 2019

I returned to my old role as a presenter for the BBC News Channel. I felt well again, and happy to be back at work among colleagues I like and respect. The BBC had not appointed a new China Editor.

10 January 2019

BBC presenter Dianne Oxberry died. Dianne was a committed and generous member of BBC Women. Of her own equal pay fight she once wrote, 'They made it difficult at every step.' And she warned other women in the group, 'Don't underestimate what this will do to you.'

17 January 2019

Glasgow City Council agreed in principle to payments to resolve historic equal pay claims. Stefan Cross, the lawyer representing many of the claimants, said: 'Since the strike there has been real and constructive negotiation.'

31 January 2019

Supermarket giant Asda lost another appeal, this time at the Court of Appeal. The decision means that lower-paid shop staff, who are mostly women, can compare themselves with higher-paid warehouse workers, who are mostly men – unless Asda appeals to the Supreme Court and wins there.

8 March 2019

In a tweet titled 'Equal pay for equal play', sports company Adidas announced that the players it sponsors on the winning 2019 FIFA Women's World Cup team will receive the same performance bonus as their male counterparts. The announcement followed news that the US women's soccer team was suing their federation over gender discrimination with all 28 members of the squad named as plaintiffs in federal court.

12 March 2019

The city of Berlin offered women tickets on public transport at a 21 per cent discount to highlight the gender pay gap. The operator BVG apologised to any men who felt discriminated against but added, 'Who apologises to the women who on average earn 21 percent less?'

12 March 2019

The Equality and Human Rights Commission launched a formal investigation into pay discrimination at the BBC, saying it suspected some women at the organisation 'have not received equal pay for equal work'. The EHRC said it hoped to conclude its investigation by the end of the year.

27 March 2019

Vice Media agreed to pay $1.87 million to settle an equal pay class action. The claimants had alleged that the company relied on prior salaries and perpetuated pay gaps as women moved within the organisation.

3 April 2019

Drinks giant Diageo UK announced it would allow men and women fifty-two weeks of parental leave, with the first twenty-six weeks fully paid. Mairéad Nayager, chief HR officer said: 'True gender equality in the working world requires fundamental changes to a broad range of working practices, including a shake-up of the policies and cultural norms around parental leave.'

5 April 2019

The second year of gender pay gap reporting in the UK showed that fewer than half the country's biggest employers had made progress on narrowing their gender pay gaps.

24 April 2019

The BBC entered itself for an award in the 'leading transformation' category at the HR Excellence Awards.

22 May 2019

A manager in BBC News, Karen Martin, wrote to hundreds of colleagues explaining that she would not take up an appointment as deputy editor of the radio newsroom because the BBC had refused to pay her equally with a man who was appointed to the same role. The BBC acknowledged that the roles were equal, but insisted that a difference in experience justified a pay disparity. Many BBC staff, men as well as women, disagreed. Several hundred signed a protest letter to the Director-General, making the point that women can never catch up if historical inequalities in promotion and pay are not corrected.

29 May 2020

The fiftieth anniversary of the UK's Equal Pay Act.

=

Dear reader, wherever you are in the world, wherever you are in life, please put your shoulder to this wheel and push – in whatever way you can.

ADVICE

=

I t is hard to give advice. Every individual and every workplace is different, and the way we respond to workplace inequality may be different at different stages of our lives. But here are my suggestions, divided into three lists, for employers, men and women respectively. I start with employers because they have the greatest power to make change fast.

Advice for employers

On pay

- Run a pay structure with clear and consistent rules. Do not rely on the barriers to justice which may protect a discriminatory pay structure.
- Keep pay under regular review. Discrimination can creep in unintentionally.
- Make equal pay your default principle. Instead of finding 'material factor' defences for paying women less for equal work, pay them the same unless the justification for paying them less makes sense to them too.
- Treat sceptically any defence of pay disparities on grounds of 'experience'. Your recruitment, promotion and pay structure may have gender biases that have cumulatively advantaged some employees and disadvantaged others over years or even decades. If experience has not been an equal opportunity, it cannot now

justify pay gaps between women and men who are doing the same work. Ask your legal team whether such a defence would be upheld by an employment tribunal. If the honest answer is no, then it's unethical to deploy it.

- Likewise, be careful about using a 'market' defence to justify inequality. It may not wash in a tribunal.
- Use the data at your fingertips to track all departures from pay parity. Measure what you intend to manage. Are men clumped at the top of a given pay band and women at the bottom? Are men getting big bonuses and women small ones? If so, ask your pay decision-makers why. Establish objective, transparent criteria for awarding bonuses.
- Explain to women what is negotiable around pay.
- If you're not confident about whether your pay structure is compliant with equality legislation, commission an independent equal pay audit and task it with identifying problems rather than giving you full marks.
- Avoid pay secrecy clauses. Promote transparency around pay. Explain the benefits of a workplace where everyone knows what is valued and sees that what is valued gets rewarded fairly.

On bias

- Keep signalling that you're committed to a workplace which values women equally. Talk openly about the ways you are trying to avoid bias.
- Demand monitoring and feedback from your managers. In progression and pay decisions, avoid practices that embed bias through advantaging 'Reference Man', and avoid confusing confidence with competence. Measure carefully who delivers what value.
- De-bias recruitment and progression by making your procedures as 'blind' as possible. The EHRC website has much advice on

anonymised applications, structured interviews and other ways to avoid the Mark/Elizabeth-type problems I mention on page 47.

- Tackle the 'motherhood penalty'. Don't penalise flexible working. Instead set an example by working flexibly yourself or inviting other senior staff to do so. Engage with women about how to avoid imposing a 'motherhood penalty' on progression and pay.
- Open up senior roles to flexible and part-time working.
- Enhance shared parental leave pay to the same level as enhanced maternity leave pay.
- Encourage men in your workforce to feel proud of belonging to an organisation that takes gender equality seriously. Support them to be advocates for equality at work. Explain why a diversity agenda cannot mean promoting women while paying them less.

On being challenged

- Do not treat women who raise equal pay issues as the enemy. They are often the canaries in your coal mine. Do not victimise them but listen, and listen particularly hard to those who have become so frustrated that they have resigned.
- Run your complaints process in good faith. Do not blank complainants. Correct injustice fast. If equal pay complaints do go to grievance, do not abuse your advantage in information and resources to defeat your employee. Wherever you feel an employment tribunal would uphold the grievance, uphold it immediately to make the point that you're serious about righting wrongs. If you don't trust your internal process to judge this impartially, appoint an outsider to adjudicate.
- Allow employees access to audio recordings of their own grievance hearings.
- If you leave the actions on this list too late and suddenly face pent-up anger from a large group of female employees, act swiftly before that anger has time to harden into collective action.

- When you publish your gender pay gap, don't resort to the defence that the gap is only there because more men do more senior jobs. Set a target for narrowing the gap and publish a clear plan for how you intend to reach that target.
- Communicate with your staff and show them that you value them.

Advice for men

- If you believe in equal pay for women, do something to show it. If you suspect a female colleague is earning less for doing similar work, alert her.
- If a female colleague is struggling to win equal pay, and asks for your pay and bonus details, be generous with the information. (In law, this is a 'protected disclosure', which means that even if you have signed a pay secrecy clause in your employment contract, such a clause is unenforceable by your employer.)
- If a female colleague doing the same or similar work asks you to attend a pay hearing with her, do so. Equal pay is a snakes and ladders board. A male comparator can help a woman move from square 9 to square 90 by saying her work is equal.
- Explain to other male colleagues that there are often stubborn structural impediments to equal pay.
- Encourage your employer to introduce a gender-equal policy on parental leave and pay for parental leave.
- If and when you become a parent, take your leave, and support your partner if she wants to retain her relationship with the workplace.
- Press your employer to make flexible working a meaningful choice for women and men.

Advice for women

Practical

- Acknowledge any inhibitions you have in talking about pay. Start – gently – to overcome them. It may be easier to open the conversation with friends and family than with colleagues, especially if yours is a workplace with taboos around the subject. When you do move to talking about pay with male colleagues, begin with someone who is leaving or has just left the organisation.
- Be patient with those who don't want to discuss their pay. Not all women want to talk about money either. Set an example and others may follow.
- Remind yourself that every pay negotiation counts. From the first job in your working life to the last, try to represent yourself to the best of your ability. Do your research. Ask the employer for the relevant pay range. Discuss it with a recruitment agency or visit a website like Glassdoor. Talk to male colleagues in the same organisation or in comparable workplaces. Don't forget to ask about bonuses and other benefits.
- In any pay discussion, take notes at the time, or immediately afterwards. Share your notes the same day, and forward the message to your private email address.
- Give any new boss an up-to-date copy of your CV so they know what skills you offer and what you might take to a rival.
- Take performance evaluations seriously. Keep a running list of the things you do that might otherwise go unnoticed and unmentioned but add value nonetheless.
- Discuss these with your boss and check whether they are reflected in your pay. Talk about how you'd like to advance. If you have a specific pay rise in mind, say so. Support your case with as much data as you can muster. Don't expect an answer on the spot. Allow your boss time to think and respond.

- If this conversation doesn't initially go according to plan, don't be impatient. Be proud of yourself for making a start.

Strategic

- If you work for a large UK employer, read its gender pay gap report and its ethnicity pay gap report. Read those of similar organisations. Note whether they have a concrete plan to narrow or close these gaps. Offer ideas. Observe how your ideas are received.
- If and when you do raise the issue of unequal pay with your employer, choose your moment carefully. Remember that even Oprah didn't fight back when first a victim. Winning demands the self-discipline to fight only when you're ready.
- Avoid raising a formal grievance except in the circumstances I mention on page 93.
- Take a look at the people who run your organisation. Do they look like you? If not, does anyone in the management chain look like you – whether on gender, ethnicity, sexual orientation, disability, age or socioeconomic class? If 'success' in your organisation never looks like you, does your organisation seem to notice or care? Is it walking the talk on diversity? If not, think about moving on.
- Use your experience of gender discrimination to sensitise you to other forms of structural disadvantage. There may well be people in your workplace who face discrimination on grounds of ethnicity, disability, age, class or sexual orientation.
- If your organisation suffers from entrenched patterns of discrimination, but you feel you can't move at present, think long-term. Ask yourself what a plan B would look like and when and how you might be able to put it into effect.
- Don't ever allow yourself to internalise disrespect or the biased evaluation of a discriminating employer. Remember the identical performance of Elizabeth and Mark and the gendered response

of many employers. The world has many bosses who are blind to their own bias and to the bias entrenched in their pay structure. If you can't yet speak your truth to your boss, speak it to yourself, your colleagues, your friends or your family. Get it into the world.

- If and when you make an equal pay complaint, be ready for a boss to suddenly find your performance wanting, or suddenly declare you 'in development'. Try not to take this personally. Remember that when it comes to demanding gender equality, you are in a long line which stretches back to the early feminists and forward to your granddaughters. Grasp your moment in history. If your employer says the man at the next desk is worth more than you, hold your ground and suggest that they prove it.

- Press your MP for new legislation to make employers and not women responsible for enforcing equal pay law, to strengthen regulation, to impose meaningful penalties.

- Take control. Aspire to run your workplace, your union or your government. Run your own company and run it equal.

Strong

- If you intend to make change from the inside, sister up. For support, advice, information exchange, self-esteem, sanity, safety from victimisation and strength in numbers, solidarity is a vital force multiplier. Start by noticing the talent and work of other women. Stay alive to the ways that unacknowledged competition can erode female solidarity.

- If you are not in a union, join one.

- Talk to female colleagues about the structural factors that underpin gender pay in your workplace, from unconscious bias to policies on parental leave and flexible working.

- If your workplace doesn't have many women, or if its culture is very competitive, reach out to other women in an occupational network or a union. Find ways to be less alone.

- If you start a sisterhood on a messaging app, keep it safe, legal and polite. But don't be afraid of disagreement. Arguments within safe boundaries can build trust and make you stronger.
- If your confidence falters, bring to mind a powerful woman: Serena Williams, Millicent Fawcett, Emmeline Pankhurst, Taylor Swift, Rosa Parks.
- Know that feminism is a long game. It was here when you were born and it will be here when you die. You can only play your part. So don't get rigid in warrior pose and don't let fighting swallow your life. Laugh at it all whenever possible. Laughter makes you brave.

RESOURCES

=

In a matter of minutes

Watch the capuchin throw her cucumber to remind yourself that even monkeys abhor injustice
https://www.youtube.com/watch?v=L2ui97YPPsg

Watch the sweet jar redistribution to see that children understand equal pay
https://www.youtube.com/watch?v=snUE2jm_nFA

Start identifying your own inbuilt biases by taking a few short tests
https://implicit.harvard.edu/implicit/

Key resources

https://www.equalityhumanrights.com/en

The Equality and Human Rights Commission website is a rich source of information and advice for women and their employers alike.

http://www.acas.org.uk/index.aspx?articleid=1461

The website of the Advisory, Conciliation and Arbitration Service has a lot of information about navigating the workplace. For those in the UK, Acas can also help you with specific advice on grievances and equal pay claims through its online help tool and its telephone helpline.

https://www.fawcettsociety.org.uk/equal-pay-advice-service

The Fawcett Society campaigns for gender equality every day in every way. And since November 2018, it has been working in partnership with legal charity YESS Law to offer free legal support to women on lower incomes facing unequal pay.

Makes you think

I've learned so much from other writers. Some books I've already mentioned, but here are more that broadened my mind:

Slay In Your Lane: The Black Girl Bible by Yomi Adegoke and Elizabeth Uviebinené

The Guilty Feminist: From Our Noble Goals to Our Worst Hypocrisies by Deborah Frances-White

Equal Pay: Law and Practice by Daphne Romney, QC

Why I'm No Longer Talking to White People About Race by Reni Eddo-Lodge

Work Like a Woman: A Manifesto for Change by Mary Portas

Brit(ish): On Race, Identity and Belonging by Afua Hirsch

Grace and Grit: My Fight for Equal Pay and Fairness at Goodyear and Beyond by Lilly Ledbetter

And because it's worth remembering that we stand on the shoulders of giants:

A Vindication of the Rights of Woman by Mary Wollstonecraft

China

To close this list of resources, something personal. An equal pay battle is all about the value of a woman's work, and I fought for my China work. At the point of resigning my post as BBC China Editor, I created a website with some of my favourite pieces. It also celebrates the great BBC team who made that work with me.

https://carriegracie.com/

ACKNOWLEDGEMENTS

=

I've never written a book before and I found it a daunting task. I don't think I'd have finished at all without the steady encouragement and advice of my brilliant editor Sarah Savitt or without the wisdom and good humour of my literary agent Rebecca Carter. In their different ways, they gave me the confidence to go on at the same time as challenging me to make the book better. That's skill.

Many other great people read the manuscript in draft form. Their insights, suggestions and questions improved it immeasurably. Some readers were old friends, like Cathy Sampson, Maria Byrne, James Gordon, Duncan Thomas, Jackie Kemp, Lucy Kynge and Katharine Hodgson. Others were friends I'd made during the equal pay struggle: Jennifer Millins, Sam Smethers, Sam Walker, Emma Webster, Rosie Campbell, Laura Jones. Several BBC Women read the text, including Martine Croxall, Razia Iqbal, Kriszta Satori and Kate Silverton. All of my readers in draft were generous with their expertise on myriad things, from pinning down the timeline to narrative structure and advice for readers.

When I started out on this journey, I knew far more about Chinese security legislation than I did about UK equality legislation. For my understanding of equal pay law and how it operates, the list of those who helped me is also long. Special mention must go to Camilla Palmer, QC, Stefan Cross, Daphne Romney, QC, and Linda Wong. Sheila Wild illuminated my understanding of the history of equal pay. Margaret Heffernan was invaluable on business culture. Economists Paul Seabright and Gabriel Ulyssea explained equal pay and labour markets. Sir David Spiegelhalter and Nigel Marriott helped me out of the maze on statistics.

This book could not have been written unless I'd won my own equal pay fight. Jennifer Millins and Hannah Laszlo at Mishcon de Reya played no small part in that! Jane Mulcahy, QC, and Dr George Molyneaux at Blackstone Chambers were there at critical moments. Michelle Stanistreet and Roy Mincoff of the NUJ were unstinting with their support. I can't name all the BBC Women who helped me, but they know who they are. I would not have won my case without them.

There are many people in this story who are shy of taking credit, and that's how it must remain. And on the subject of unsung heroes, I would also like to thank all the women and men who wrote to me, posted support on social media or stopped me in the street. You helped me more than you can know. You gave me faith that we were not alone and that change was possible.

In many ways, I have found the past two years a difficult journey. But without the equal pay fight I would not have had the opportunity to meet some very great people. So I find myself unable to regret it.

I think I do owe some thanks to my bosses at the BBC. There is much we don't agree on and some passages in this book will make hard reading for them. But they have a tough job trying to modernise a venerable national institution for turbulent times. Gender pay is just one of many fronts on which they find themselves fighting. In some workplaces, bosses victimise women who raise equal pay problems. This has not happened to me. Tony Hall told Parliament I'd done a brave thing in speaking out. Fran Unsworth apologised to me for BBC failings. Jonathan Munro put me forward as RTS Specialist Journalist of the Year even as I was mounting an equal pay grievance. And James Harding publicly commended me for turning the same determined gaze on gender pay that I had turned on China: 'She calls it as she sees it.' I am grateful to all of them for keeping the argument separate from the person making it.

Returning to my publisher, I would like to thank copy-editor Zoe Gullen for her subtle and penetrating eye and her scrupulous attention to detail. Duncan Spilling designed the awesome jacket for the book and Marie Hrynczak ensured there were pages in between. I am also very blessed in the publicity team of Susan de Soissons, Grace Vincent and Kimberley Nyamhondera. Editor Ailah Ahmed picked up seamlessly when Sarah Savitt went on maternity leave, and piloted the book through the last stages to publication: a privilege to have not just one great editor but two. This book might not have reached shore without the wise counsel of legal director Maddie Mogford or the steady commitment of Clare Smith and Little, Brown's managing director Charlie King.

My biggest thanks go to my close friends, work colleagues and family for love and sanity. The longest march has been for my children, Rachel and Daniel. They put up with a lot during the living of this story, and then they put up with a lot all over again during the writing of it. But you'll be relieved to read that none of it has dented their sense of humour.

Thank you, Rachel. Thank you, Daniel.

NOTES

=

Preface

1   *'Trust is the foundation of the BBC . . .'*: Editorial Guidelines,
    https://www.bbc.co.uk/editorialguidelines/guidelines.

Prologue: Up Over the Top

7   *a suspiciously large element that is 'unexplained'*: International
    Labour Organization, *Global Wage Report 2018/19: What lies
    behind gender pay gaps* (Geneva: International Labour Office,
    2018), https://www.ilo.org/wcmsp5/groups/public/---dgreports/---
    dcomm/---publ/documents/publication/wcms_650553.pdf.

7   *discrimination accounted for a full 38 per cent*: 'Why Australian
    women are still being paid less than men', KPMG media release,
    27 October 2016, https://home.kpmg/au/en/home/media/press-
    releases/2016/10/economics-gender-pay-gap-28-oct-2016.html.

7   *outright gender discrimination at 38 per cent*: Francine D. Blau and
    Lawrence M. Kahn, 'The gender wage gap: extent, trends, and
    explanations', NBER Working Paper No. 21913, January 2016,
    https://www.nber.org/papers/w21913.

8   *only six countries have legislation*: 'Women, business and the
    law 2019: a decade of reform' (Washington DC: World Bank
    Group, 2019), https://openknowledge.worldbank.org/bitstream/
    handle/10986/31327/WBL2019.pdf/.

8   *an average woman will make nearly $600,000 less*: Chris Wilson,
    'Just how bad is the gender pay gap? Brutal, when you look at a
    lifetime of work', *Time*, 2 April 2019, http://time.com/5562269/
    equal-pay-day-women-men-lifetime-wages/.

8   *women receive nearly 40 per cent less from pensions*: 'Tackling the
    gender pension gap', Prospect, https://www.prospect.org.uk/help-
    at-work/pensions-retirement/pension-gender-pay-gap.

8   *companies with strong female leadership*: CS Gender 3000, Credit
    Suisse, 2014.

8   *In 2015 one major study estimated*: Jonathan Woetzel et al., *The*

Power of Parity: How Advancing Women's Equality Can Add $12 Trillion to Global Growth, McKinsey Global Institute report, September 2015, https://www.mckinsey.com/~/media/McKinsey/ Featured%20Insights/Employment%20and%20Growth/ How%20advancing%20womens%20equality%20can%20 add%2012%20trillion%20to%20global%20growth/MGI%20 Power%20of%20parity_Full%20report_September%202015. ashx.

8–9 *'In a "full potential" scenario ...'*: Ibid.

9 *global gender economic parity was 202 years off*: World Economic Forum, *Insight Report: The Global Gender Pay Gap Report 2018* (Geneva: World Economic Forum, 2018), http://www3.weforum. org/docs/WEF_GGGR_2018.pdf.

9 *'The overall picture is that gender equality has stalled'*: Quoted in Rupert Neate, 'Global pay gap will take 202 years to close, says World Economic Forum', *Guardian*, 18 December 2018, https:// www.theguardian.com/world/2018/dec/18/global-gender-pay-gap- will-take-202-years-to-close-says-world-economic-forum.

Chapter 1: Get Real

17 *this pay list said the North America Editor was earning*: 'BBC pay: How much do its stars earn?', BBC News, 19 July 2017, https:// www.bbc.co.uk/news/entertainment-arts-40653861.

18 *'It's complicated ...'*: Quoted in Jane Martinson, 'The road to gender parity in BBC, paved with bad intentions', *Guardian*, 19 July 2017, https://www.theguardian.com/media/2017/jul/19/the- road-to-gender-parity-in-bbc-pay-paved-with-bad-intentions.

18 *'I'm looking forward to presenting @BBCWomansHour ...'*: @ janegarvey1, 11:34 p.m., 18 July 2017, https://twitter.com/ janegarvey1/status/887561218441039874?lang=en.

18 *'We've seen the way the BBC is paying women less ...'*: Quoted in 'BBC pay: Male stars earn more than female talent', BBC News, 19 July 2017, https://www.bbc.co.uk/news/entertainment- arts-40661179.

18 *'It is very important that the lid ...'*: Quoted in Rebecca Flood, '"Pay women more!" Theresa May condemns BBC as she wades into gender pay gap row', *Daily Express*, 19 July 2017, https:// www.express.co.uk/news/uk/830631/Theresa-May-BBC-pay-gap- gender-row-discrimination-equality.

18–19 *'How has this situation arisen at the BBC ...'*: Quoted in 'BBC women let the gender pay gap happen, government adviser says', BBC News, 27 July 2017, https://www.bbc.co.uk/news/ uk-40744426.

21 *'On gender and diversity, the BBC . . .'*: Quoted in Katie Scott,
    'BBC spends £193.6m on talent pay bill', employeebenefits.co.uk,
    19 July 2017, https://www.employeebenefits.co.uk/issues/july-
    online-2017/bbc-spends-193-6m-talent/.

21 *'As the UK's largest broadcaster . . .'*: 'Diversity of UK television
    industry revealed', Ofcom media release, 14 September 2017,
    https://www.ofcom.org.uk/about-ofcom/latest/media/media-
    releases/2017/diversity-uk-television-industry.

21 *In one survey, 83 per cent of respondents*: Ian Griggs, 'Public does
    not understand BBC's reasons for top earnings or gender pay gap,
    survey finds', *PRWeek*, 26 July 2017, https://www.prweek.com/
    article/1440318/public-does-not-understand-bbcs-reasons-top-
    earnings-gender-pay-gap-survey-finds.

22 *'If it's happened to us . . .'*: @janegarvey1, 3:15 a.m.,
    6 September 2017, https://twitter.com/janegarvey1/
    status/905373961705443328.

22 *a letter signed by forty-four of the BBC's most senior on-air women*:
    'Female BBC stars' letter to Tony Hall demanding equal pay
    in full', *Telegraph*, 22 July 2017, https://www.telegraph.co.uk/
    news/2017/07/22/female-bbc-stars-letter-demanding-equal-pay-
    tony-hall-full/.

24 *'Across the BBC, our provisional figures show . . .'*: Quoted in Jessica
    Elgot, 'Director-General says he hopes BBC can close gender
    pay gap before 2020', *Observer*, 23 July 2017, https://www.
    theguardian.com/society/2017/jul/23/director-general-says-he-
    wants-bbc-at-forefront-of-change-on-equal-pay.

25 *'1970: Equal Pay Act. 2010: Equality Act . . .'*: @clarebalding, 12:44
    a.m., 23 July 2017, https://twitter.com/clarebalding/status/889028
    506314788864?lang=en.

26 *'incandescent with rage'*: Sarah Montague, 'Sarah Montague on
    her gender pay gap: I'm furious at being paid less than men at the
    BBC', *Sunday Times*, 8 April 2018, https://www.thetimes.co.uk/
    article/sarah-montague-on-her-gender-pay-gap-im-furious-about-
    being-paid-less-than-men-at-the-bbc-t9vkfjqk0.

26 *'as though bosses had naked pictures of you . . .'*: Quoted in
    NUJ briefing to the DCMS session on pay at the BBC, 31
    January 2018, http://data.parliament.uk/writtenevidence/
    committeeevidence.svc/evidencedocument/digital-culture-media-
    and-sport-committee/bbc-pay/written/77588.html.

26 *'It's difficult for everybody, but . . .'*: 'BBC pay: Anita Rani
    "disappointed" by race and class gap', BBC News, 4 August 2017,
    https://www.bbc.co.uk/news/entertainment-arts-40824357.

26 *'Being underpaid in relation to your peers . . .'*: Margaret Heffernan,
    'How I demanded – and won – equal pay', *Financial Times*, 30

July 2017, https://www.ft.com/content/6277d252-7048-11e7-93ff-99f383b09ff9.

36 *In the UK, people are much more willing*: Zachary Davies Boren, 'Talking about money is Britain's last taboo', *Independent*, 19 September 2015, https://www.independent.co.uk/news/science/talking-about-money-is-britains-last-taboo-10508902.html.

36 *But recent research suggests*: 'Fawcett launches equal pay advice service as research reveals 1 in 3 workers are unaware pay discrimination is illegal', Fawcett Society press release, 9 November 2018, https://www.fawcettsociety.org.uk/news/fawcett-launches-equal-pay-advice-service-as-research-reveals-1-in-3-workers-are-unaware-of-rights

36 *'Pay discrimination is able to thrive . . .'*: Quoted in ibid.

38–9 *'The cycles of poverty, discrimination and sexism . . .'*: Serena Williams, 'Serena Williams: How black women can close the pay gap', Fortune.com, 31 July 2017, http://fortune.com/2017/07/31/serena-williams-black-women-equal-pay/.

Chapter 2: Stop, Think

45 *an experiment in Norway*: 'What do these kids understand that your boss doesn't?', Finansforbundet, https://www.facebook.com/watch/?v=10156793637468273.

46 *'It is difficult to get a man . . .'*: Upton Sinclair, *I, Candidate for Governor: And How I Got Licked* (1934)

47 *In an illuminating study*: Dr Christopher Begeny, Professor Michelle Ryan et al., 'Gender discrimination in the veterinary profession: A brief report of the BVA Employers' Study 2018', BVA Public Affairs, November 2018. https://www.bva.co.uk/uploadedFiles/Content/News,_campaigns_and_policies/Policies/Future_of_the_profession/Gender%20discrimination%20in%20the%20vet%20profession.%20BVA%20workforce%20report%20Nov%202018.pdf.

48 *One labour market study found*: Valentina Di Stasio and Anthony Heath, 'Are employers in Britain discriminating against ethnic minorities? Summary of findings from the GEMM project', GEMM project briefing note, January 2019, http://csi.nuff.ox.ac.uk/wp-content/uploads/2019/01/Are-employers-in-Britain-discriminating-against-ethnic-minorities_final.pdf.

49 *black women of African descent have seen virtually no progress*: 'Many minority ethnic women "left behind" by pay gap progress', Fawcett Society press release, 6 March 2017, https://www.fawcettsociety.org.uk/news/minority-ethnic-women-left-behind-pay-gap-progress.

49 *'They justified their decisions . . .'*: Iris Bohnet, *What Works: Gender Equality by Design* (Cambridge, MA: The Belknap Press of Harvard University Press, 2016).

49 *management students were asked to evaluate*: Kathleen L. McGinn and Nicole Tempest, 'Heidi Roizen', Harvard Business School Case Collection, January 2000 (revised April 2010), http://www.hbs.edu/faculty/Pages/item.aspx?num=26880.

49–50 *'What is celebrated as entrepreneurship . . .'*: Bohnet, *What Works*, p. 22.

50 *'Not only did employers counter . . .'*: Ibid.

50 *the evidence suggests people who don't press for better pay*: See Linda Babcock and Sara Laschever, *Women Don't Ask: The High Cost of Avoiding Negotiation – and Positive Strategies for Change* (New York: Bantam, 2003).

50 *When the Sony hack happened . . .*: Jennifer Lawrence, 'Jennifer Lawrence: "Why do I make less than my male co-stars?"', Lenny Letter, 13 October 2015, https://www.lennyletter.com/story/jennifer-lawrence-why-do-i-make-less-than-my-male-costars.

50 *even women who ask mostly still don't get*: Benjamin Artz, Amanda H. Goodall and Andrew J. Oswald, 'Do women ask?', *Industrial Relations*, 57:4 (9 May 2018), https://onlinelibrary.wiley.com/doi/abs/10.1111/irel.12214.

51 *'In extreme cases . . .'*: Bohnet, *What Works*.

51 *a study of American MBA graduates*: Hannah Riley Bowles, Linda Babcock, and Kathleen L. McGinn, 'Constraints and triggers: situational mechanics of gender in negotiation', *Journal of Personality and Social Psychology*, 89:6 (2005), 951–65, https://projects.iq.harvard.edu/files/hbowles/files/situational_mechanics.pdf.

51–2 *'Historically, in my experience . . .'*: Hannah Hope, '"Women are timid": Piers Morgan blames gender pay gap on women being "scared" to ask their bosses for salary increases', *Sun*, 26 February 2018, https://www.thesun.co.uk/tvandshowbiz/5678314/piers-morgan-timid-women-gender-pay-gap/.

52 *a study of US bankers*: Fiona Greig, 'Propensity to negotiate and career advancement: evidence from an investment bank that women are on a "slow elevator"', *Negotiation Journal*, 24 (2008), https://onlinelibrary.wiley.com/doi/abs/10.1111/j.1571-9979.2008.00200.x.

52 *'because we (people in general) . . .'*: Tomas Chamorro-Premuzic, 'Why do so many incompetent men become leaders?', *Harvard Business Review*, 22 August 2013, https://hbr.org/2013/08/why-do-so-many-incompetent-men.

53 *The more people know*: Dave Smith, 'Most people have no idea

whether they're paid fairly', *Harvard Business Review*, December 2015, https://hbr.org/2015/10/most-people-have-no-idea-whether-theyre-paid-fairly.

54   *I recall being instructed . . .*: Robin Allen, QC, 'The oldest problem: Establishing equal work', Second Hamlyn Lecture 2018 in the series 'Why does equality seem so difficult?'

54   *'It's not possible to know . . .'*: 'What is equal pay?', EHRC, https://www.equalityhumanrights.com/en/advice-and-guidance/what-equal-pay.

55   *'We, at the Ministry for Women . . .'*: 'New research identifies causes of gender pay gap', Ministry for Women, 7 March 2019, https://women.govt.nz/news/new-research-identifies-causes-gender-pay-gap.

55   *'the unexplained element should not be interpreted . . .'*: 'Understanding the gender pay gap in the UK', ONS release, 17 January 2018, https://www.ons.gov.uk/employmentandlabourmarket/peopleinwork/earningsandworkinghours/articles/understandingthegenderpaygapintheuk/2018-01-17.

56   *For women of previous generations*: See Professor Pat Hudson, 'Women's work', BBC History, 29 March 2011, https://www.bbc.co.uk/history/british/victorians/womens_work_01.shtml.

56   *'The low wages of women . . .'*: *Pioneer*, 5 April 1834, quoted in Mary Davis, 'An historical introduction to the campaign for equal pay', Winning Equal Pay: The Value of Women's Work, http://www.unionhistory.info/equalpay/roaddisplay.php?irn=820.

56   *'equal remuneration for work of equal value'*: Article 427 of the Treaty of Versailles. *International Labour Office Official Bulletin*, vol. 1 (April 1919–August 1920).

57   *From 1941 British women were conscripted*: Carol Harris, 'Women under fire in World War Two', BBC History, 17 February 2011, http://www.bbc.co.uk/history/british/britain_wwtwo/women_at_war_01.shtml.

57   *The trend was global*: See D'Ann Campbell, 'Women in combat: the World War II experience in the United States, Great Britain, Germany, and the Soviet Union', *Journal of Military History*, 57:2 (April 1993), 301–23, http://americanhistoryprojects.com/downloads/ww2/combat.pdf; see also Kazimiera Janina Cottam, *Soviet Airwomen in Combat in World War II* (Manhattan, KS: Military Affairs/Aerospace Historian, 1983).

57   *'Unequal pay was not new . . .'*: Professor Mary Davis, 'Women at work', Britain at Work: Voices from the Workplace 1945–1995, http://www.unionhistory.info/britainatwork/narrativedisplay.php?type=womenatwork.

58   *'A lot of women jeered us . . .'*: Quoted in Simon Goodley,

'Dagenham sewing machinists recall strike that changed women's lives', *Guardian*, 6 June 2013, https://www.theguardian.com/politics/2013/jun/06/dagenham-sewing-machinists-strike.

58 *'It made me realise that women can fight ...'*: Quoted in Maureen Paton, 'The Dagenham girls: Meet the four women whose crusading work inspired a new film', *Daily Mail*, 11 September 2010, https://www.dailymail.co.uk/home/you/article-1310482/The-Dagenham-girls-Meet-friends-pioneering-fight-equal-rights-inspired-new-film.html.

58 *'This meant that they had nearly six years ...'*: Davis, 'Women at work'.

59 *I'm thinking to myself 70 per cent ...*: Quoted in 'Catch of the day: Hull fish packers win equal pay', Winning Equal Pay: The Value of Women's Work, http://www.unionhistory.info/equalpay/display.php?irn=779.

60 *it wasn't just speech therapists who earned less*: Anthony Browne, 'Nurses set for £35m equal pay triumph', *Observer*, 15 July 2001, https://www.theguardian.com/society/2001/jul/15/equality.nhsstaff.

62 *'The number one priority was to protect the pay ...'*: Simon Hattenstone, 'The most hated lawyer in Britain', *Guardian*, 1 May 2010, https://www.theguardian.com/society/2010/may/01/stefan-cross-female-pay-birmingham.

63 *an epic battle for female council workers in Glasgow*: 'Campaigners hail Glasgow City Council equal pay ruling', BBC News, 18 August 2017, https://www.bbc.co.uk/news/uk-scotland-glasgow-west-40975929.

63 *the largest equal pay action in the UK private sector*: 'Asda workers win major step in equal pay claim battle', BBC News, 14 October 2016, https://www.bbc.co.uk/news/business-37658027.

63 *'Pay rates in stores differ from pay rates in distribution centres ...'*: 'Equal pay: Asda loses appeal in court case', BBC News, 31 January 2019, https://www.bbc.co.uk/news/business-47072013.

65 *'create a huge barrier to access to justice ...'*: The Law Society, 'Access to justice – making the legal system accessible to all', General Election 2017 briefing, https://www.lawsociety.org.uk/Support-services/documents/access-to-justice/.

65 *Australia's was 15.2 per cent and New Zealand's 9.4 per cent*: See: 'Australia's Gender Pay Gap Statistics', Workplace Gender Equality Agency, 22 February 2019, https://www.wgea.gov.au/data/fact-sheets/australias-gender-pay-gap-statistics; 'Gender pay gap is second-smallest', Stats NZ, 14 August 2018, https://www.stats.govt.nz/news/gender-pay-gap-is-second-smallest.

65 *a 2017 survey by the Pew Research Center*: Kim Parker and Cary Funk, 'Gender discrimination comes in many forms for today's

working women', Pew Research Center, 14 December 2017, https://www.pewresearch.org/fact-tank/2017/12/14/gender-discrimination-comes-in-many-forms-for-todays-working-women/.

66 *'In our view, the Court does not comprehend...'*: Quoted in Linda L. Barkacs and Craig B. Barkacs, 'The time is right – or is it? The Supreme Court speaks in *Ledbetter v. Goodyear Tire & Rubber Co.*', *Journal of Legal, Ethical and Regulatory Issues*, 12:1 (2009), https://www.academia.edu/8230205/THE_TIME_IS_RIGHT_OR_IS_IT_THE_SUPREME_COURT_SPEAKS_IN_LEDBETTER_V._GOODYEAR_TIRE_and_RUBBER_CO.

66 *'The Court's insistence on immediate contest...'*: 'Ledbetter v Goodyear Tire & Rubber Co. (No. 05-1074): Ginsburg, J., dissenting', via LII Cornell University Law School, https://www.law.cornell.edu/supct/html/05-1074.ZD.html.

67 *In 2017, 82 per cent of wealth created*: Katie Hope, '"World's richest 1% get 82% of the wealth", says Oxfam', BBC News, 22 January 2018, https://www.bbc.co.uk/news/business-42745853; 'Richest 1 percent bagged 82 percent of wealth created last year – poorest half of humanity got nothing', Oxfam International, 22 January 2018, https://www.oxfam.org/en/pressroom/pressreleases/2018-01-22/richest-1-percent-bagged-82-percent-wealth-created-last-year.

68 *'Every good economist should also be a feminist...'*: Luigi Zingales, 'Why every good economist should be feminist', Pro-Market, 2 August 2018, https://promarket.org/every-good-economist-feminist/.

68 *'motherhood penalty'*: Damian Grimshaw and Jill Rubery, 'The motherhood pay gap: a review of the issues, theory and international evidence', International Labour Officer Working Paper No. 1/2015, 2015, https://eige.europa.eu/resources/wcms_371804.pdf; Henrik Kleven, Camille Landais and Jakob Eghold Søgaard, 'Children and gender inequality: evidence from Denmark', NBER Working Paper No. 24219, January 2018, https://www.henrikkleven.com/uploads/3/7/3/1/37310663/kleven-landais-sogaard_nber-w24219_jan2018.pdf.

69 *Research conducted over several decades suggests*: Dave Heller, 'FSU research finds troubling disadvantages, including bias, against women in business', Florida State University News, 1 September 2018, https://news.fsu.edu/news/2018/09/01/fsu-research-finds-troubling-disadvantages-including-bias-against-women-in-business/.

70 *The difference in earnings widens steadily*: See Monica Costa Dias, Robert Joyce and Francesca Parodi, 'Mothers suffer big long-term pay penalty from part-time working', Institute for Fiscal

Studies press release, 5 February 2018, https://www.ifs.org.uk/
publications/10364.

70 *Research for the UK's Equality and Human Rights Commission*:
'Pregnancy and maternity-related discrimination and
disadvantage: experiences of mothers', EHRC report, 2016,
https://www.equalityhumanrights.com/sites/default/files/
mothers_report_-_bis-16-146-pregnancy-and-maternity-related-
discrimination-and-disadvantage-experiences-of-mothers_1.pdf.

70 *Usually it is men who reap the overwork premium*: Kim A. Weeden,
Youngjoo Cha and Mauricio Bucca, 'Long work hours, part-time
work, and trends in the gender gap in pay, the motherhood wage
penalty, and the fatherhood wage premium', *RSF: The Russell
Sage Foundation Journal of the Social Sciences*, 2:4 (August 2016),
71–102, https://muse.jhu.edu/article/630321/pdf.

70 *'The gender gap in pay would be considerably reduced . . .'*: Claudia
Goldin, 'A grand gender convergence: its last chapter', *American
Economic Review*, 104:4 (2014), 1091–119, https://scholar.harvard.
edu/files/goldin/files/goldin_aeapress_2014_1.pdf.

71 *One study showed managers could not tell the difference*: Erin Reed,
'Why some men pretend to work 80-hour weeks', *Harvard Business
Review*, 28 April 2015, https://hbr.org/2015/04/why-some-men-
pretend-to-work-80-hour-weeks.

72 *'Overall, women ranked lack of flexibility . . .'*: PwC, 'Time to talk:
What has to change for women at work', 2018, https://www.pwc.
com/gx/en/about/diversity/iwd/international-womens-day-pwc-
time-to-talk-report.pdf.

72 *'It's time we stop treating childcare . . .'*: 'State of the Union
2015: full transcript', 21 January 2015, https://edition.cnn.
com/2015/01/20/politics/state-of-the-union-2015-transcript-full-
text/.

72 *Research in the US suggests fathers*: See: 'Parenting in America',
Pew Research Center, 17 December 2015, https://www.
pewsocialtrends.org/2015/12/17/2-satisfaction-time-and-
support/#parenting-matters-to-overall-identity; Kim Parker
and Gretchen Livingston, '7 facts about American dads', Pew
Research Center, 13 June 2018, https://www.pewresearch.org/fact-
tank/2018/06/13/fathers-day-facts/.

73 *'each month that the father stays on parental leave . . .'*: Elly-Ann
Johansson, 'The effect of own and spousal parental leave on
earnings', Institute for Labour Market Policy Evaluation Working
Paper, 2014:4. https://www.ifau.se/globalassets/pdf/se/2010/wp10-
4-The-effect-of-own-and-spousal-parental-leave-on-earnings.pdf.

73 *'paternity leave in Australia is almost a token policy'*: Quoted
in Emelie Watkins, 'All genders lose out under the parental

leave scheme', Honi Soit, 30 November 2018, https://honisoit.
com/2018/11/all-genders-lose-out-under-the-parental-leave-
scheme/.

73 *less than 2 per cent of eligible fathers*: 'Shared parental leave take-up
may be as low as 2%', BBC News, 12 February 2018, https://www.
bbc.co.uk/news/business-43026312.

73 *Aviva introduced an equal parental leave policy*: 'Equal parental
leave shows men are eager to share childcare', Aviva, 20 November
2018, https://www.aviva.com/newsroom/news-releases/2018/11/
avivas-paid-parental-leave-shows-men-are-eager-to-share-childcare-
duties/.

74 *'If fathers were to be offered the same . . .'*: Duncan Fisher,
'Want men to share parental leave? Just give them equality',
Guardian, 15 February 2018, https://www.theguardian.com/
commentisfree/2018/feb/15/men-share-parental-leave-entitlement-
women-equality-fathers.

74 *'That's an excellent suggestion, Miss Triggs . . .'*: © Punch Limited.
https://punch.photoshelter.com/image/I0000eHEXGJ_wImQ.

75 *'In my career so far, I've needed . . .'*: 'Emma Stone, Andrea
Riseborough & Billie Jean King on tennis, equality & the *Battle
of the Sexes*', Out.com, 26 July 2017, https://www.out.com/
out-exclusives/2017/7/06/emma-stone-andrea-riseborough-billie-
jean-king-tennis-equality-battle-sexes.

75 *even fake money*: Lisa Miller, 'The money-empathy gap', *New York
Magazine*, 29 June 2012, http://nymag.com/news/features/money-
brain-2012-7/.

75 *Another study, at the University of Utah*: Maryam Kouchaki, 'Dirty
money: mere exposure to money motivates to think business, cheat
and lie', Harvard University Edmond J. Safra Center for Ethics
blog, 22 January 2013, https://ethics.harvard.edu/blog/dirty-
money.

75 *'Thinking about money leads people to think "business" . . .'*: Ibid.

Chapter 3: Get Mad

78 *Primatologists at Emory University*: Sarah F. Brosnan and Frans B.
M. de Waal, 'Monkeys reject unequal pay', *Nature*, 425 (2003),
297–9, https://www.nature.com/articles/nature01963.

78 *'an effect amplified if the partner received . . .'*: Ibid.

79 *'During the evolution of cooperation . . .'*: Ibid.

79 *'reply in a reasonable time . . .'*: 'Asking and responding to questions
of discrimination in the workplace: Acas guidance for job
applicants, employees, employers and others asking questions
about discrimination related to the Equality Act 2010', Acas, 2014,

http://m.acas.org.uk/media/pdf/m/p/Asking-and-responding-to-questions-of-discrimination-in-the-workplace.pdf.

81 *'in a better place than many organisations'*: Quoted in 'BBC's 9% gender pay gap revealed', BBC News, 4 October 2017, https://www.bbc.co.uk/news/entertainment-arts-41497265.

81 *an equal pay audit*: 'BBC Equal Pay Audit Report', October 2017, https://downloads.bbc.co.uk/aboutthebbc/insidethebbc/reports/equal_pay_audit.pdf.

81 *'no evidence of "systemic discrimination . . .'*: Sir Patrick Elias, quoted in 'BBC's 9% gender pay gap revealed'.

81 *more immediate questions*: For example, some of the job groups analysed showed men paid more and some showed women paid more. But the audit did not explain the size of the groups in which men were paid more against the size of groups in which women were paid more. Moreover, EHRC guidance says recurring differences of over 3 per cent merit further investigation but the audit examined average differences of more than 5 per cent (see 'Equal pay audit for larger organisations', https://www.equalityhumanrights.com/en/multipage-guide/equal-pay-audit-larger-organisations). The BBC claimed the audit followed EHRC guidance.

81 *'does not, and could not, categorically establish . . .'*: Quoted in 'BBC's 9% gender pay gap revealed'.

81 *'A lack of consistency or transparency . . .'*: Quoted in Matthew Moore, 'Mixed-sex job panels to close BBC pay gap', *The Times*, 5 October 2017, https://www.thetimes.co.uk/article/mixed-sex-job-panels-to-close-bbc-pay-gap-n8fzxxtx5.

82 *'While today's reports show . . .'*: 'BBC publishes Equal Pay Audit and Pay Gap Report', BBC Media Centre, 4 October 2017, https://www.bbc.co.uk/mediacentre/latestnews/2017/equal-pay-audit-pay-gap-report.

82 *'The idea that gender in any way would reflect . . .'*: Rosamund Urwin, 'Radio 2's new boss Lewis Carnie: "We're smack-them-over-the-head entertainment"', *Evening Standard*, 5 October 2017, https://www.standard.co.uk/lifestyle/london-life/lewis-carnie-we-re-smackthemoverthehead-entertainment-a3651441.html.

84 *Only two years earlier*: Patrick Foster, 'BBC News boss: Women lack confidence to apply for top reporting jobs', *Telegraph*, 12 June 2016, https://www.telegraph.co.uk/news/2016/06/12/bbc-news-boss-women-lack-confidence-to-apply-for-top-reporting-j/.

86 *'lack of awareness, not deliberate discrimination'*: 'Risky practices', EHRC, 'Risky practices', https://www.equalityhumanrights.com/en/advice-and-guidance/risky-practices.

87 *A recent US study found teenage girls*: Sandra Hofferth and Frances

Goldscheider, 'Reflections on the future of the second half of the gender revolution', *PAA Affairs* (summer 2017), http://www.populationassociation.org/wp-content/uploads/PAA-Summer17-Final.pdf.

87 *A study of twelve-year-olds*: Gwyther Rees, 'Children's daily activities: age variations between 8 and 12 years across 16 countries', *Journal of International and Comparative Social Policy*, 33:2 (2017), 114–35, https://www.tandfonline.com/doi/abs/10.108 0/21699763.2017.1307778.

87 *some research suggests girls internalise negative emotion more*: Tara M. Chaplin, 'Gender and emotion expression: a developmental contextual perspective', *Emotion Review*, 7:1 (January 2015), 14–21, https://www.ncbi.nlm.nih.gov/pmc/articles/PMC4469291/

88 *'informal policy' to discriminate against older women*: 'Communications Committee – Second Report: Women in news and current affairs broadcasting', 7 January 2015, https://publications.parliament.uk/pa/ld201415/ldselect/ldcomuni/91/9102.htm

90 *'I feel a lot of sadness, but I can't help but laugh . . .'*: 'Reflecting on one very, very strange year at uber', www.susanjfowler.com, 19 February 2017, https://www.susanjfowler.com/blog/2017/2/19/reflecting-on-one-very-strange-year-at-uber.

91 *'As much as I loved my work, I knew . . .'*: Margaret Heffernan, 'How I demanded – and won – equal pay', *Financial Times*, 30 July 2017, https://www.ft.com/content/6277d252-7048-11e7-93ff-99f383b09ff9.

101 *In 2016 an independent review*: 'The Dame Janet Smith Review', BBC Trust, https://www.bbc.co.uk/bbctrust/dame_janet_smith.

101 *'A serial rapist and a predatory sexual abuser . . .'*: Savile and Hall: BBC "missed chances to stop attacks", BBC News, 25 February 2015, https://www.bbc.co.uk/news/uk-35658398. After Savile's death the BBC shelved a TV investigation of his crimes and instead broadcast tributes to Savile over the Christmas period. It was left to rival broadcaster ITV to air a documentary the following year examining allegations of sexual abuse. A subsequent inquiry criticised BBC management but found no evidence of a cover-up: 'BBC criticised for Newsnight axed Jimmy Savile report', BBC News, 19 December 2012, https://www.bbc.co.uk/news/uk-20778261.

101 *'turned a blind eye, where it should have shone a light'*: 'Savile and Hall: BBC "missed chances to stop attacks".

102 *overhauled its bullying and harassment policy*: 'BBC to overhaul bullying and harassment policy following the publication of Respect at Work Review. "Gagging clauses" also set to be

dropped', BBC Media Centre, 2 May 2013, https://www.bbc.
co.uk/mediacentre/latestnews/2013/respect-at-work-review.html.

102 *'an atmosphere of fear still exists today in the BBC'*: 'Jimmy Savile
and the BBC: Dame Janet Smith report's key sections', BBC News,
25 February 2016, https://www.bbc.co.uk/news/uk-35657868.

Chapter 4: Sister Up

105 *'If I've learnt anything . . .'*: @janegarvey1, 3:10 a.m.,
6 September 2017, https://twitter.com/janegarvey1/
status/905372537579810816.

106 *'ultimately it could have led to none of us playing . . .'*: Judith
Brumley and Romy Oltuski, 'How the US women's hockey team
tripled their salaries by banding together', *InStyle*, 6 April 2018,
https://www.instyle.com/news/us-womens-national-hockey-team-
tripled-salaries-banding-together.

106 *'We always found ways to stick together . . .'*: Ibid.

107 *'she shook society into a new pattern . . .'*: Marina Warner, 'The
Agitator: Emmeline Pankhurst', *Time*, 14 June 1999, http://
content.time.com/time/magazine/article/0,9171,991250,00.html.

107–8 *'Originally articulated on behalf of black women . . .'*: Kimberlé
Crenshaw, 'Why intersectionality can't wait', *Washington Post*, 24
September 2015.

108 *'It takes a lot of work to consistently challenge ourselves . . .'*: Kimberlé
Crenshaw, 'Kimberlé Crenshaw on intersectionality: "I wanted to
come up with an everyday metaphor that anyone could use"', *New
Statesman*, 2 April 2014.

109–10 *'In the employment sphere . . .'*: Kathleen L. McGinn, Mayra
Ruiz Castro and Elizabeth Long Lingo, 'Learning from Mum:
cross-national evidence linking maternal employment and adult
children's outcomes', *Work, Employment and Society*, 30 April
2018, https://doi.org/10.1177/0950017018760167.

110 *Another study found that seeing fathers*: Mick Cunningham, 'The
influence of parental attitudes and behaviors on children's attitudes
toward gender and household labor in early adulthood', *Journal
of Marriage and Family*, 63(1), 2001 111–122, http://dx.doi.
org/10.1111/j.1741-3737.2001.00111.x.

110 *'There is no question at the BBC . . .'*: 'Revised transcript of evidence
taken before the Select Committee on Communications: Inquiry
into News and Current Affairs Broadcasting', 28 October 2014,
http://data.parliament.uk/writtenevidence/committeeevidence.svc/
evidencedocument/communications-committee/women-in-news-
and-current-affairs-broadcasting/oral/15038.html.

110 *'The men continue to function . . .'*: See 'Revised transcript of

evidence taken before The Select Committee on Communications: Inquiry on Women in News and Current Affairs Broadcasting', Evidence Session No. 3, 4 November 2014, http://data.parliament. uk/writtenevidence/committeeevidence.svc/evidencedocument/ communications-committee/women-in-news-and-current-affairs-broadcasting/oral/15195.html.

111 *'There's a special place in hell ...':* Madeleine Albright, 'Madeleine Albright: my undiplomatic moment', *New York Times*, 12 February 2016. https://www.nytimes.com/2016/02/13/opinion/ madeleine-albright-my-undiplomatic-moment.html.

111 *'I'm not a person who thinks the world ...':* As at 'Verbatim: Jul. 24 2006', *Time*, 18 July 2006. http://content.time.com/time/ magazine/article/0,9171,1215791,00.html.

111 *'queen bees preening ...':* Chris Smyth, 'Female bosses in NHS are queen bees, says medical chief Dame Sally Davies', *The Times*, 17 December 2014, https://www.thetimes.co.uk/article/ female-bosses-in-nhs-are-queen-bees-says-medical-chief-dame-sally-davies-xdqglj590dd.

111 *'Women aren't any meaner to women ...':* 'Opinion: Sheryl Sandberg on the myth of the catty woman', *New York Times*, 23 June 2016, https://www.nytimes.com/2016/06/23/opinion/sunday/ sheryl-sandberg-on-the-myth-of-the-catty-woman.html.

111 *audio tape in which he bragged*: Ben Jacobs, Sabrina Siddiqui and Scott Bixby, '"You can do anything": Trump brags on tape about using fame to get women', *Guardian*, 8 October 2016, https:// www.theguardian.com/us-news/2016/oct/07/donald-trump-leaked-recording-women.

112 *'feminism' was the most-looked-up word*: 'Merriam-Webster's 2017 Words of the Year', https://www.merriam-webster.com/words-at-play/word-of-the-year-2017-feminism.

112 *'Right now with so many campaigns ...':* Comments at the Royal Foundation Forum, 28 February 2018. As at Caroline Hallemann, 'Meghan Markle weighs in on #MeToo and Time's Up', *Town & Country*, 28 February 2018, https://www.townandcountrymag. com/society/tradition/a18921806/meghan-markle-comments-me-too-times-up/.

112–13 *'It was wrong. If I walked away ...':* Ginny Dougary, '"I spent £20k dyeing my hair but now I'm glad to be grey": from Miriam O'Reilly, the TV star who battled the BBC over ageism, a defiant celebration of her dramatic new look', *Daily Mail*, 24 April 2019, https://www.dailymail.co.uk/femail/article-6956177/TV-star-MIRIAM-OREILLY-spent-20k-dyeing-hair-Im-glad-grey.html.

114–15 *The individual stories that BBC Women later submitted*: All quotes in 'BBC Women: Their pay gap stories', BBC News,

30 January 2018, https://www.bbc.co.uk/news/entertainment-arts-42872377.

115 *'Women usually have no idea how good they are'*: Conversation with the author, 12 November 2018.

115 *'If you tell me I'm rubbish …'*: Lauren Collins, 'How the BBC Women are working toward equal pay', *New Yorker*, 16 July 2018, https://www.newyorker.com/magazine/2018/07/23/how-the-bbc-women-are-working-toward-equal-pay.

115 *the evidence is clear that they are strong*: See Emily T. Amanatullah and Michael W. Morris, 'negotiating gender roles: gender differences in assertive negotiating are mediated by women's fear of backlash and attenuated when negotiating on behalf of others', *Journal of Personality and Social Psychology*, 92:2 (February 2010), 256–67, https://www.researchgate.net/publication/41087504_Negotiating_Gender_Roles_Gender_Differences_in_Assertive_Negotiating_Are_Mediated_by_Women's_Fear_of_Backlash_and_Attenuated_When_Negotiating_on_Behalf_of_Others.

119 *A report by the Social Mobility Commission*: *State of the Nation 2016: Social Mobility in Great Britain*, Social Mobility Commission report, November 2016, https://assets.publishing.service.gov.uk/government/uploads/system/uploads/attachment_data/file/569410/Social_Mobility_Commission_2016_REPORT_WEB__1__.pdf.

120 *When the* Sunday Times *asked … Steph McGovern about pay*: Sian Griffiths, 'Steph McGovern: I'm not posh – so the BBC pays me less', *Sunday Times*, 25 February 2018, https://www.thetimes.co.uk/article/steph-mcgovern-im-not-posh-so-bbc-pays-me-less-d9mhfj98k.

120 *'We talk a lot in the BBC about how to …'*: @stephbreakfast, 12:11 p.m., 25 February 2018, https://twitter.com/stephbreakfast/status/967854559778476034.

120 *'posh women are paid a hell of a lot more than me'*: Phoebe Southworth, 'Working class BBC presenter Steph McGovern says "posh women are paid a hell of a lot more than me" as she slams corporation for caring more about ethnic diversity than the class divide', *Mail on Sunday*, 25 February 2018, https://www.dailymail.co.uk/news/article-5432551/Steph-McGovern-says-posh-women-BBC-paid-her.html.

120 *conditioned to compare themselves*: Belinda Weber, 'Exploring female competition and aggression', Medical News Today, 28 October 2013, https://www.medicalnewstoday.com/articles/268012.php.

122 *'almost eight out of ten women journalists …'*: 'Eight out of ten women at the BBC believe they are paid less than male

counterparts', NUJ, 10 November 2017, https://www.nuj.org.uk/news/eight-out-of-ten-women-at-the-bbc-believe-they-are-paid-less/.

122 *Men are often paid more than women ...*': Quoted in ibid.

124 *The equality regulator specifically warns*: 'Equal pay audit step 1: deciding the scope', Equality and Human Rights Commission, https://www.equalityhumanrights.com/en/multipage-guide/equal-pay-audit-step-1-deciding-scope.

125 *'The reasonable man adapts ...*': George Bernard Shaw, *Man and Superman: A Comedy and a Philosophy* (1903).

127 *a website of my best China work*: https://carriegracie.com/.

127 *'too tough an environment for novices*': Ceri Thomas, quoted in Sue MacGregor, 'Why women are tough enough for Today', *Telegraph*, 31 March 2010, https://www.telegraph.co.uk/culture/tvandradio/7541856/Why-women-are-tough-enough-for-Today.html.

Chapter 5: Speak Your Truth

131 *This was how I spoke mine*: Carrie Gracie, 'Carrie Gracie: secretive BBC made us feel trapped', *The Times*, 8 January 2018, https://www.thetimes.co.uk/article/carrie-gracie-secretive-bbc-made-us-feel-trapped-tcbndnfdw.

Chapter 6: Fight to Win

139 *'A revolution is not a dinner party ...*': Mao Tse Tung, *Report on an Investigation of the Peasant Movement in Hunan*.

140 *'Just cultures aim specifically ...*': Margaret Heffernan, *Beyond Measure: The Big Impact of Small Changes* (New York: TED Books, 2015).

141 *Public whistle-blowing*: Public Interest Disclosure Act 1998, https://www.legislation.gov.uk/ukpga/1998/23/contents.

141 *correct whistle-blowing procedures*: See 'Whistle-blowing – Public Interest Disclosure', Acas, http://www.acas.org.uk/index.aspx?articleid=1919.

142 *'Speaking your truth ...*': Transcript at 'Read Oprah Winfrey's rousing Golden Globes speech', CNN Entertainment, 10 January 2018, https://edition.cnn.com/2018/01/08/entertainment/oprah-globes-speech-transcript/index.html.

143 *'I knew he didn't hear nor see me ...*': Ali Montag, 'Here's what Oprah did when she found out her male co-worker was making more money than her', CNBC.com, 1 June 2018, https://www.cnbc.com/2018/06/01/what-oprah-winfrey-did-

when-her-male-co-worker-was-making-more-money.html.

143 *'He actually said to me . . .'*: Jennifer Calfas, 'The time Oprah Winfrey refused to work until her female producers got raises', money.com, 7 September 2017, http://money.com/money/4923704/oprah-winfrey-women-raises/.

143 *'transcends any culture, geography . . .'*: 'Read Oprah Winfrey's rousing Golden Globes speech'.

144 *'I'm not going to let you or your client . . .'*: Quoted in Eva Wiseman, 'Taylor Swift's punch-the-air moment for girls', *Observer*, 20 August 2017, https://www.theguardian.com/lifeandstyle/2017/aug/20/taylor-swift-do-not-feel-guilty-about-a-man-being-punished.

144 *'People always say that I didn't . . .'*: Quoted in *Congressional Record: Proceedings and Debates of the 109th Congress – Second Session*, vol. 152, part 11, 13 July 2006–24 July 2006, (Washington DC: United States Government Printing Office, 2006).

145 *Many things in this life are complicated . . .*: @SusanCalman, 1:05 a.m., 8 January 2018, https://twitter.com/SusanCalman/status/950292361799749632.

145 *Women in every broadcaster, boardroom . . .*: @pennymitv, 11:56 p.m., 7 January 2018, https://twitter.com/pennymitv/status/950275038208552960.

145 *'Nobody wants to be the buzzkill'*: Stephanie Zacharek, Eliana Dockterman and Haley Sweetland Edwards, '*Time* Person of the Year 2017: The Silence Breakers', *Time*, 18 December 2017, http://time.com/time-person-of-the-year-2017-silence-breakers/.

146 *'Superb journalist, great China Editor . . .'*: @wrobinson101, 2:41 p.m., 7 January 2018, https://twitter.com/wrobinson101/status/950135253103988738?lang=en. 'Radio 4 host Winifred Robinson taken off air after tweet backing Carrie Gracie', BBC News, 9 January 2018, https://www.bbc.co.uk/news/entertainment-arts-42623068.

147 *'[A]s a treasured national institution, the BBC must . . .'*: *Hansard*, vol. 634, 9 January 2018, https://hansard.parliament.uk/commons/2018-01-09/debates/4022E5C8-F2B6-4A43-89DF-4DB793534A79/BBCPay.

148 *'placated by a BBC-funded internal review . . .'*: *Hansard*, vol. 634, 9 January 2018, https://hansard.parliament.uk/commons/2018-01-09/debates/4022E5C8-F2B6-4A43-89DF-4DB793534A79/BBCPay.

149 *What other news organisation . . .*: @BBCCarrie, 7:29 p.m., 10 January 2018, https://twitter.com/BBCCarrie/status/951294997390856192.

149   *'daring to pit his infinitely tiny ...'*: Henry Fairlie, *Daily Mail*, August 1957.

149   *'I regard servile acceptance of its faults as a form of neglect'*: In 'The monarchy today', *National and English Review*, August 1957.

150   *The conversation went like this*: Transcript at Roisin O'Connor, 'John Humphrys and Jon Sopel: Hot mic audio of conversation about Carrie Gracie leaked', *Independent*, 13 January 2018, https://www.independent.co.uk/arts-entertainment/tv/news/john-humphrys-jon-sopel-leaked-audio-bbc-today-programme-carrie-gracie-what-did-they-say-reaction-a8157761.html.

151   *'Silly banter'*: Sofia Petkar and Paul Revoir, 'Caught out: Shocking audio catches BBC's John Humphreys and Jon Sopel joking about gender pay gap debacle', *Sun*, 13 January 2018, https://www.thesun.co.uk/news/5334719/john-humphrys-jon-sopel-bbc-today-show-gender-pay-gap-jokes-audio-listen/.

151   *'This was what I thought ...'*: Matthew Moore, 'Humphrys' BBC pay joke shows what we're up against, says Jane Garvey', *The Times*, 12 January 2018, https://www.thetimes.co.uk/edition/news/women-fume-as-john-humphrys-jokes-with-jon-sopel-about-bbc-pay-in-wake-of-carrie-gracie-resignation-nkmdmcdwf.

151   *'It was not meant for any other ears ...'*: 'Recording of John Humphrys' "jokey" off-air equal pay comments leaked', *Telegraph*, 14 January 2018, https://www.telegraph.co.uk/news/2018/01/14/recording-john-humphrys-jokey-off-air-equal-pay-comments-leaked/.

151   *'I think two things ...'*: Interviewed on Channel 4 News. As at 'BBC director-general Tony Hall: I've not had a pay cut', *Belfast Telegraph*, 30 January 2018, https://www.belfasttelegraph.co.uk/entertainment/news/bbc-directorgeneral-tony-hall-ive-not-had-a-pay-cut-36548670.html.

151   *'the court of King John'*: Helena Horton, 'Jon Sopel says he tried to shut down "nuts" off-air conversation with John Humphrys but was "in the court of King John"', *Telegraph*, 29 July 2018, https://www.telegraph.co.uk/news/2018/07/29/jon-sopel-says-tried-shut-nuts-off-air-conversation-john-humphrys/.

152   *'this was an ill-advised off-air conversation ...'*: Quoted in Tom Batchelor, 'John Humphrys joked about gender pay gap after BBC China editor Carrie Gracie resigned, leaked tape reveals', *Independent*, 12 January 2018, https://www.independent.co.uk/arts-entertainment/tv/news/john-humphrys-bbc-pay-gap-carrie-gracie-radio-4-today-jon-sopel-leaked-recording-gender-equality-a8154771.html.

152   *the BBC said John had not campaigned*: Helena Horton, 'John Humphrys is impartial on equal pay, BBC rules, amid outcry over

Carrie Gracie comments', *Telegraph*, 12 January 2018, https://www.telegraph.co.uk/news/2018/01/12/john-humphrys-will-allowed-present-statements-equal-pay-widespread/.

152 *Anita Anand had tweeted about equal pay*: Chris Hastings and Sanchez Manning, 'Fury as BBC temporarily drops Anita Anand from presenting Radio 4's Any Answers because of her criticism of pay gap', *Mail on Sunday*, 3 February 2018, https://www.dailymail.co.uk/news/article-5348761/BBC-temporarily-drops-Anita-Anand-presenting-Radio-4.html.

152 *'There is a time for everything ...'*: Ecclesiastes 3:1–8.

Chapter 7: Listen Up

155 *'only line of accountability to licence fee payers'*: 'Conclusions and recommendations', BBC Annual Report and Accounts 2017-18, parliament.uk, https://publications.parliament.uk/pa/cm201719/cmselect/cmcumeds/993/99308.htm.

155 *'intentionally and knowingly'*: 'Disinformation and "fake news": Final Report published', parliament.uk, 18 February 2019, https://www.parliament.uk/business/committees/committees-a-z/commons-select/digital-culture-media-and-sport-committee/news/fake-news-report-published-17-19/.

155 *Facebook denied any illegality*: See Digital, Culture, Media and Sport Committee, Oral evidence: Disinformation and 'fake news', HC 363, 27 November 2018, http://data.parliament.uk/writtenevidence/committeeevidence.svc/evidencedocument/digital-culture-media-and-sport-committee/disinformation-and-fake-news/oral/92923.html.

155 *In January 2018, the Committee invited*: See Digital, Culture, Media and Sport Committee, Oral evidence: BBC Pay, HC 732, 31 January 2018, http://data.parliament.uk/writtenevidence/committeeevidence.svc/evidencedocument/digital-culture-media-and-sport-committee/bbc-pay/oral/77888.html.

156 *In the US, judges with daughters*: Adam N. Glynn and Maya Sen, 'Identifying judicial empathy: does having daughters cause judges to rule for women's issues?', *American Journal of Political Science*, 59:1 (January 2015), https://ash.harvard.edu/files/identifying_judicial_empathy_does_having_daughters.pdf.

156 *in Denmark there is a positive correlation*: Michael S. Dahl, Cristian L. Dezső and David Gaddis Ross, 'Fatherhood and managerial style: how a male CEO's children affect the wages of his employees', *Administrative Science Quarterly*, 57:4 (2012), 1–25, https://pdfs.semanticscholar.org/ea8a/b3a2c5370e4158bdda7f98367527065560f1.pdf.

160 *'typically driven by material and justifiable factors ...'*: Quoted at Matthew Moore, 'Controversial pay review finds no unlawful gender bias at BBC', *The Times*, 30 January 2018, https://www.thetimes.co.uk/article/bbc-stars-will-discover-who-earns-what-as-new-pay-system-unveiled-zgtfvq5kq.

160 *'In all sampled cases ...'*: PwC, 'On-air review', 30 January 2018, https://downloads.bbc.co.uk/aboutthebbc/insidethebbc/howwework/reports/pdf/on_air_talent_review.pdf.

161 *'I don't believe there has been illegality ...'*: Comment on *Channel 4 News*, 30 January 2018, quoted in Matthew Moore, 'BBC pay review will give men more rises than women', *The Times*, 31 January 2018, https://www.thetimes.co.uk/article/bbc-pay-review-will-give-men-more-rises-than-women-plsgjpf6z.

161 *'lack of clarity and openness ...'*: 'Pay and equality at the BBC', BBC Media Centre, 30 January 2018, https://www.bbc.co.uk/mediacentre/latestnews/2018/pay-and-equality-at-the-bbc?lang=gd.

161 *'far from perfect'*: 'BBC review finds "no gender bias in on-air pay decisions"', BBC News, 30 January 2018, https://www.bbc.co.uk/news/entertainment-arts-42872363.

161 *'a period of significant pay restraint'*: 'Pay and equality at the BBC'.

161 *'a complex and bureaucratic system ...'*: Quoted in Eleanor Rose, 'Former BBC Africa correspondent reveals how she quit over pay gap', *Evening Standard*, 4 February 2018, https://www.standard.co.uk/news/uk/former-bbc-africa-correspondent-reveals-how-she-quit-over-pay-gap-a3757401.html.

161 *'Paying men more than women @BBC ...'*: @HarrietHarman, 10:17 a.m., 30 January 2018, https://twitter.com/harrietharman/status/958403734849097729?lang=en.

161–2 *'It's really hard to not reach ...'*: Quoted in Alexandra Topping, '"Same old fudge": BBC women hit out at equal pay review', *Guardian*, 30 January 2018, https://www.theguardian.com/media/2018/jan/30/bbc-women-hit-out-equal-pay-review-gender-bias.

162 *'The BBC has led every radio news bulletin ...'*: @afneil, 12:27 p.m., 30 January 2018, https://twitter.com/afneil/status/958436558390128640.

163 *In 2015, the Director-General himself*: Tony Hall, 'Next to the global giants the BBC is a minnow', *The Times*, 23 July 2015, https://www.thetimes.co.uk/article/next-to-the-global-giants-the-bbc-is-a-minnow-3st3rz6x8nt.

163 *Murder in the Lucky Holiday Hotel* had been singled out: *BBC Annual Report and Accounts 2016/17*, 2017, https://downloads.bbc.co.uk/aboutthebbc/insidethebbc/reports/pdf/bbc-annualreport-201617.pdf.

164 *'In effect, the BBC is saying they selected men ...'*: 'Equal pay', BBC

Annual Report and Accounts 2017–18: Equal pay at the BBC, parliament.uk, https://publications.parliament.uk/pa/cm201719/cmselect/cmcumeds/993/99305.htm.

166 *'I still have a little impostor syndrome . . .'*: 'Michelle Obama: "I still have impostor syndrome"', BBC News, 4 December 2018, https://www.bbc.co.uk/news/uk-46434147.

166 *'a stricken trawler that's lost its catch'*: Jan Moir, 'The day Radio 4's flagship show imploded in a soggy morass of smuggery: Jan Moir listens as guest host Carrie Gracie cannot talk about her own story', *Daily Mail*, 9 January 2018, https://www.dailymail.co.uk/debate/article-5248631/JAN-MOIR-Carrie-Gracie-talk-story.html.

166 *'flouncing out'*, *'whingeing'*: Gary Oliver, 'Blimey, O'Reilly, are you still whingeing', The Conservative Woman, 16 January 2018, https://www.conservativewoman.co.uk/blimey-oreilly-still-whingeing/.

166–7 *'shrieking culture of victimhood'*, *'self-righteous lynch mobs'*, *'grievance-seeking betrayal'*: Trevor Kavanagh, 'Master of impartiality John Humphrys has been betrayed by a cowardly sneak – and must not be sacked at all costs', *Sun*, 14 January 2018, https://www.thesun.co.uk/news/5339413/john-humphrys-betrayed-by-cowardly-sneak/.

170 *'It is unacceptable to talk . . .'*: Digital, Culture, Media and Sport Committee, Oral evidence: BBC Pay, HC 732, 31 January 2018, http://data.parliament.uk/writtenevidence/committeeevidence.svc/evidencedocument/digital-culture-media-and-sport-committee/bbc-pay/oral/77888.html. See also 'Carrie Gracie tells MPs the BBC is in real trouble over equal pay – video', *Guardian*, 31 January 2018, https://www.theguardian.com/media/video/2018/jan/31/carrie-gracie-tells-mps-bbc-real-trouble-over-equal-pay-video.

170 *'If you try to humiliate me . . .'*: Ibid.

170 *'When you have this notion . . .'*: Ibid.

171 *'looking at the equity . . .'*: Ibid.

171 *'I think that would have been done . . .'*: Ibid.

173 *'I think that is the point . . .'*: Ibid.

173 *'It is a little bit more than an oversight . . .'*: Ibid.

173 *Fran Unsworth told the Committee*: Ibid.

173 *Anne Bulford said*: Ibid.

173 *'the worst get out of jail free card . . .'*: Ibid.

174 *'We dealt largely through the editors . . .'*: Ibid.

Chapter 8: Laugh, Endure and Dare to Hope

178 *'Fun disables fear. It makes people feel braver'*: Conversation with the author, 12 November 2018.

178 *'Back at work and feeling undervalued? . . .'*, *'open to misinterpretation'*: 'BBC deletes tweet advising women: "Why not start the year by asking for a pay rise?"', *Telegraph*, 11 January 2018, https://www.telegraph.co.uk/news/2018/01/11/bbc-deletes-tweet-advising-women-not-start-year-asking-pay-rise/.

185 *two huge management initiatives on pay*: 'BBC Public Service Transparency Review', http://downloads.bbc.co.uk/aboutthebbc/insidethebbc/howwework/reports/pdf/bbc_transparency_review_the_hutton.pdf.

186 *new terms and conditions for the entire workforce*: 'BBC welcomes unions vote for Terms and Conditions changes', BBC Media Centre, 12 June 2018, https://www.bbc.co.uk/mediacentre/latestnews/2018/terms-and-conditions.

187 *'As I've spent a lot of time hammering the BBC . . .'*: @anitathetweeter, 7:58 a.m., 26 March 2018, https://twitter.com/anitathetweeter/status/978285085819658242.

188 *'We're employed to ask tough questions . . .'*: Cathy Newman, 'I'm angry that my female ITN colleagues are still having to argue for the top roles and pay', *Telegraph*, 15 March 2018, https://www.telegraph.co.uk/women/work/angry-female-itn-colleagues-still-having-argue-top-roles-pay/.

188 *in a separate story about union pay*: 'General Secretary's remuneration', NUJ, 21 February 2018, https://www.nuj.org.uk/news/general-secretarys-remuneration/.

188 *'We've got the rhetoric very nicely developed . . .'*: Decca Aitkenhead, 'Harriet Harman on exposing the pay gap: "This is kind of . . . revolutionary"', *Guardian*, 12 January 2018, https://www.theguardian.com/politics/2018/jan/12/harriet-harman-gender-pay-gap-equal-act-saturday-interview.

189 *'By making this information public . . .'*: Theresa May, 'We must make the gender pay gap a thing of the past', *Telegraph*, 3 April 2018, https://www.telegraph.co.uk/politics/2018/04/03/must-make-gender-pay-gap-thing-past/.

189 *'The low number of employers . . .'*: 'Closing the gender pay gap', EHRC, December 2018, https://www.equalityhumanrights.com/sites/default/files/closing-the-gender-pay-gap_0.pdf.

190 *A study published in 2000*: Claudia Goldin and Cecilia Rouse, 'orchestrating impartiality: the impact of "blind" auditions of female musicians', Harvard Kennedy School Women and Public Policy Program, 2000, http://gap.hks.harvard.edu/orchestrating-impartiality-impact-%E2%80%9Cblind%E2%80%9D-auditions-female-musicians.

190 *The EHRC has published lots of ideas*: See, for example: 'Good equality practice for employers: equality policies, equality training

and monitoring', https://www.equalityhumanrights.com/en/publication-download/good-equality-practice-employers-equality-policies-equality-training-and; Duncan Brown, Catherine Rickard and Andrea Broughton, 'Tackling gender, disability and ethnicity pay gaps: a progress review', https://www.equalityhumanrights.com/sites/default/files/research-report-110-tackling-gender-disability-ethnicity-pay-gaps.pdf.

190 *for nudges to drive change*: Iris Bohnet, *What Works: Gender Equality by Design* (Cambridge, MA: The Belknap Press of Harvard University Press, 2016)

191 *'We don't play shenanigans . . .'*: Comments in an interview on *60 Minutes*. Transcript at Lesley Stahl, 'Leading by example to close the gender pay gap', CBS News, 15 April 2018, https://www.cbsnews.com/news/salesforce-ceo-marc-benioff-leading-by-example-to-close-the-gender-pay-gap/.

192 *'CEOs, with one button on one computer . . .'*: Ibid.

192 *'No matter the size of your company . . .'*: Quoted in Nick Bastone, 'Salesforce's Chief People Officer explains how and why the company has spent $8.7 million to close its gender pay gap', Business Insider, 15 December 2018, https://www.businessinsider.com/cindy-robbins-salesforce-equal-pay-2018-11?r=US&IR=T#robbins-says-salesforce-effort-around-equal-pay-is-a-call-to-action-for-other-companies-to-start-doing-the-same-8.

192 *'systemic gender anomaly'*: 'Salary Anomaly Working Group: Analysis & Findings (26 May 2016)', University of Waterloo, https://uwaterloo.ca/provost/sites/ca.provost/files/uploads/files/salaryanomalyworkinggroup.pdf.

193 *'The pay gap was hidden . . .'*: Quoted in Jon Henley, '"Equality won't happen by itself": how Iceland got tough on gender pay gap', *Guardian*, 20 February 2018, https://www.theguardian.com/world/2018/feb/20/iceland-equal-pay-law-gender-gap-women-jobs-equality.

193 *one fatality for every 287 million passengers*: 'Aviation safety: a look a the regulation and procedures that make aviation one of the safest forms of travel', Civil Aviation Authority, https://www.caa.co.uk/Consumers/Guide-to-aviation/Aviation-safety/.

194–5 *'I am not in work . . .'*: 'Female chef paid up to £6k a year less than male colleague for same work wins equal pay case', leighday.co.uk, 11 June 2018, https://www.leighday.co.uk/News/News-2018/June-2018/Female-chef-paid-up-to-6k-a-year-less-than-male-c.

195 *'At Compass Group . . .'*: 'Our Gender Pay Report – Compass Group UK', 2017, https://www.compass-group.com/content/dam/compass-group/corporate/Acting-responsibly/GenderPayGap/Gender_Pay_Report_2017_FINAL.PDF.

195 *'mainly due to us having more men . . .'*: 'We've published our gender pay gap report today', Co-op Colleagues, 28 February 2018, https://assets.ctfassets.net/5ywmq66472jr/7Lko8TEyPaG buOLZUvDceB/7aa232969e92a8c157981f639bd19acd/Co-op_ Gender_Pay_Gap_Report_2018.pdf.

196 *'It's two weeks of my life . . .'*: Quoted in Lauren Collins, 'How the BBC Women are working toward equal pay', *New Yorker*, 16 July 2018, https://www.newyorker.com/magazine/2018/07/23/how-the-bbc-women-are-working-toward-equal-pay.

197 *'he is widely considered . . .'*: Quoted in Nicolas Slawson, 'Navratilova: BBC pays McEnroe 10 times more for Wimbledon role', *Guardian*, 19 March 2018, https://www.theguardian.com/sport/2018/mar/19/navratilova-bbc-pays-mcenroe-10-times-more-for-wimbledon-role.

197 *'opened [her] eyes to a lot'*: Quoted in Rebecca Lawrence, 'The Crown pay gap: Claire Foy admits "embarrassing" scandal "opened her eyes" to sexism in the industry', *Daily Mail*, 24 April 2018, https://www.dailymail.co.uk/tvshowbiz/article-5653475/The-Crown-pay-gap-Claire-Foy-admits-embarrassing-scandal-opened-eyes-sexism.html.

201 *Employers have a legal duty of care*: 'Defining an employer's duty of care', Acas, http://www.acas.org.uk/index.aspx?articleid=3751.

Chapter 9: Enlist Good Men

205 *'ghastly on a personal level'*, *'I was quietly minding my own business . . .'*: Rachel Cooke, 'Jon Sopel: "I wake up at six every morning to see if Trump has tweeted"', *Observer*, 29 July 2018, https://www.theguardian.com/media/2018/jul/29/jon-sopel-bbc-trump-gener-pay-gap-interview.

205 *In the US, nearly half of men*: Katy Steinmetz, 'Nearly half of men believe the pay gap is "made up," survey finds', *Time*, 2 April 2019, http://time.com/5562171/pay-gap-survey-equal-pay-day/.

205 *A 2019 global study on attitudes*: 'Global study reveals what world thinks about women's equality', King's College London news centre, 5 March 2019, https://www.kcl.ac.uk/news/global-study-reveals-what-world-thinks-about-womens-equality.

206 *'maintain their subordination . . .'*: John Stuart Mill, *The Subjection of Women* (1869).

206 *If men had ever been found in society . . .*: Ibid.

207 *'Both the principal oboe and principal flute . . .'*: Jeremy Eichler, 'The BSO's principal flutist says she is paid far less than the man who is the principal oboist', *Boston Globe*, 6 July 2018, https://www.bostonglobe.com/

arts/2018/07/05/bso-principal-flutist-sues-for-equal-pay/
Mx9KncUJ0P2wXqOUaTJUlJ/story.html.

207   *'every bit my match in skills, if not more so'*: Geoff Edgars, 'Elizabeth
      Rowe has sued the BSO. Her case could change how orchestras
      pay men and women', *Washington Post*, 11 December 2018, https://
      www.washingtonpost.com/graphics/2018/entertainment/music/
      orchestra-gender-pay-gap/?noredirect=on&utm_source=reddit.
      com&utm_term=.bf0ab47fc9f1.

207   *'Ever looked at a flute part? . . .'*: Ibid.

207–8 *'Equal pay and a place at the table . . .'*: Matt Bagwell,
      'Benedict Cumberbatch says he won't take on a role
      unless his female co-stars are paid the same', HuffPost,
      8 May 2018, https://www.huffingtonpost.co.uk/entry/
      benedict-cumberbatch-equal-pay-me-too-feminism-radio-times-
      interview_uk_5af1a4c4e4b041fd2d2b1ba9.

208   *Sandi Toksvig revealed*: 'Sandi Toksvig "paid fraction" of Fry's QI
      hosting fee', BBC News, 8 September 2018, https://www.bbc.
      co.uk/news/entertainment-arts-45460322.

208   *'He approached me and said . . .'*: Bruce Dessau, 'Katherine Ryan:
      "Men are like dolphins, best enjoyed on holiday"', *The Times*, 13
      October 2018, https://www.thetimes.co.uk/article/katherine-ryan-
      men-are-likedolphins-best-enjoyed-onholiday-p09kpwvh8.

209   *encourages them to sign up*: As at https://mbaallies.com/sign-the-
      pledge/.

Chapter 10: Get Equal

212   *the journey in figures*: See also 'BBC pay: The 2018–19 list of star
      salaries', BBC News, 2 July 2019, https://www.bbc.co.uk/news/
      entertainment-arts-48839428.

212   *Jon Sopel's annual salary for 2017/18*: James Gill, 'BBC pay
      2018: full list of the highest paid stars revealed', *Radio Times*,
      11 July 2018, https://www.radiotimes.com/news/tv/2018-07-11/
      bbc-pay-2018-full-list-top-earners-talent-salaries-how-much-do-
      bbc-stars-get-paid/.

225   *there would be £361,000*: Anna Behrmann, 'BBC's Carrie Gracie
      £360k payout to charity', *The Times*, 10 November 2018.

225   *'Women need real pay transparency . . .'*: Quoted in 'YESS
      Law to work with Fawcett Society following Carrie Gracie
      announcement', YESS Law press release, 29 June 2018, https://
      www.yesslaw.org.uk/news/yess-law-to-work-with-fawcett-society-
      following-carrie-gracie-announcement/.

226   *'Our aim at YESS is to try to resolve . . .'*: Ibid.

230   *'my mum, Jennifer's mum and mothers and daughters everywhere'*:

@BBCCarrie, 1:42 p.m., 29 June 2018, https://twitter.com/bbccarrie/status/1012798448108752896.

Epilogue: Are We Nearly There Yet?

232 *'It's 2018 and we should be rewarding people fairly . . .'*: Kate Palmer, 'WSP Opus closes gender pay gap', WSP Opus, 20 August 2018, https://www.wsp-opus.co.nz/news-and-publications/news-2018-2020/wsp-opus-closes-gender-pay-gap/.

232 *The British government launched a consultation*: 'Ethnicity pay gap: Firms may be forced to reveal figures', BBC News, 11 October 2018, https://www.bbc.co.uk/news/business-45818234.

233 *reported that the BBC was failing to live up to its duty*: 'End culture of "invidious, opaque decision-making" on pay, report says', DCMS Select Committee, 25 October 2018, https://www.parliament.uk/business/committees/committees-a-z/commons-select/digital-culture-media-and-sport-committee/news/bbc-report-published-17-19/.

233 *'clearly spelling out . . .'*: Quoted in Matthew Moore, 'BBC heads for court as angry staff sue over pay "inequality"', *The Times*, 26 October 2018, https://www.thetimes.co.uk/article/bbc-heads-for-court-as-angry-staff-sue-over-pay-inequality-zp5k525pb.

233 *'Ms Gracie deserves great credit . . .'*: 'Conclusions and recommendations', BBC Annual Report and Accounts 2017–18: Equal pay at the BBC, parliament.uk, https://publications.parliament.uk/pa/cm201719/cmselect/cmcumeds/993/99308.htm.

233 *Google staff in offices across the world*: Dave Lee, 'Google staff walk out over women's treatment', BBC News, 1 November 2018, https://www.bbc.co.uk/news/technology-46054202?ocid=wsnews.chat-apps.in-app-msg.whatsapp.trial.link1_.auin.

234 *Stella Creasy, MP, issued invitations*: Alexandra Topping, 'Save the date, but party to mark end of gender pay gap not until 2235', *Guardian*, 20 November 2018, https://www.theguardian.com/world/2018/nov/10/save-the-date-but-party-to-mark-end-of-gender-pay-gap-equal-pay-day.

234 *investigation on pay discrimination*: Rianna Croxford, 'Ethnic minority academics earn less than white colleagues', BBC News, 7 December 2018, https://www.bbc.co.uk/news/education-46473269.

235 *'Where people take on significant extra responsibilities . . .'*: Nick Craven, Jonathan Bucks and Miles Goslett, 'The Big Bucks Corporation: Bumper pay rises for BBC's top brass . . . as it threatens to scrap free TV for viewers over 75', *Mail on Sunday*, 15 December 2018, https://www.dailymail.co.uk/news/

article-6499983/Bumper-pay-rises-BBCs-brass-threatens-scrap-free-TV-viewers-75.html.

236 *'Since the strike ...'*: Quoted in Libby Brooks, 'Women win 12-year equal pay battle with Glasgow City Council', *Guardian*, 17 January 2019, https://www.theguardian.com/society/2019/jan/17/glasgow-council-women-workers-win-12-year-equal-pay-battle.

236 *Supermarket giant Asda lost another appeal*: 'Equal pay: Asda loses appeal in court case', BBC News, 31 January 2019, https://www.bbc.co.uk/news/business-47072013.

236 *'Equal pay for equal play'*: @adidas, 3:30 p.m., 8 March 2019, https://twitter.com/adidas/status/1104162465703739396.

236 *news that the US women's soccer team was suing*: 'Adidas to pay equal bonuses for women's World Cup winners', Reuters, 9 March 2019, https://uk.reuters.com/article/uk-soccer-usa-adidas/adidas-to-pay-equal-bonuses-for-womens-world-cup-winners-idUKKBN1QQ08X.

236 *'Who apologises to the women ...'*: Joshua Posaner, 'Berlin offers women 21 percent metro ticket discount to highlight pay gap', politico.eu, 12 March 2019, https://www.politico.eu/article/berlin-offers-women-21-metro-ticket-discount-to-highlight-pay-gap/.

237 *'have not received equal pay for equal work'*: 'Investigation: Does the BBC pay women and men equally for equal work?', EHRC, https://www.equalityhumanrights.com/en/ymchwiliadau-ac-archwiliadau/investigation-does-bbc-pay-women-and-men-equally-equal-work.

237 *Vice Media agreed to pay $1.87 million*: Eriq Gardner, 'Vice Media Agrees to $1.87 Million Settlement for Paying Female Staffers Less Than Men', *Hollywood Reporter*, 27 March 2019, https://www.hollywoodreporter.com/thr-esq/vice-media-agrees-187-million-settlement-paying-female-staffers-men-1197427?sfns=mo.

237 *'True gender equality in the working world ...'*: Quoted in 'Paternity leave: "All my dad friends were incredibly jealous"', BBC News, 3 April 2019, https://www.bbc.co.uk/news/business-47792269.

238 *The BBC entered itself for an award*: Anita Singh, 'BBC nominated for HR award despite investigation into alleged pay discrimination', *Telegraph*, 24 April 2019, https://www.telegraph.co.uk/news/2019/04/24/bbc-nominated-hr-award-despiteinvestigation-alleged-pay-discrimination/.

238 *A manager in BBC News, Karen Martin*: 'Female BBC manager rejects job over equal pay', BBC News, 22 May 2019, https://www.bbc.co.uk/news/entertainment-arts-48364081.

238 *Several hundred signed a protest letter*: See @mattkmoore, 7:00 a.m., 23 May 2019, https://twitter.com/mattkmoore/status/1131560410975543296.

It's okay to talk about pay.

www.yesslaw.org.uk

Carrie Gracie made a donation to
The Fawcett Society so that we could set up an
Equal Pay Advice Service in partnership with YESS Law.

This Service is here to help you work out if you are being
paid unfairly, and will give you **free legal advice** on what to
do about it. In particular we want to hear from those whose
gross income is £30,000 a year or less, and do not have
access to legal advice.

Your conversations with us are free and confidential. You
are in control of the process and can decide what to do
based on our advice. Your employer will never need to know
you took advice from us if you don't want them to.

Visit our website and fill out a short survey to get in touch:

www.fawcettsociety.org.uk

We can stop unfair pay for good.
Stand in solidarity with Carrie by giving a woman the
support and access to justice she deserves.

Donate towards our Equal Pay Advice Service today at
www.gofundme.com/equalpaynow